DATE DUE

Demco, Inc. 38-293

PERSONALIZED INSTRUCTION

The Key to Student Achievement

Second Edition

James W. Keefe
John M. Jenkins

Rowman & Littlefield Education
Lanham, Maryland • Toronto • Plymouth, UK
2008

Published in the United States of America
by Rowman & Littlefield Education
A Division of Rowman & Littlefield Publishers, Inc.
A wholly owned subsidiary of The Rowman & Littlefield Publishing Group, Inc.
4501 Forbes Boulevard, Suite 200, Lanham, Maryland 20706
www.rowmaneducation.com

Estover Road
Plymouth PL6 7PY
United Kingdom

British Library Cataloguing in Publication Information Available

Library of Congress Cataloging-in-Publication Data
Keefe, James W.
  Personalized instruction : the key to student achievement / James W. Keefe,
John M. Jenkins. — 2nd ed.
      p. cm.
  Includes bibliographical references.
  ISBN-13: 978-1-57886-755-4 (cloth : alk. paper)
  ISBN-10: 1-57886-755-X (cloth : alk. paper)
  ISBN-13: 978-1-57886-756-1 (pbk. : alk. paper)
  ISBN-10: 1-57886-756-8 (pbk. : alk. paper)
  1. Individualized instruction–United States. 2. School management and
organization–United States. I. Jenkins, John M. II. Title.

  LB1031.K383 2008
  371.39'4–dc22   2007040000

∞™ The paper used in this publication meets the minimum requirements of
American National Standard for Information Sciences—Permanence of Paper
for Printed Library Materials, ANSI/NISO Z39.48-1992.
Manufactured in the United States of America.

We dedicate this book to the members of the Learning Environments Consortium International (LEC) who have long been advocates for the kind of education that is described in these pages. We also dedicate this book to the principals and teachers in schools throughout the United States and the rest of the world who have implemented personalized approaches to instruction, despite pressures from powerful external forces to the contrary. They, along with the members of LEC, are motivated by a vision that places students at the center of the educational process.

CONTENTS

FOREWORD

It is an inconvenience, but nonetheless a reality, that no two of us are quite the same or that any one of us is the same over a long period of time. Mercifully, we vary. Yes, there are patterns—early readers often make the same sorts of errors in similar texts—but idiosyncrasy of style, inclination, and commitment inevitably intrude. Each of us is a jumble of complexity, both as biological beings and as people pressed into particular environments.

In most modern cultures, each of us glories in this individuality. Indeed, we value it. I *am* somebody. I am *special*. I bring something new to my community. There is, obviously, arrogance in these self-proclamations. Few of us are wholly different. Although I try differently, I react to some situations, all too often, as my five older sisters or my best buddies might. We are creatures of our environments. But there is stubborn truth in our individuality as well.

Not surprisingly, and whatever the nobility of our intentions, standardized educational approaches are inevitably inefficient, indeed often unfair and cruel. There is not and can never be One Best System of learning (to use David Tyack's [1995] wonderful phrase). As a people, we might agree that there should be a system of schools to instill in each young citizen the ideas, habits, and skills that our community respects.

At the same time, we must also agree that such a system will fail unless it attends carefully and respectfully to the specialness in each of us—a system, indeed, but a system that accommodates to what each of us is as a distinct person.

In practice, there will be tradeoffs. To provide each of us with tutors for every subject—each of us, as it were, on one end of a log with the great educator Mark Hopkins on the other end—is practically unattainable. We must make full use of what we know about the patterns of learning and maturation among us. But we must also provide for the specialness in each person.

That is what "personalized instruction" is all about. For over 150 years, American educators have struggled to design schools that are both communities with common structures and routines and are places that respect and nurture specialness. Yet, at times, we stray from this ideal with unproductive forays, such as back-to-basics and No Child Left Behind (NCLB).

The effects of NCLB continue to spread, with both the good and the bad present. The "good" is that no child is to be shuffled off by districts or schools just because he or she is "difficult to handle" or is somehow off the district's radar screen. The "bad" is that serious education is (once again) reduced to a "score" on, usually, a single battery of tests, and that decisions affecting that youngster are made largely on that basis. That the profession has not risen as one to strenuously resist this policy is an embarrassment. We appear to be in thrall to the federal definitions of educational excellence. Shame on us!

Given new insights into what makes individuals unique, the goal of personalization seems more salient than ever and demands commitment from all educators. James Keefe and John Jenkins have sorted through the research and all of the varied attempts to personalize instruction and have drawn some important lessons. The necessary complexity of effective schools—however simple they may appear in their design—is inconvenient, costly, and demanding of parents, teachers, counselors, and principals. It is also imperative that we accept that complexity—and glory in the richness of humanity that it represents.

Theodore R. Sizer

INTRODUCING
PERSONALIZED INSTRUCTION

Most American schools are average. They are neither excellent nor poor. As we start a new millennium, our educational system as a whole is neither at risk nor exemplary. In fact, it exhibits more lingering signs of the past than hopeful cues of the future. It is, regrettably, merely holding its own.

David Tyack and Larry Cuban (1995) commented on this stubborn persistence of the traditional ways of American schooling:

> The basic grammar of schooling, like the shape of classrooms, has remained remarkably stable over the decades. Little has changed in the ways that schools divide time and space, classify students and allocate them to classrooms, splinter knowledge into "subjects," and award grades and "credits" as evidence of learning.

American schools today are much as they have been since the middle of the nineteenth century. They seem to defy—really, to absorb and render neutral—any significant change in the way they are organized, in the way their teachers teach, and in the ways their students learn.

From the mid-nineteenth century to the mid-twentieth, schoolhouses were locked in their own Cartesian grids of standard classrooms, each accommodating a standard number of children to be instructed by one teacher of, it was hoped, standard credentials. The teacher's mission was to transmit the predominant culture for a year. In a secondary school, bells would ring at regular intervals, signaling students, and sometimes teachers, to change boxes.

Because the process of schooling consisted mostly of a talking teacher and a learner who rarely stirred from his place, the learner was provided with a "pupil station," consisting of a chair and desk fixed to the floor. Not until well into the twentieth century were the chair and desk free-standing and rearrangeable (Gores, 1976).

This unchanging structure fostered a highly standardized approach to teaching and learning that resembled the nineteenth-century factory structure on which it was modeled. Teachers taught (talked and supervised); students learned (listened and responded). The curriculum was largely standardized and only "normal" students regularly passed the periodic examinations, while the slower or "retarded" were held back. Instead of abandoning this rigid grading system, most reformers attempted to modify or "fine-tune" it. But because the system had been developed to provide a standard approach to teaching and learning, it tended to absorb or discard attempts to improve or "soften" it.

The *Washington Post*'s former critic-at-large and current op-ed columnist Richard Cohen recalled his own experiences at "curriculum night" for parents in a 1987 essay on "High (School) Anxiety":

> When I was a student, I believed in the conspiracy theory of parenthood. I thought all parents had gotten together to lie about school, to say it was the best time of their lives. They would pretend envy at Christmas and Easter vacations, a 9-to-3 day, and two months off in the summer. They would depict life after school (real life) as being infinitely tougher—a vocational treadmill, a chore in which the rewards were what little money they could make. School they said would be the happiest time of my life. What were these people talking about?
>
> As adults, we structure our lives to avoid precisely the sort of pain school routinely inflicted. Only politicians and athletes, who either win or lose, still pass or fail . . . . Most of us learn to avoid situations in which we cannot cope, to master something, and never to do what we cannot do.

Schooling may not be as bad as that, but for countless students, it is still a never-ending chore, unmatched to their interests, ill suited to their needs. Recent international comparisons of student achievement (although methodologically flawed) have shown American students to be average on the whole, good in some areas and only fair in several others. Reform and restructuring efforts have become commonplace over the past four decades in response to these kinds of reports. New graduation requirements, better textbooks and materials, different school schedules, year-round schooling, new professional development programs for teachers, and attempts at systemic or whole-system reorganization have dominated state and some national efforts. Yet, much of this is still fine-tuning, an attempt to modify or regulate the existing structure of schooling.

Robert Sternberg (1996) pointed out that one of the greatest temptations we face is falling victim to our own prejudices (confirmation bias). We have a bias of whatever kind, and we set out to uncover and/or interpret evidence to support our point of view. Both scholars and practitioners have fallen victim to such biases. Suppose, for example, we believed that all differences in educational attainment between and among groups are a result of IQ differences or socioeconomic differences, or even instructional strategies. If we believed strongly enough, we might find evidence of what we believed—and live to regret it. Schooling is complex and demands well-thought-out, systematic, and even complex strategies—not simplistic policies and solutions.

John Dewey (1902) thought of the child as an active organism in search of stimuli that will promote its growth. He stressed the experiential nature of learning as problem solving and the local nature of schooling, emphasizing active community participation in the process. He stated that "the manner in which the machinery of instruction bears upon the child really controls the whole system."

A controversial study of American education commissioned by the U.S. Department of Energy and conducted by the Sandia National Laboratories (Carson, Huelskamp, and Woodall 1992) drew on existing national databases to profile the current status of the enterprise. The Sandia Report found that adjusted aggregate SAT scores had risen since the late 1970s, that high school dropout rates were declining (except for Hispanics), that college Graduate Record Examination scores had risen significantly since the late 1970s, and that the United States led the world in the proportion of its population graduating from college, particularly in science and engineering. Sandia also documented that striking changes had occurred in school-age populations (one-third minority) because of immigration. The report pointed out that many of the current recommendations for educational reform are in conflict, such as local autonomy and empowerment versus national testing and a national curriculum. The report urged that our educational priorities should emphasize improving the education of minority and inner-city students, adjusting to immigration and demographic changes, and enhancing the status of teachers. These recommendations suggested a more focused and personalized approach to schooling in America. They argued for more attention to inner-city and rural schools, to learner differences, and to the developmental needs of teachers.

Then, along came the federal No Child Left Behind (NCLB) legislation of 2002. This reauthorization of the Elementary and Secondary Education Act of 1965 mandated higher educational standards, annual state-sponsored testing, disaggregated analysis of testing data, and sanctions for schools not achieving "adequate yearly progress" (AYP). The goal was for all students to be at grade level in reading and math by 2014. Reeves (2004) pointed out that "the federal law requires only that states use tests based upon their own academic content standards. Some states have embraced standards that are rich in analytical reasoning and complex thinking requirements." Some have not.

From the beginning, the act has had its proponents and detractors. Politicians typically have been strong supporters of the legislation, and many educators are among its most outspoken critics. Educational writer Gerald Bracey (2006) called it an "Orwellian double-speak program" even before it was voted into law. Many others simply tried to make it work.

But NCLB has made it both more and less difficult to personalize instruction: less difficult because the intent of the legislation is certainly good—to reach all students and enhance their learning skills, which only a personalized approach to instruction can achieve, and more difficult because NCLB is tied to high-stakes state testing with the following potential negative consequences (Smith, 1993):

- Loss of instructional time due to additional test preparation focus
- Narrowing of the curriculum because schools redefine course content to raise test scores
- Restricting the modes of instruction to more test-like strategies

- Diminishing teacher effectiveness because of undue pressure and invidious comparisons
- Harm to students without offsetting benefits, including stress, burn-out, misbehavior, and so on

Some studies have shown positive results under NCLB, especially in states where systemic renewal efforts have been initiated, but the Harvard University–based Civil Rights Project (CRP) released a study in 2006 that reported NCLB, in comparison with the findings of the National Assessment of Educational Progress (NAEP), had not improved reading and math achievement or reduced racial and poverty gaps. NCLB seems, in balance, to be another well-intentioned but flawed attempt to substitute testing for instruction.

We know quite a bit today about what makes schools exemplary and what makes instruction more successful. And we know that exemplary schools support exemplary learning environments. Deborah Meier (1998) has written extensively about the features of exemplary schools. She asserts that the foundations of school excellence are smallness, sufficient self-governance, and choice of alternatives. "It helps if schools are of a reasonable size, small enough for faculty members to sit around a table and iron things (such as standards) out, for everyone to be known well by everyone else, and for schools and families to collaborate face-to-face over time." It helps if the local school community has sufficient authority "to make decisions about staffing, leadership, and the full use of their budget as well as about the particulars of scheduling curriculum, pedagogy, and assessment." It also helps if schools can be sufficiently different from one another to provide choices for parents, students, and teachers.

We also know that the most promising schools target the quality of learning opportunities available to all students in the school by:

- Setting attainable goals with long time lines for accomplishing them
- Focusing explicitly on particular aspects of the curriculum and instructional practice while targeting professional development to these changes
- Putting in place a school-level process for considering changes in practice while refraining from making school governance the main preoccupation of the reform effort

- Encouraging collaborative engagement of staff members with one another and using professional development resources to further this end (Shields and Knapp, 1997)

In other words, exemplary schools set out deliberately to design or re-design themselves with an eye toward providing the most supportive learning environments for all their students. These schools are reasonable in size, have some control over staff, budget, and curriculum, with a shared vision and opportunities for professional development, workable communication and reward structures, good leadership and adequate resources, and a push for curricular and instructional renewal. They have committed teachers and engaged students. They have visionary cultures focused on student success.

Jerome Bruner said that "culture is probably biology's last great evolutionary trick. It frees *Homo sapiens* to construct a symbolic world flexible enough to meet local needs and to adapt to a myriad of ecological circumstances" (1998, p. 184). The best schools redesign themselves with teachers acting as guides and resources in a process of shared exploration with students who are active in thinking about their own learning and in planning and implementing their own projects. Bruner argues that this kind of learning requires the active construction of knowledge through social interaction—a culture of reflection, collaboration, and personalization.

Kenneth Sirotnik and John Goodlad cautioned us to think in terms of school "renewal" rather than "reform." Sirotnik (1999) wrote that reform is usually preoccupied with accountability rather than evaluation. Much of high-stakes reform, for example, is aimed at rewarding or punishing schools and educators. Renewal, on the other hand, urges a new accountability more akin to "responsibility." Goodlad pointed out that, "The language of reform carries with it the traditional connotations of things gone wrong that need to be corrected, as with delinquent boys or girls incarcerated in reform schools. This language is not uplifting. It says little or nothing about the nature of education, the self, or the human community. . . . School renewal is a much different game. . . . The language and the ethos of renewal have to do with the people in and around schools improving their practice and developing the collaborative mechanisms necessary to better their schools" (1999, pp. 574, 575).

Renewal is concerned primarily with what Sarason (1989) called "creating new settings" that reflect critical inquiry about educational practice. Renewal is all about learner growth in knowledge and self-awareness leading to wisdom, personal happiness, and collective responsibility.

Only a minority of schools achieve these kinds of reflective and exploratory environments. Most schools are average and are satisfied with maintaining or perhaps fine-tuning traditional school organizational patterns and pedagogy. Doing more is risky in many communities and requires long-range vision and above-average knowledge of learning theory and practice. Better to leave well enough alone.

But time marches on and the world changes. And it has changed dramatically from the time of the Second World War. We have gone from a late industrial era to an information era to the beginnings of a McLuhanesque global village. If lagging schools in the inner cities and poor rural areas are to rescue their students from the relatively permanent "underclass" of society, and average schools (the majority) are to improve, and good schools are to move to a higher level, personalization of instruction and learning must become a local, state, and even national priority.

The school learning process is an interaction of three elements: (1) student prior knowledge, style, and engagement; (2) teacher competence, style, and commitment; and (3) the organization of the learning environment. *Personalization of instruction and learning is the effort on the part of a school to take into account individual student characteristics and needs, and flexible instructional practices in organizing the learning environment.* Teachers committed to personalizing instruction help their students develop personal learning plans, assist in diagnosing their cognitive strengths and weaknesses and learning style characteristics, help adapt the learning environment and instruction to learner needs and interests, and mentor authentic and reflective learning experiences for their students.

There are an increasing number of elementary, middle, and secondary schools—both public and private—that are working assiduously to redesign themselves for the challenges of the twenty-first century. In this book, we discuss the types of school environments and the organizational, pedagogical, and evaluative strategies that can encourage and support the personalization of instruction and learning in schools of the new millennium.

❶

THE SCHOOL
LEARNING ENVIRONMENT

When a school is really successful, how can we know that it prepares all of its students appropriately for subsequent schooling and/or for adult life? Too often, schools with fine reputations merely have the best teachers and advantaged students. Nor are standardized test scores really much help. In addition to a high correlation with socioeconomic status, test scores do not predict what students will achieve in real life.

What makes for a good school? Deborah Meier (1992), former principal of the Central Park East Secondary School in New York's inner city of East Harlem, said that it starts with teachers. Teachers must exhibit a self-conscious reflectiveness about their own learning, a sympathy and appreciation for others, a desire for collaborative work, an urge to have others share their interests, and a great deal of perseverance and commitment to getting the job done. Meier also thinks that a good school is one: (1) where everyone feels safe; (2) where people know you (hence, small in size and scale); (3) where teachers are experts and coaches but not judges and juries; (4) where students are able to make sense of things (making meaning of life's puzzles); and (5) where learning is social and interactive.

Talk and reflection are at the heart of this kind of school, the kind of conversation that seems hardly to exist in many schools. Good schools favor dialogue and discussion among students and among teachers—a give and take about ideas and issues, books and films, reality and fantasy—about life itself.

Such a school is a different kind of place from most schools that we know. The corridors and bulletin boards and display cases are filled with student work and projects. Administrators and teachers are friendly and supportive, clearly partners and guides for their students. The learning spaces are purposeful and suited to the task. The desks or tables are rarely arranged in rows, but systematically, either for private work or groups, depending on the activity. The students are friendly and interactive, involved in doing things—not listening to or watching others. They are more often in groups, or twos or threes, only occasionally alone. They are engaged in discussions, cooperative small groups, project work, writing, producing things, and in serious research. These are schools with very different cultures and learning environments than typical institutions. They are places for learning and growing.

NEW SCHOOL CULTURE

Culture is the way people or institutions do things and the ways they learn to do them. Geertz (1973) called culture a system of meaning encompassing the beliefs, rituals, and ceremonies of a particular group of people. Culture is what people believe guides their way of life and their actions. In the natural environment, to survive, humans must provide for their material, emotional, and intellectual needs. These are satisfied by a culture, a complex system that includes tools, language, arts, and beliefs. Cultures vary because they must be compatible with their supporting environments. Thus, different climates, terrains, and sources of food evoke different cultural responses.

School culture is described by Stolp and Smith (1995) as "historically transmitted patterns of meaning that include the norms, values, beliefs, traditions, and myths understood, maybe in varying degrees, by members of the school community." These and other authors maintain that the concept of culture is very important to educational reform. Usually organizational factors, such as block scheduling or site-based management or performance assessment, are the focus of reform, not culture and its best measures: climate and satisfaction. Climate measures how groups of people *in general* view a culture—their perceptions of various aspects of an organization and its members. Satisfaction measures how *individuals* view their own *personal* places in the culture.

Culture is "the key to administrative practice and organizational improvement" (Cunningham & Gresso, 1993). "What we have learned from a long history of structural change is that it does not work! . . . Structure should not be used to change organizational performance and effectiveness. It should be vice versa—focus on the culture of excellence and the structures will evolve to support the culture." For the past forty years, educators have been concentrated on modifying the structures of schooling, the staffing and schedules, the buildings and programs, with only modest success. But the traditional culture of schools has been quite resilient. It has resisted piecemeal tampering and even comprehensive change efforts when the initial focus of change ignored its pervasive influence. *To change the traditional ways of schooling, educators must concentrate on the cultures of schools first and deal with the organizational issues later.*

Supportive school cultures are distinguished by common practices and subcultures that encourage a learning community in the school (Keefe & Jenkins, 1997). Common practice in these schools supports mutual respect, caring, integrity, equity, and academic excellence. All cultural subgroups support the mission, goals, and preferred learning environment of the school. All rituals and ceremonies of the school reinforce respect for each individual and the value of learning.

Cunningham and Gresso (1993) proposed a list of correlates of effective school culture derived from the Danforth Foundation's School Administrators Fellowship Program. These basic tenets have enabled schools and districts to develop effective and efficient cultures and to mount appropriate structures and programs.

- The Vertical slice: Individuals across all levels of a district or school form a *team* that meets regularly to communicate about differing values, views, and issues. The team "slices" across all the horizontal cultures that exist in the organization (i.e., board members, administrators, teachers, students, parents, community members, etc.).

- Vision, not deficiencies: The team focuses on what the district or school *should be* like (the design) and *not* on the problems and deficiencies (a deficit model).
- Collegial relationships: Team members develop a sense of community—a learning community—and learn to trust one another on the way to creating a learning organization in the district or school.
- Trust and support: A sense of community depends on team members striving to trust and support one another in their mutual quest.
- Values and interest, not power and position: Team members put aside personal desires for power and "winning," and concentrate on dialogue toward common values and goals.
- Access to quality information: An efficient common culture is built on ready access to accurate information so that the group can make sound enabling decisions and help individuals improve their performance.
- Broad participation: The culture is strengthened when everyone participates and adds their strengths to the emerging whole ("the whole is greater than its parts").
- Lifelong growth: The culture encourages individuals to redefine themselves—to engage in a process of personal inquiry and development.
- Individual empowerment: The culture empowers individuals to pursue personal mastery in support of the emerging organizational design or redesign.
- Continuous and sustained innovation: Pursuing a common vision and realizing a new school design demands a long time line and a commitment to substantial improvement. Changing districts or schools is a continuing process, not a short-term project.

If a school's culture is to support comprehensive and long-term redesign, it must first regenerate itself as a learning organization through reflective dialogue, improved communication among all cooperating members, and new relationships that help all individuals cooperate and grow.

Sergiovanni (1987) reminded us that "all schools have cultures, but successful schools seem to have strong and functional cultures aligned with a vision of quality schooling. Culture serves as a compass setting to steer people in a common direction . . . but the shaping and establishment of such a culture doesn't just happen. It is, instead, a negotiated product of the shared sentiments of school participants" (p. 59). Unfortunately, this product is not easy to achieve and flies in the face of much of what we know about actual school environments. Recent organizational theorists describe schools as "organizational anarchies" (Cohen, March, & Olsen, 1972) or "loosely coupled" organizations (Weick, 1982). Conventional wisdom sees schools as self-correcting rational systems, with goal consensus, ample resources, good information dissemination, and predictable problems and solutions. In fact, *none* of these conditions is typical. Most schools are not unified organisms, but are loose collections of parallel systems, frequently operating on their own. A unified culture must be developed, with administrators providing the "glue" and a school design team providing the vehicle (Keefe & Howard, 1997).

TYPES OF LEARNING ENVIRONMENTS

At the beginning of the twentieth century, educators were particularly concerned with individual differences among learners. Theorists, researchers, and practitioners all focused on measuring and understanding group and individual intelligence, student abilities, personality traits, and vocational aptitudes and interests. By the early 1930s, a large body of knowledge emerged on individual differences and learning. Apart from early studies on theories of learning and personality, however, little attention was paid to the study of learning environments. The logical step was to determine the relationship between individual learning characteristics and the nature of the learning environment.

In 1936, Kurt Lewin postulated that all human beings operate in a "life space" and that all behavior is a function of the person (P) and the environment (E). His simple and elegant equation, $B = f(P, E)$, argued that individual differences in behavior are a result of the interaction of persons with the environment and that behavior can best be understood by investigating these interactions and the relative contributions of different variables to them. To explain how individuals behave and learn, then, we must study the characteristics of individual persons in interaction with the environment.

We can easily extend Lewin's equation to include the primary factors in learning and instruction. The personal characteristics most pertinent to the equation are the student's prior learning history (existing knowledge and skills), learner style (how he or she learns and prefers to learn), and learner engagement (motivation to learn and persistence). Primary environmental variables include teacher competence, style (especially flexibility), and commitment, as well as the quality and flexibility of the learning environment itself.

The key here is the person–environment interaction. When the match between student and learning environment is a good one, learning is facilitated. Most American classrooms are heterogeneous situations with many students and a mix of aptitudes. A match is not easily achieved with so many individuals. The teacher must strive for alternative paths.

Three general organizational patterns have shaped the learning environments of American schools during the past century. The *traditional* pattern has been the dominant pattern and still influences much of what goes on in American elementary, middle, and secondary classrooms. *Transitional* and *interactive* patterns have become more common during the most recent three decades.

Traditional Environments

The organizational pattern found most often in American schools is based on nineteenth-century factory models, scientific management theory, the behavioral research of Thorndike and Skinner, and the learning hierarchies of Gagne and Bloom. The focus is on uniform behavior, administrator and teacher control, and measurement. The behavioral approach stresses assessment (everything must be measured), specific objectives, curricular scope and sequence, explicit teaching and direct instruction, and reinforcement strategies of reward and punishment (Keefe & Jenkins, 1997). English and Hill (1990) describe this pattern as the "custodial school," with these features:

- The concept base is scientific management (efficiency and cost-effectiveness).
- The organization is hierarchical, from school board and superintendent, through the principal, to the teachers at the base.

- Communication is generally formal and one-way, with highly structured faculty and parent meetings.
- Decision making is autocratic with the superintendent and principal having the legal responsibility and final word.
- Teaching is talking, with teachers doing most of the talking and students in a passive or largely responsive role (listen, remember, and respond).
- The curriculum is subject discipline based, organized in separate fields, and textbook oriented (not all discipline-based curriculum, of course, is necessarily traditional in organization).
- Accountability is external and rigid, with quiet classrooms, orderly hallways, strict student discipline, and efficient school buildings.

The classroom scene is familiar. Egg-crate classrooms and desks lined up in neat rows. Students face the teacher, organized, very likely, in alphabetical order. The teacher talks and talks and talks. Or the teacher asks questions and the students try to give the answer the teacher has in mind. Or the students work quietly on seatwork under the watchful eye of the teacher. The teacher's desk and the chalkboard are the center of attention. The bulletin board has a commercial display, not student work. There are few resources except textbooks. The students are orderly and passive. The teacher is in control. Little real interaction takes place—the kind of discussion or dialogue or probing questions and thoughtful answers that get to the core of issues and problems.

Various attempts have been made throughout this century to change or modify this dominant pattern, but usually back-to-basics (over)reactions have forced schools back into familiar practices. Some schools however, have broken the barrier.

Transitional Environments

Since the 1930s, many schools have attempted to restructure: to provide a more flexible curriculum (as in the Eight-Year Study), or to better meet the needs of large urban populations (as in the Effective Schools Movement), or simply to provide a more responsive learning environment for today's children (as in Individually Guided Education). The intent usually has been to *modify* the existing behaviorist pattern of traditional schooling. The stimulus has been a growing concern for the needs of immigrant children, or low achievement among minority youth, or the results of new research.

English and Hill (1990) characterize the transitional environment as the "effective school" and list these features:

- The concept base is school effectiveness research.
- The organization is consultative with the principal and an advisory cabinet relating to individual teachers.
- Communication is one-way (leader initiated), but with more feedback and discussion.
- Decision making is consultative with the leadership team making final decisions and informing others.
- Teaching is "effective telling," with large group, small group, and other appropriate interventions for student mastery.
- The curriculum is objectives-based, retaining separate subject fields, but with mastery standards.
- Accountability is more objective, based on indicators of school effectiveness (e.g., improved standardized test scores, better attendance, fewer dropouts).

The transitional school environment may reflect organizational changes, instructional changes, or both. Mastery learning (Bloom, 1984) is a well-known instructional approach that is anchored in behaviorism, but attempts to modify the lockstep procedures of the traditional classroom. It takes the form of either: (1) *individualized instruction* based on the premise of continuous progress through a sequence of planned units (or workbooks) geared to mastery criteria or (2) *group-based mastery learning* employing short daily units, teaching to lesson objectives, pretest, retest, and posttest assessment, and re-teaching and correctives as necessary. Both approaches are teacher-managed and involve the use of reinforcement strategies and monitoring of student work. Units are teacher-planned and directed. Flexibility comes with continuous progress (the pacing element) in individualized instruction and re-teaching/correctives in both individualized and group approaches. The learning environment is notably changed but rarely interactive and authentic (characterized by higher-order thinking, deep knowledge, substantive conversations, or real-world connections).

The research base for both individualized instruction and group-based mastery learning is impressive. Various meta-analyses from the 1970s and 1980s consistently found positive results (Ellis & Fouts, 1993). Bloom's research showed that group mastery learning regularly produced a strong effect size of 1.0 (one standard deviation). It seems that this modified behaviorist approach is successful if raising student test scores is a major goal.

The effective schools movement is another transitional approach based on the so-called effective schools research of the 1970s and 1980s. This research defined school effectiveness in terms of high test scores and good attendance and completion rates, and rated school success according to these criteria. Edmonds' (1982) listing—principal leadership, academic focus, orderly and safe climate, teacher expectations for student mastery, and program evaluation based on measures of student achievement—is typical of the factors important to the approach.

This research spawned a movement that recommended lists of effective school characteristics as templates for school improvement, particularly in troubled urban schools. Lezotte and Bancroft (1985) summarized the most common attributes of the movement:

- Focusing on the individual school as the unit for improvement
- Using a building-based improvement team of administrators and teachers
- Adopting a long-term orientation (3–5 years) for planning and implementation
- Organizing according to the concepts of effective schools research
- Accepting as basic assumptions the importance of student outcomes and the primacy of academic learning

The effective schools programs were concerned primarily with how a school was organized, and how changes would be monitored and assessed. Much of the research is descriptive and exploratory, concerned with comparing school test scores with leadership, curricular, and instructional characteristics. Case studies and program evaluations typically detail how changes have been implemented and how schools have changed. Controlled studies are lacking. But the movement has helped many schools to review their organization and structure and to make significant changes in their school and classroom environments.

Ellis and Fouts (1993) noted that the effective schools movement has "its roots in the efficiency movement, which first appeared in American school literature coincident with the rise of industrialism. One could safely exchange the word 'efficient' for the word 'effective' with little loss of meaning. Its main attraction seems to be the compelling correlation between high test scores (which everybody wants) and certain lists of characteristics" (p. 86). The movement failed to move schools toward the authentic and reflective environments that the new century seems to demand.

Interactive Environments

We use the term "interactive" to describe school environments that are communities of learning characterized by reflective and thematic curricular organization, authentic pedagogy and assessment, and personalized instruction. A small number of schools have been working by design for the past two decades to achieve these learning environments. English and Hill (1990) described this pattern as the "restructured school." Some of the features they assign to this pattern include:

- The concept base is school-as-a-learning-organization, a "Theory Z" approach.
- The organization is participative with a leadership/design team linked to teaching teams, school committees, and community organizations.
- Communication is two-way: vertically for policy and horizontally for consultation.
- Decision making is collaborative, with decisions made at the appropriate level of implementation and with feedback to all those involved.
- Teaching is guiding, telling, showing, intervening, and coaching.
- The curriculum is core-based, but thematic to encourage reflective problem solving; it may be discipline based (rather than interdisciplinary), but organized around essential or generative questions.
- Accountability is performance based, geared to learner effectiveness criteria (e.g., mastery of skills; social or community service or participation; career preparation).

Interactive environments may incorporate behaviorist or cognitive paradigms of instruction. We have already mentioned some of the most effective behaviorist practices. Cognitive approaches (developmental and apprenticeship) began to have a greater influence on instructional practice in the 1970s. Cognitive developmental models emphasize the complexity of learning, the need for meaning and understanding, holistic learning environments with long-term projects, and performance assessment. The essence of the developmental model is a learning environment designed to involve students and teachers in a total learning experience. "Cognitive apprenticeship models marry the principles of John Dewey's laboratory school and contemporary computer learning with the craft apprenticeship. Experts and novices collaborate on common projects. The experts (teachers) show the novices (students) what to do" (Keefe & Jenkins, 1997, p. 41). In a cognitive apprenticeship, teachers share their thinking and decision-making processes with their students, mentoring, admitting mistakes, and even beginning again if needed. The activities gradually become longer and harder as students evidence the capability. Assessment is talking about what has happened.

Interactive schools and environments are different. Interactive primary classrooms are packed with learning materials, not just textbooks, but children's books, blocks, construction paper, paints, rocks, and various theater props (Wood, 1992). Middle and high schools have multiple print and nonprint resources, tools of learning like audio-visual and computer equipment, cameras and art objects, science equipment, and many kinds of hands-on manipulatives. The learning spaces are flexible but purposive. Tables and perhaps desks are arranged by task for small groups or learning stations or research/independent study. There may be open space for a wide variety of activities and dedicated spaces for small group or for subject area or thematic resource centers. Teachers and students work together on real products.

Wood (1992) describes experiences in schools with interactive learning environments:

> Observe the work going on. It is seldom quiet and not often teacher-centered either. Children are doing things, not just watching someone else.

These are schools where learning is not a spectator sport. You will find class meetings going on, with kids planning the next class project or working out class rules. They are more likely to be working in groups than alone, collaborating to solve a difficult math problem or gathering historical information for a presentation. They are busy writing their own books, newsletters, and newspapers, or producing their own videotapes. Or they are very carefully putting the finishing touches on the next display for public consumption of what they have learned about houses, trees, the solar systems, Steinbeck, geometric equations, or the Constitution. (p. xv)

These schools and classrooms are ones that make learning come alive. Kids can't wait to get in them, often arriving well before school to begin project work or to seek help from a teacher. And they are places that no one is in a hurry to leave at the end of the day.

These places are more likely to be elementary schools and classrooms than middle or high schools. They can be found all over the country, indeed all over North America, in all kinds of communities. They are not in large number, but they are on the increase. Generally, they are not part of national reform projects, but some are. And, they can be found in large urban centers and poor rural communities as well as in "average" places. They offer no uniform or routinized solutions to school improvement. They are often unique. But, they can be imitated or at least what they have accomplished can be adapted to other circumstances. Wood (1992) likens them to laboratories rather than the museums that many traditional schools have become.

How can you recognize them? Wood (1992) again suggests that you look around in a school or classroom and ask yourself a few pertinent questions:

- Is the focus of attention the teacher's desk or places where students work?
- Is the room set up for just whole-group activity or for a variety of tasks?
- Whose space is it—the teacher's, dominated by his or her work, or the students', with their work proudly on display?
- What can you do with the "stuff" in the room—just look at it, or touch it, move it, use it to find out something new?

Interactive schools focus on active learning and a climate of reflection and collaboration. They are student-oriented environments. They are spaces for personalized instruction and learning (pp. 131–132).

SYSTEMS THINKING

An optimal learning environment must be both fluid and well organized if it is to make best use of the limited time available each day for formal schooling. Systems thinking can provide the template for this design. A system is a group of parts that operate together and influence the operation of the whole. Deming (1993) called a system "a network of independent components that work together to accomplish the aim of the system. . . . A system must have an aim. Without an aim there is no system. The aim must be clear to everyone in the system. . . . Optimization is a process of orchestrating the efforts of all components towards the achievement of the stated aim. . . . Anything less than optimization of the whole system will bring eventual loss to every component of the system."

The essential characteristics of a system are properties of the whole and not of the individual parts. Human bodies are systems. A building is a system. An automobile is a system. "The essential property of an automobile is that it can take us from one place to another. No single part of an automobile—a wheel, an axle, a carburetor—can do that. Once we take a system apart, it loses that fundamental characteristic. If we were to dissemble a car, even if we kept every single piece, we would no longer have a car. Why? *Because the automobile is not the sum of its parts; it is the product of their interactions*" (Wardman, 1994, p. 2; emphasis in original).

Schools can be like that. If you analyze the elements of many schools, you may find that they do not fit together very well. They are merely loose collections of parts that do not really mesh. They were never designed to work together. They just *happened* that way because of long tradition and periodic addition or subtraction of components. Schools, like all systems, operate according to the first principle of systems thinking: *structure influences behavior*. A system functions in a certain way because of its structure. In a very real sense, a system causes its own behavior. Conventional schools function in traditional ways because their system components make it hard to do otherwise. Their systemic structure is the pattern of interactions—the relationships—not among people, but among the key components of the school organization (Keefe & Jenkins, 1997). Urban schools, for example, are thought to be the victims of poor teachers and unruly students, but the reality is that the structures and processes of these schools do not support learning for their particular students. The schools are frequently dysfunctional, not the students or the teachers.

Hamilton and Zelden (1987) argued that a system differs from a mere program. An interactive learning environment, for example, is more than a series of programs or projects. It is an integrated enterprise. These authors describe a system as:

- Inclusive—providing a place for everyone who needs one
- Comprehensive—addressing a full range of issues
- Integrated internally—linking its internal components closely (i.e., curriculum, instruction, schedule, building organization, and student services)
- Connected externally—building external communication linkages and working relationships with community, business, and political agencies outside the school
- Comprehensible—capable of being understood and utilized with the help of appropriate facilitators and advisers

The medium of systems thinking is *synthesis*, not analysis. The purpose of analysis is to take things apart, to see *how* it works, to fix whatever might not be working. Synthesis is the exact opposite. Synthesis first attempts to identify the larger system, then to understand it as a whole, and only then to break down the understanding of the whole in order to understand the relationship and functioning of the parts to the whole. Synthesis reveals *why* a system works the way that it does. "The automobile, for example, was originally developed for six passengers. But no amount of analysis will help you find out why. The answer lies in the fact that cars were designed for the average American family, which happened to be 5.6 at the time. Cars are now smaller because the average family size is 3.2" (Wardman, 1994, p. 3).

School aims today are defined in mission and vision statements and in student outcome statements. Historically, school aims were outlined in statements of philosophy, purpose, and goals and objectives. The aims of public schooling at the turn of the twentieth century were to socialize and provide basic skills training for scores of immigrants, using factory-line technology to produce standard products. Teachers were the workers; students, the products.

> Based on faith in rationalistic management, in the power of rules to direct human behavior, and in the ability of administrators to discover and implement common procedures to produce desired outcomes, twentieth-century education policy has assumed that continually improving the design specifications for schoolwork—required courses, textbooks, testing instruments, and management systems—will lead to student learning. Knowledgeable teachers were not part of the equation because the bureaucratic model assumed that important decisions would be made by others in the hierarchy and handed down in the form of rules and curriculum packages. (Darling-Hammond, 1997, pp. 16–17)

One could argue that such schools were functional 100 years ago, but the circumstances for which they were designed no longer exist today. Yet, many contemporary schools still operate according to this design. And because structure influences behavior, many of these schools are highly dysfunctional in the contemporary environment. The old factory metaphor saw teaching as the transmission of organized knowledge ("just give me the facts"), the curriculum as a delivery system, and the core functions of teaching as lecturing, questioning, giving assignments and homework, correcting papers and giving tests, awarding grades, and so forth. Peel and McCary (1997) argued that a more functional metaphor for the contemporary school is a "knowledge-work organization." Under this conceptualization, teaching involves presenting students with opportunities to do high-quality work. Teaching provides information but also ways to apply it to relevant tasks. Learning is an active process, beginning with basic skills, but leading to effective problem solving, productive teamwork, and the skills of lifelong learning. Peel and McCary see teachers in this kind of system as: (1) designers of high-quality work, (2) decision makers, (3) facilitators, and (4) performance coaches. Students are workers and learning apprentices. They engage in active learning geared to creating intellectual or physical products like those of adults in the "real world."

Conceptualizing the school as a knowledge-work organization invokes a new systems design for schooling, one better suited to the needs of twenty-first-century students. Because the structure is very different, a school as a knowledge-work system encourages teachers to act very differently:

- To design work for students that will capture their interest and motivate them to persevere if they do not have immediate success
- To assist students in decision making with suitable tasks, successful solutions to problems, and appropriate timetables for the work to be performed
- To serve as facilitator and motivator of students, using their knowledge as subject matter experts, academic advisers, and personal mentors to suggest ways to complete the learning tasks
- To act as student performance coaches, demonstrating ways to improve learning and providing feedback so that students can judge and improve their own performance

Teaching and learning in a school designed as a knowledge-work system might well utilize a thematic curriculum organized around a core of essential ideas based on the realities of adult life. In the Francis W. Parker Charter Essential School (Parker Annual Report, 1996–1997), for example, the activities in all curricular domains are centered on an annual schoolwide "essential question," such as "What is community?" or "What is change?" While reading and writing about Steinbeck's *The Pearl* and McCullers' *Member of the Wedding,* Parker students recently proceeded from investigating personal change to documenting change over time in a particular object, then to a case study of South Africa, and finally to reading and analyzing Sophocles' *Antigone* for ways in which individuals can bring about change in society. This junior-senior high school's 1996–1997 science and math curriculum focused on an integrated approach to physics and applied science, studying motion and forces, electricity, and optics, with "math challenge of the week" problems linked to the science topics. Spanish classes emphasized communication skills, cross-cultural comparisons, and the "immigrant experience." Teaching at Parker is an authentic, reflective, and challenging experience concerned with higher-order thinking, deep rather than superficial knowledge, substantive conversation among teachers and students, and connections to the world beyond the classroom. Teachers are encouraged and expected to participate in a learning community that emphasizes collaboration with colleagues, parents, students', and the wider community in setting school standards and norms, assessing student progress, and pursuing school improvement.

In a conversation with *Educational Leadership* editor John O'Neil (1995), learning organization guru Peter Senge said, "Significant changes in the process and content of education require coordinated efforts throughout the school: you cannot implement 'learner-directed learning,' for example, in one classroom and not others . . . . So there's absolutely no choice but trying to create change on multiple levels . . . . You have to be working simultaneously to create a totally different environment in the classroom, in the school, in the school system, and eventually with the community. And that's why it's not easy" (p. 21). Such a comprehensive change process requires a systems approach to school design or redesign. Keefe and Howard (1997) proposed an 11-stage design process for the total school beginning with specifications for three *basic* design components—mission and vision statements, school culture and climate statements, and a student outcomes statement. The school design/redesign is then fleshed out in specifications for eight *systems* components—curriculum; instructional programs and instructional techniques; school structure and organization; school leadership, management, and budgeting; school staffing and staff development; communication and political structures; school resources, physical plant, and equipment; and an evaluation plan. These eight components provide a template for the design of any school and define a systematic plan for developing a desirable school of the future—the school that a local learning community deems necessary for the growth of its students.

PERSONALIZATION

The earliest formal use of the term "personalized" can be found in the Personalized System of Instruction (PSI) introduced in 1962 by Fred S. Keller,

J. Gilmore Sherman, and two other psychologists at the University of Brasilia. Many universities still use the method, but now more often in group-based or computer-aided variations. The method was first reported by Keller (1968) in the first issue of *The Journal of Applied Behavior Analysis*. PSI is a neo-behaviorist, systems-based approach to instruction, designed to utilize what was then known about the relationship between student behavior, the environment, and reinforcement theory. In Keller's words, "those features which seem to distinguish [PSI] from conventional teaching procedures are:

1. The go-at-your-own-pace feature, *which permits a student to move through the course at a speed commensurate with his ability and other demands upon his time.*
2. The unit-perfection requirement for advance, *which lets the student go ahead to new material only after demonstrating mastery of that which preceded.*
3. The use of lectures and demonstrations as vehicles of motivation, *rather than sources of critical information.*
4. The *related stress* upon the written word *in teacher-student communications.*
5. The use of proctors, *which permits repeated testing, immediate scoring, almost unavoidable tutoring, and a marked enhancement of the personal-social aspect of the educational process."* (1968, p. 83; italics in original)

PSI is based on behaviorist principles of operant conditioning such as reinforcement, shaping, and fading. Clark (1999) described PSI in this way: "It is composed of small self-paced modularized units of instructions where study guides direct learners through the modules. Unit tests are given on each module where learners must show mastery by scoring at least a 90%. PSI combines 'mastery learning' with principles of reinforcement theory." Student proctors are used to help with individual problems and lectures are given for motivational problems only. Kulik, Kulik, and Cohen (1979, 1990) found—in meta-analyses of more than 300 studies reported over 25 years of the outcomes of many different methods of instruction—that PSI is superior to other forms of instruction, not just to other behaviorist forms.

PSI was a landmark in the development of personalization. More behaviorist than its contemporary successors and subject to the noncomputerized workload problems of its era, it unmistakably moved the focus in education from the teacher to the student. It shifted the emphasis from rigid group processing of instruction to self-pacing, and set the stage for more personal contact between mentors and their charges and a truly performance-based approach to student assessment and progress reporting. Individualized instruction and direct instruction are its direct descendants. The National Association of Secondary School Principals (NASSP) Model Schools Project used a variation of PSI as its instructional model from 1969 to 1974.

In the mid-1970s, University of Denver special educator Anne Welch Carroll proposed a new look at the relationship between general and special education. Her solution was "Personalized Education," an instructional philosophy and a set of strategies based on ecological theory, Piaget's concepts of assimilation and accommodation, and Festinger's theory of cognitive dissonance. Ecological theory argues for the integration of the individual and the environment; teacher, student, and environment interact as a whole. Piaget contends that this relationship is reciprocal. The student is both reactor and contributor to his or her own learning process. If a student cannot learn within a given environment nor adapt to its requirements, the environment will produce inappropriate consequences for the student. Festinger warns that if the environment is too demanding, the student will embrace "dissonance reduction." If the environment pushes too hard, the student will try to slow down or block the input (Carroll, 1975).

Carroll proposed three broad characteristics of a personalized approach to education.

1. *The learner must be actively involved.* The learner must be engaged in the production of knowledge, not just passively absorbing information from the teacher or other sources. Students must be involved in the planning of instruction, the goals and objectives of the program or project, the learning activities, the assessment of progress, and in opportunities for relearning when progress is slow.
2. *The teacher must be a learning facilitator.* The teacher in a personalized approach is not so much presenter as troubleshooter—a

resource person, a mentor, and a guide to the novice learner. This kind of teacher spends less time lecturing to a classroom of students and more time working with learners in small groups or individually. The teacher's focus is on student development, motivation, and success.

3. *A student's program must be success-oriented.* Personalized instruction builds on the child's strengths, with real skill development that enhances cognitive deficiencies so that the learner can experience satisfaction and success. The system engages both students and teachers in working together toward mutually agreed upon and productive goals.

Carroll's approach to personalized education helped students attain a sense of balance in the learning environment between what is challenging and productive and what is beyond the student's present capabilities. Her approach moved personalization away from the behavioral and toward the cognitive dimension. It is still very much representative of best practice in special education today.

In the mid-1970s, NASSP Model Schools Project principal and later NASSP director of research James W. Keefe formulated a systematic model of personalization for the Learning Environments Consortium International. Keefe's model fleshed out the paradigm of diagnosis, prescription, instruction, and evaluation (DPIE) used in the Model Schools Project and later adopted by LEC International. This expansion of the DPIE model was a bridge between earlier behavioral systems and newer strategies arising from cognitive psychology. Keefe's model of personalized education begins with what is known about the learner and builds the learning environment on learner needs and interests.

Personalization under the Keefe model is still employed by LEC International (with refinements to be detailed later) and is widely used in self-directed Canadian schools. Many of the elements of NASSP's 1996 report, *Breaking Ranks: Changing an American Institution*—although with some different names—are derived from NASSP's Model Schools Project and the Keefe/LEC model of personalization. Moreover, in the first edition of this book, Keefe and John Jenkins (2000), both former NASSP Model Schools Project principals, published an update of the LEC personalized education model focusing specifically on its instructional component.

Along with LEC International, the Coalition of Essential Schools spearheaded personalization through the final decades of the twentieth century and beyond. The Coalition's Common Principles developed by its founder, Theodore R. Sizer, require that "teaching and learning should be personalized to the maximum extent possible." The Coalition attempted to combine the rigor of serious learning with the kinds of structure and strategies that really engage children and young people. It emphasized student intellectual development, essential knowledge and skills, student-as-worker and teacher-as-coach, demonstration of student mastery by "exhibition" (standards-based product or performance), and, of course, personalization of teaching and learning.

In 1996, NASSP put its considerable weight behind the movement for personalization. In that year it released a report entitled *Breaking Ranks: Changing an American Institution*, which proposed that American high schools commit themselves to substantive renewal guided by six main themes and 13 interrelated sets of recommendations. These recommendations included those dealing with: (1) priorities for renewal, (2) a school's web of support, and (3) leadership. First among the report's main themes is: "Personalization—High schools must break into units of no more than 600 students so that teachers and students can get to know each other better. Then, teachers should use a variety of instructional strategies that accommodate individual learning styles and engage students. This will be helped by every student having a Personal Adult Advocate and a Personal Plan for Progress" (NASSP, 1996, p. 5). Interspersed among the recommendations are 16 dealing specifically with personalization.

NASSP followed this report with *Breaking Ranks II: Strategies for Leading High School Reform* (NASSP, 2004) in collaboration with the Education Alliance at Brown University and its Center for Secondary School Design. This second NASSP report offered a second definition of personalization, a "working definition linked to the *Breaking Ranks* call for a more student-centered, personalized experience in high schools:" Personalization is "a learning process in which schools help students assess their own talents and aspirations, plan a pathway toward their own purposes, work cooperatively with others on challenging tasks, maintain a record of their explorations, and demonstrate their learning against clear standards in a wide variety of media, all with the close support of adult mentors and guides" (Clark, 1991). This definition strongly reflects the Coalition of Essential Schools' emphasis on authentic assessment and accountability, but it also incorporates elements derived from earlier conceptualizations.

Breaking Ranks II focuses on student success and improved performance through the interaction of "three touchstones: (1) collaborative leadership and professional learning communities, (2) personalization of the learning environment, and (3) renewal of curriculum, instruction and assessment" (NASSP, 2004). *Breaking Ranks II* is a comprehensive handbook of strategies and school-site examples intended to flesh out the report's thirty-one core recommendations. Many of these recommendations require or imply aspects of personalization.

It is not our intent to examine the total redesign of schooling but only its instructional component and issues related to personalization. We will limit our discussion to instructional techniques and strategies that can be linked to a comprehensive plan of school design or redesign. We begin by summarizing several historical attempts to develop more personalized student learning environments.

EARLIER INITIATIVES

Various school renewal initiatives have been mounted over the past 100 years to provide a "child-centered," "humanistic," "individualized," or "personalized" approach to instruction and learning at the elementary, secondary, and college levels. The early history of modern education— from Johann Comenius (1592–1670) through Jean Jacques Rousseau (1712–1728), Johann Pestalozzi (1746–1827), and Fredrich Froebel (1782–1852)—saw more and more insistent attempts to portray knowledge as dynamic (rather than changeless), education as personal growth, human nature as flexible, and learners as partners in the learning process. Nevertheless, as Tanner and Tanner (1990) pointed out, "Nineteenth-century educational reformers were concerned about time, sometimes years, spent by children in reviewing and repeating what they had studied before. It seemed that there was motion but not much progress." But, there were some notable exceptions.

John Dewey's Laboratory School

Francis Parker's Quincy System was the first in a series of nineteenth-century efforts to improve private and public schools. These new programs were as varied as their proponent's philosophies, but most contributed very little. Others proved to be of seminal value. Of particular interest were the laboratory schools connected with teacher-training institutions. The John Dewey Laboratory School was typical and perhaps the most significant of this group.

John Dewey (1859–1952) was a philosopher, psychologist, and educator at the University of Chicago and later at Columbia University. In 1896, two years after he came to the University of Chicago, Dewey opened an experimental school with the help of his wife. The school was guided by Dewey's educational theories and, in particular, by three general principles:

1. Instruction must concentrate on developing students' minds, not on subject matter.
2. Instruction must be project-oriented and integrated, not segmented into short units of time (i.e., 40 or 50 minutes per subject).
3. Curriculum must progress through the years of schooling from practical experiences (like gardening or cooking) to formal subjects (such as botany or homemaking) to integrated studies (such as agriculture or home economics).

In the Dewey school, projects were organized to stress hands-on activities, scientific processes (observing, analyzing, investigating, quantifying, and predicting), social cooperation, and exchange of ideas. Reading and writing were emphasized from the early days of schooling, and drill and practice were embedded in real tasks in language and mathematics. Formal instruction in the symbol systems was delayed until children could understand why it was needed. The curriculum was organized around occupations to encourage students to begin with what interested them and then to progress to more formal academic topics linked to their interests.

Dewey wanted creative new ways of communicating subject matter. His teachers describe discussion and field trips in their reports (innovations at that time), as well as class conversation, dramatizations and class readings, the study of pictures, and experimental work in science. The teachers were responsible for the selection of subject matter, the courses of study, the actual instruction, as well as the day-to-day conduct and administration of the school. Dewey (1900/1990) said that "the teachers started with question marks, rather than with fixed rules, and if any answers have been reached, it is the teachers in the school who have supplied them."

The John Dewey Laboratory School was committed to relating school to everyday life and involving teachers actively and continuously in devising curriculum and instructional strategies. The implications of his school for today's schools are straightforward, if difficult to realize. Laurel Tanner (1988) expresses it this way: "Opportunities to solve problems should be present throughout the curriculum. Students should be engaged in problem solving in the real sense, as opposed to mechanically using a model problem with model procedures." The concept behind the Dewey school was the idea of a school as a small cooperative society where children, with adult guidance, could solve problems at any stage of their development, and learn to become caring and knowledgeable adults (Tanner, 1997). Dewey (1900/1990) aptly sums up the purpose and value of his school in these words: "The everyday work of the school shows that children can live in a school as out of it, and yet grow daily in wisdom, kindness, and the spirit of obedience—that learning may, even with little children, lay hold upon the substance of truth that nourishes the spirit, and yet the forms of knowledge be observed and cultivated; and that growth may be genuine and thorough, and yet a delight" (pp. 177–178).

The Dewey school showed that subject matter could be of interest to children, that problem-solving activities and real-life projects could dominate a school curriculum, and that teachers and students could work together as collaborators in the educative process.

The NASSP Model Schools Project

Other attempts were made in the early twentieth century to change what Tyack and Cuban (1995) called the "basic grammar of schooling." Superintendent Jesse Newlon, for example, began an effort in Denver in the 1920s (persisting through the 1930s) to implement the Deweyan principles of relating school to everyday life and engaging teachers in actively developing school curriculum and instructional strategies. Progressive educators in many places criticized the domination of the high school curriculum by college entrance requirements. The Carnegie unit and graded schooling were challenged. The most significant effort early in this era was the Eight-Year Study (1933–1941) sponsored by the Progressive Education Association and bankrolled by the General Education Board and other foundations. Some 29 public and private high schools were freed from specific college entrance requirements in Carnegie units. Over time, they developed unique responses, with core curricular programs across departmental lines, teacher and student planning and decision making, more emphasis on progress in the arts and community service, and school scheduling and class-size variations. Students from Eight-Year Study schools did very well in college and, in many cases, better than students from conventional schools. Although the intervention of World War II and the subsequent cold war muted wide dissemination and application of the findings of the study, participants agreed that a new grammar of schooling was sustainable and could be more successful than traditional forms.

These and other initiatives spurred a group of influential organizations in the 1960s to work "to overthrow the Carnegie unit, the egg-crate classroom, the teacher-dominated traditional curriculum, passive styles of learning, and the isolation of teachers from each other" (Tyack & Cuban, 1995). The Ford Foundation provided millions of grant dollars to "lighthouse schools," beginning in the 1960s. In 1968, the National Association of Secondary School Principals (NASSP) and its Associate Secretary for Research and Development, J. Lloyd Trump, received a major grant of $1.03 million from the Danforth Foundation for a Model Schools Project to develop "schools of the future"—"high schools of tomorrow."

Trump (with Dorsey Baynham) had published a *Guide to Better Schools: Focus on Change* in 1961 to outline the recommendations of the NASSP Commission on the Experimental Study of the Utilization of the Staff in the Secondary School. These Staff Utilization Studies and a subsequent Administrative Internship program served as the research base for the Model Schools Project. The Staff Utilization Studies, for example, reported the results of experiments in 100 junior and senior high schools in many parts of the United States.

The Model Schools Project (1969–1974) proposed a total change in the school learning environment, a gestalt of change that included a differentiated school staff of teachers and aides, new roles for teachers and students, individualized student scheduling and evaluation, a nongraded "continuous progress" curriculum, and resource centers offering a variety of print and nonprint learning materials and activities. Thirty-four (ultimately 36 with new entrees) public and private schools in the United States and Canada, both middle/junior and senior high schools, attempted to make a major change in the grammar of schooling. The most basic goal of the project was "to provide a program with varied strategies and environments for learning through which all pupils, regardless of differences in individual talents and interests, may proceed with gains" (Trump, 1970, p. 109). The project mandated three modes of learning—large group presentation, small group discussion, and independent study—and continuous contact with eight or nine areas of learning. Each student's schedule was individualized with assistance from teacher advisers and subject-area teachers. The curriculum was organized in units and designed in learning packets/guides to provide for continuous progress. Learning resources referenced in the packets included performance objectives, books, articles, pamphlets, audio-visual materials, hands-on activities, community and work experiences, and self-, pre-, and posttests.

Individualized student learning leaned heavily on up to 22 hours of independent study each week using the self-paced learning packets. All students participated in large group and small group activities each week in each major area of learning, but spent a majority of their time working alone or with a few others in independent study. They proceeded at their own pace and chosen level of difficulty—*basic* (general program), *desirable* (college prep or vocational), or *enriching* (advanced placement, honors, International Baccalaureate). They began each year, and whenever necessary after that, by goal-setting and planning their programs with their chosen teacher advisers. Subject-area teachers acted as consultants and facilitators in each department resource center. Students tested on each unit only when they were ready. Grading was based on absolute performance standards, not on comparisons with the group. All students had to be scheduled somewhere at all times and attendance was regularly checked and reported. Students could graduate early, on time, or late depending on their maturity, commitment, and progress.

The Model Schools Project schools were variously successful in implementing the total model and in making a significant difference in the learning of individual students. Almost half of the original group failed to complete the project and only about 10 schools were highly successful. The most notable long-term success story was Bishop Carroll High School of Calgary, Alberta—a school still representative of the original "model," and one of Canada's most prestigious secondary institutions. Most of the other successful schools fell victim to administrative and/or teacher turnover. The project did not achieve the major impact on secondary education that was expected in the 1970s and beyond because of a "back-to-basics" backlash at that time and subsequent waves of reform under such mottoes as "excellence" and "quality."

The Model Schools Project clearly advanced the goal and framework of personalization. Schools found ways to increase flexibility and moved away from many of the traditional locksteps. Students achieved at least as well and often better than their traditional counterparts. Both gifted and challenged students benefited from appropriate programs. Choice and responsibility were well served. Trump (1977) put it this way: "Any school program is personalized to the extent that every student has opportunities with guidance to explore potential interests and talents in all areas of human knowledge and activities." The Model Schools Project set new standards for subsequent efforts to renew the school environment more suitably for all kinds of students with diverse needs and interests.

CONTEMPORARY INITIATIVES

The past 35 years have seen waves of restructuring movements (and counter-movements) from Competency-based Education and the Effective Schools Movement in the 1970s and 1980s to Outcomes-based Education and Quality Schools of the 1980s and 1990s. We discuss two influential initiatives from 1970 to the present. Both are important for their philosophical and practical frameworks and their impact on personalized instruction. One started out as small regional network of schools in the western part of the United States and Canada. The other is a large national coalition of schools representing every part of the United States.

Learning Environments Consortium International

Five of the most successful schools in the Model Schools Project formed a private, voluntary, and nonprofit follow-up in 1974 under the presidency of William D. Georgiades, the associate director of the Model Schools Project. This collaborative, called the Learning Environments Consortium International (LEC), initially limited its membership to the western regions of the United States and Canada. It is organized as a regional self-help network of schools and districts with its own officers and board of directors. Participating districts and schools contribute regular membership fees and make membership commitments to bring some stability to the school design/redesign process. The major goal of the Consortium has been to assist schools in developing personalized education programs. Over the years, LEC International has worked with schools in the states of California, Oregon, Washington, Nevada, Montana, Texas, and Louisiana, and in the Canadian provinces of Alberta and British Columbia.

In 1996, LEC International extended its scope from an organization of districts and schools to include individual educators committed to school design/redesign and the personalization of instruction. The resulting LEC Forum is an informal consortium of individuals with knowledge and experience in major areas of educational change and design. Members monitor changing educational policy trends, produce working papers, and continue to work with interested districts and schools on comprehensive redesign and personalization.

LEC's technical assistance model has stressed four elements (Georgiades et al., 1979; Keefe, Jenkins, & Hersey, 1992):

1. Administrative role: The principal is the primary instrument of change in schools, but only in conjunction with a supervisory-management team that acts as a steering committee and in full collaboration with teachers and the community to plan a school design and work to implement it.

2. Teacher role: Teachers cultivate personalized advising and instruction. The teacher serves a dual role in LEC schools, as a subject-area consultant and as a teacher adviser to a small group of students. Teacher consultants foster interaction among students and support them with large group presentations, small group seminars, and a variety of learning materials for independent study and community experiences. Advisement emphasizes the teacher-adviser's relationship with the student as person and learner and the value of academic and other nontechnical advice.

3. Personalized education: The LEC "personalized education concept" begins with learner needs and interests, and fashions a learning environment to meet those needs, as well as the demands of society. LEC advocates a model of personalized education formulated initially in the 1970s for LEC schools by Keefe (1989, p. 76) and updated several times since then to reflect new research (see Figure 1.1 for the current version). The model encourages the *diagnosis* of student developmental characteristics, learning style, and prior knowledge and skills; forms of *prescription* that include student advisement, goal setting and planning, and program placement; personalized *instruction* building on flexible teacher style, a variety of instructional materials, authentic pedagogy, and other

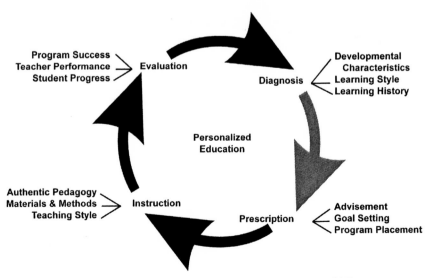

Figure 1.1.   Model of Personalized Education (Keefe: Revised, 1995)

proven strategies; and *evaluation* of student progress, teacher performance, and program success.

4. Program evaluation: LEC recommends the CIPP model of evaluation developed by Stufflebeam, et al. (1971) at Ohio State University. The model calls for evaluation of program *context* (needs, the setting, goals, and planning decisions), *input* (system capabilities, solution strategies, and structuring decisions), *process* (program design and implementation), and *product* (outcomes and recycling decisions). Several LEC schools have utilized the NASSP Comprehensive Assessment of School Environments Information Management System (CASE-IMS) to collect much of this information (see Keefe, 1994).

LEC International advocates total school design/redesign with personalized instruction as the instructional component. Personalized instruction takes place in supervised study, in small groups and in media and resource centers. Students work alone, with one other or a few others, in scheduled seminars, and in the community. Teacher coaching of students occurs on a one-to-one basis, but more often in a cluster of students who are working in the same area and topic of the curriculum. The practice of personalized instruction in LEC schools supports many learning paradigms and methodologies. It has included a modified mastery learning method, a cognitive learning style–based approach, the use of authentic pedagogy and assessment, and an apprenticeship program with guided practice, exploration, and teacher coaching.

Generally, LEC schools have successfully implemented the administrative and teacher roles and much of the personalized education component. They have found it easiest to establish a teacher-adviser role for teachers, to provide learning options and self-paced materials for students, to make school schedules more flexible, and to make greater use of the community as a learning resource. They have found it more difficult to establish a learning environment that allows individuals to proceed at their own (but reasonable) pace while also providing opportunities for reflective conversation and interactive activities. They have encountered considerable difficulty in *total* school design/redesign, in realizing the *total* evaluation component, and in conducting replicable research.

The real strength of the LEC effort, however, lies in the fact that, after some 35 years, the consortium is still active and encouraging districts and schools to search for new and productive ways to personalize the education experience.

Coalition of Essential Schools

Theodore R. Sizer mounted a large research project in 1979 to better understand the nature and effectiveness of American secondary education. This project, A Study of High Schools, culminated in three books, of which *Horace's Compromise: The Dilemma of the American High School* (1984) was the major summary statement. The Coalition of Essential Schools was established in 1984 at Brown University as a result of this study. The members of the coalition (with Sizer as chair) believed, as do members of LEC International, that no one model of schooling is good for all schools. Sizer asserts that good schools have only *shared ideas* in common about learning and schooling. These ideas are realized in different ways in different settings. Sizer summarized these ideas as a list of Common Principles in order to energize the activity of the Coalition.

The Coalition's Common Principles as recast for elementary school practice (Sizer, 1996) are broader in scope and application than the original high school list and follow in a somewhat abbreviated form:

- The school should focus on helping young people develop the habit of using their minds well. Schools should not attempt to be comprehensive if such a claim is made at the expense of the school's central intellectual purpose. Schools should be learner-centered, addressing students' social and emotional development as well as their academic progress.
- The school's academic goal should be simple: that each student masters a limited number of essential skills and areas of knowledge. The aphorism "less is more" should dominate. Students of all ages should have many opportunities to discover and construct meaning from their own experiences.
- The school's goals should apply to all students, while the means to these goals will vary.

- Teaching and learning should be personalized to the maximum extent feasible.
- The governing practical metaphor of the school should be student-as-worker rather than the more familiar metaphor of teacher-as-deliverer-of-instructional-services. Accordingly, a prominent pedagogy will be coaching and guiding.
- Teaching and learning should be documented and assessed with tools based on student performance of real tasks. The final diploma should be awarded upon a successful demonstration of mastery of gradation—an "exhibition." As the diploma is awarded when earned, the school's program proceeds with no strict age grading and with no system of "credits earned" by "time spent" in class.
- Families should be vital members of the school community. The tone of the school should explicitly and self-consciously stress values of unanxious anticipation, of trust, and of decency.
- The principal and teachers should perceive themselves as generalists first (teachers and scholars in general education) and specialists second (experts in one particular discipline). Staff should expect multiple obligations (teacher-counselor-manager) and a sense of commitment to the entire school.
- Ultimate administrative and budget targets should include substantial time for collective planning by teachers, competitive salaries for staff, and an ultimate per-pupil cost not to exceed that at traditional schools by more than 10 percent (pp. 157–159).

By the mid-1990s, the Coalition and its state partners through the Education Commission of the States (Re: Learning) counted more than 1,000 schools at varying levels of implementation. About 250 schools had moved beyond the formative stages and were playing out their insights into student intellectual development, the meaning of essential knowledge and skills, personalization of teaching and learning, student-as-worker and teacher-as-coach, and demonstration of student mastery by "exhibition." Many of the schools adopted the standards and practices of "authentic pedagogy" to achieve a basic Coalition principle: "helping young people develop the habit of using their minds well." Authentic pedagogy (Newmann, Secada, & Wehlage, 1995) is based on three criteria of intellectual achievement: (1) construction rather than mere reproduction of knowledge; (2) disciplined inquiry, using an existing knowledge base to achieve an in-depth understanding of an issue or problem and to convey it to others through real forms of communication; and (3) value beyond school, a meaning in real-life terms beyond school grades or honor rolls or scholarships. Establishing these standards has required Coalition schools to focus the curriculum on important in-depth knowledge rather than breadth of coverage, on a strong working relationship between students-as-workers and teachers-as-coaches or guides, and on personalizing the learning environment to the optimum degree possible.

In practice at the secondary school level, personalization has meant reducing teachers' daily contact from 130 to 150 students to a more manageable 80 or less, and placing virtually all instructional decisions in the hands of teachers. At both elementary and secondary levels, it has necessitated a flexible school structure that moves away from six to eight separate subjects and a school day divided into related and virtually equal time units. It also has meant that "what is essential must be grasped and the task of the Essential School is to adapt—to *personalize*—its program so that each student, or small group of students, can 'elect' the means to that essential end, however discouraging that goal may appear at first. . . . Schools must be personalized to the maximum feasible extent. Kids differ, one from the other, profoundly; and while we should make the best of commonalities, we must accommodate and capitalize on these differences" (Sizer, 1984).

Personalization and learning in-depth are often untidy, frequently noisy, and usually engrossing. The Coalition of Essential Schools has attempted to combine the rigor of serious learning with the kinds of structure and modes that involve children and young people. Students have been asked to work harder, but have come to know that self-respect and the respect of others only comes with achievement—that to achieve as adults they must learn how to learn for themselves. The Coalition, like LEC International, champions comprehensive, "all-at-once" school design and redesign. Personalization in the form of smaller class size, more student-teacher interaction, and instruction suited to the needs and interests of individual students is at the core of these efforts.

SUMMING UP

Personalized school environments have been launched very successfully
in several periods of school renewal during the past century. Yet, despite
these successes and a substantial body of supportive research and best
practice, these earlier initiatives have failed to penetrate the barricades
of traditional practice. In fairly short order, these more personalized efforts were superseded by coverage-oriented and rote-learning systems—various forms of back-to-basics or test-based initiatives. The
causes of these earlier failures are still with us today in the neglect of sophisticated teacher preservice and inservice training and the relative
complexity of the newer efforts. The current No Child Left Behind legislation has institutionalized some of the most mechanistic of these practices in too many states. On the other hand, some contemporary state
renewal efforts, such as *New Hampshire's Vision for Redesign* (New
Hampshire Department of Education, 2007), clearly reflect the influence of the NASSP, LEC, CES, and other efforts to combine personalization with accountability.

Darling-Hammond (1997, p. 12) aptly summarizes the situation in this
way:

> Perhaps the single biggest obstacle to maintaining progressive reforms is
> the extensive skill needed to teach both students and subjects well. In all
> the previous reform eras, practitioners asked to implement reforms like
> "open education" or "the project method" knew they were supposed to
> make learning relevant and attend to student needs. However, they often
> did not know how to fashion work that was rigorous as well as relevant,
> how to employ variable student-based strategies and also teach for high
> levels of disciplined understanding in content areas. And schools were of-
> ten unable to support these new pedagogies with new forms of organiza-
> tion, governance, and professional development. Many teachers lost track
> of either their students or the curriculum goals as they broke with their
> previous routines, trying to become more child-centered by letting go of
> subject-matter standards or more subject-centered by ignoring students
> while the curriculum marched on ahead. In the 1960s, many educators'
> inability to manage both sets of goals led to the perception that schools
> had lost academic rigor in their eagerness to be relevant.

Teaching practice that succeeds in developing deep understanding of challenging content for a wide range of learners is highly complex: it maintains dialectic between students and subjects, allowing neither to overwhelm the other. Such teaching presses for mastery of content in ways that enable students to apply their learning and connect it to other knowledge as they develop proficient performances in the field of study. Because students will necessarily come to any learning experience with different strategies and prior experiences—and thus with different starting points for the material to be learned—successful teachers must know how to create experiences that let students access ideas in a variety of ways, yet always press for deeper and more disciplined understanding.

Such teaching requires a strong knowledge of subject matter, substantial pedagogical skill, a commitment to helping individual students beyond simple routines and test-based formulas, and the deep desire to make instruction both thoughtful and interactive.

In the next two chapters, some of the methodological forerunners of personalized instruction are reviewed and its most basic elements are determined.

2

BASIC ELEMENTS
OF PERSONALIZED
INSTRUCTION: CULTURE

Personalized education is a systemic effort on the part of a school to take into account individual student characteristics and effective instructional practices in organizing the learning environment (Keefe, 1989). Special educator Anne Welch Carroll (1975) called personalized education, "An attempt to achieve a balance between the characteristics of the learner and the learning environment. It is the match of the learning environment with the learner's information, processing strategies, concepts, learning sets, motivational systems achieved and skills acquired. It is a continual process" (p. 19). The teacher, acting as adviser and coach, helps students attain a sense of balance in the learning environment between what is challenging and productive and what is beyond the student's present capabilities. In William Glasser's terms, the student is able to engage in freely chosen and meaningful learning with assistance from caring adults resulting in real, life-related performance.

SOME ANTECEDENTS OF PERSONALIZED INSTRUCTION

In the past, antecedents of personalization have been known under different names: nongraded education, continuous progress education, individualized instruction, individually guided or prescribed education, and so forth. Each of these concepts is concerned with personalized education but in a limited way. Personalization is broader in scope, more systematic in organization, and more authentic in its goals and strategies.

Nongraded education is primarily a *grouping practice.* American schools began as ungraded or nongraded organizations. Students of different ages gathered in one classroom (i.e., the one-room schoolhouse) and worked together largely at their own rates using the available materials. By 1870, however, virtually every school had become graded. Even before 1900, efforts were under way to develop alternatives to grouping by age.

Nongraded education was first introduced in Bronxville, New York, in 1925. The cross-age grouping of this approach makes possible progress in school predicated on skill levels and achievement rather than year of birth. Not using grades, however, does not actually introduce any substantive change in instructional planning or methodology. Whole class instruction usually remains the norm. Grouping is based on similar ability, achievement, or a combination of both.

Continuous progress (CP) *education* is a *scheduling strategy*, a way of organizing the school program to facilitate self-pacing and individual student learning plans. It begins with the identification of performance goals and criteria that describe what students should be able to do upon completion of their education. Sequenced instructional materials are developed to provide a variety of ways for students to accomplish the school learning goals. Each learning sequence is a continuum of learning experiences that permits students to progress at their own pace and according to their own individual needs. At its best, continuous progress is *a management system* designed to help students progress in an orderly fashion. Continuous progress is concerned with removing time and failure from the learning equation.

The main difficulty with CP programs is the complexity of organization required to monitor variable student grouping and progress reporting arrangements. Scheduling and grade reporting can be nightmarish unless a systematic approach is adopted. An additional CP pitfall is the likelihood that students will experience little real interaction in their schooling. Some CP programs have turned into giant study halls with students working the majority of time *alone*.

Individualized instruction conveys more of the reality of personalization. Individualization is a *teaching methodology* that generally focuses
on behaviorally stated instructional objectives, content sequences, multiple learning activities and materials, arrangements for individual learning differences, and differential use of staff. An attempt is usually made
to diagnose the learning status of each student through standardized
testing or subject pretests. Considerable use is made of autoinstruc-
tional techniques, such as learning packages, contracts, and programmed instruction. Independent study and small group work receive
as much attention as large group activities.

Individualized instruction can be very effective, depending primarily
on the balance achieved in the instructional setting. Programs that
overemphasize one or another element usually falter. For example, too
much slavish adherence to behavioral objectives, too much independent
study, or too little structure can doom an otherwise effective effort.
Most individualized programs are linear; that is, all students follow virtually the same course of study. Only the pace and, to a degree, the
learning activities vary. Individual help for students in the form of
coaching or advisement oftentimes is lacking.

Systematic individualized programs, such as *Individually Guided Ed-
ucation/Secondary* (Klausmeier, Lipham, & Daresh 1980), approach
personalization. But IGE/Secondary lacks a strong diagnostic component, an emphasis on interactive and reflective learning environments,
the elements of authentic pedagogy, and truly flexible *scheduling* like
continuous progress arrangements. Its strength lies in the gestalt it
brings to the learning environment.

Adaptive Instruction (Wang & Lindvall, 1984) is another systematic
individualized approach "that incorporates alternative strategies for instruction and resource utilization and has built-in flexibility to permit students to take various routes to, and amounts of time for, learning." Adaptive instruction is the current heir to individualized instruction and
mastery learning and, like these earlier initiatives, attempts to accommodate individual student differences by means of multiple learning outcomes and flexible program characteristics. Wang and Lindvall (1984)
advocate that adaptive programs include these essential components:

- Instructional content that is essential to further learning, is useful
  for functioning in society, and is clearly specified and organized to
  facilitate learning

- Assessment and diagnosis that provide appropriate placement in the curricula and regular assessment of progress
- Student learning experiences in which ample time is provided for essential content, student use of effective learning skills, alternative assignments and activities, and success in mastering content
- Management of instruction that permits independent study, student schedule planning, self-selection of some goals and activities, and self-monitoring of progress
- Collaboration among students that enables them to both provide and obtain help from peers and to work in group activities

Adaptive instruction has been associated with "equal access" education for the handicapped and is particularly well suited for students from diverse cultural/ethnic backgrounds. It has experienced success when implementation is systematic and broadly supported. It labors under many of the liabilities of its predecessors, with an overly behaviorist orientation, a lack of authentic and reflective emphasis, relatively rigid scheduling arrangements, and the usual problems that come with a complex system.

Style-Based Instruction (Kolb, 1976; Gregorc, 1978; Dunn & Dunn, 1978; Hunt, et al., 1978; Letteri, 1980; Silver & Hanson, 1980; Keefe et al., 1986) is a contemporary diagnostic-prescriptive instructional system that grew out of research on cognitive controls, personality types, and aptitude-treatment interaction analyses. Virtually all current style-based systems reflect one or more of these three lines of research: on information processing styles, personality-related learning tendencies, and the relationship of individual differences to instructional method. A task force on learning style, commissioned by the National Association of Secondary School Principals in the 1980s, agreed on three basic principles of style-based learning (Keefe, 1991b):

1. All students can benefit both from a responsive learning environment and the enhancement of their learning (cognitive) skills.
2. Some students first require cognitive skills development ("augmentation") rather than a modified learning environment ("adaptation").
3. Other students with sound cognitive skills can profit from matching the learning environment to their learning styles (p. 3).

Style-based instruction features many useful elements. Its strengths are its diagnostic component, the potential for flexible learning arrangements, and the use of performance-based assessment. Unfortunately, some style-based programs are little more than enhanced individualized instruction. But those style-based systems that embrace student advisement, interactive learning, and a culture of collaboration do border on truly personalized instruction.

BASIC ELEMENTS OF PERSONALIZED INSTRUCTION

Darling-Hammond (1997) argued that we must put students first, that all children have a right to learn. Darling-Hammond (1996) cited four factors that are important for powerful teaching and learning:

1. *Structures for caring and structures for serious learning*, structures that enable teachers to know students well and to work with them intensely (i.e., smaller school size, student interdisciplinary clusters, multiyear advisories, extended time with individual students, etc.).
2. *Shared exhibitions of student work* that make it clear what the school values and how students are doing. Teachers set standards, create authentic assessments, and display student work in every way possible to provide a basis for what works and what needs to be improved.
3. *Structures that support teacher collaboration focused on student learning*, in particular, teacher teams for curriculum planning, student advisement, and accountability for student success.
4. *Structures for shared decision making and dialogue about teaching and learning* with other teachers, students, and parents. Teachers, often in collaboration with students and parents, recommend hiring their colleagues, agree on professional development, formulate curriculum, and design evaluation systems. These structures support a workable decentralization of authority and operation.

These structures are not a model to be imposed on schools, but rather are a broad blueprint for ongoing improvement in school organization and good practice.

What, then, are the basic elements of a personalized approach to instruction? If we consider the implications of historic efforts to renew schooling and take into account the most flexible of recent efforts to make learning more personal, a direction begins to emerge. We believe that there are *six basic elements of personalized instruction* that should be present if a school wishes to develop powerful teaching and learning for student success. These elements or structures produce a challenging, integrative, but child-centered learning environment, one that is interactive and meaningful, but with reasonably structured learning activities, flexible use of time and space, and authentic, performance-based assessment of student progress. We think of these six basic elements as constituting the *culture* and *context* of personalized instruction. The cultural components—teacher role, student learning characteristics, and collegial relationships—establish the foundation of personalization and ensure that the school prizes a caring and collaborative environment, student diversity, and individual development. The contextual factors—interactivity, flexible scheduling, and authentic assessment—promote and support student engagement, thoughtful growth, and proficient performance. The following six elements of personalized instruction are detailed in this chapter and the following chapter:

1. A dual teacher role of coach and adviser
2. The diagnosis of relevant student learning characteristics, including:
   - Developmental level
   - Cognitive/learning style
   - Prior knowledge/skills
3. A culture of collegiality in the school, characterized by:
   - A constructivist environment
   - Collaborative learning arrangements
4. An interactive learning environment characterized by:
   - Small school or small group (class) size
   - Thoughtful conversation
   - Active learning activities
   - Authentic student achievement
5. Flexible scheduling and pacing, but with adequate structure
6. Authentic assessment

DUAL TEACHER ROLE

The indispensable catalyst in the personalized instructional environment is the teacher, the instructional specialist who is closest to the learning situation and best understands the needs and interests of students, as well as the policies of the school and the district. Personalized instruction demands that the teacher assume the dual roles of subject-matter coach, consultant and facilitator, and teacher-adviser to a select group of students. As learning coach, the teacher collaborates with other teachers, student peer tutors, and community resource persons to guide student learning. As teacher-adviser, the teacher provides advice, counsel, and guidance to 15 to 20 students on academic and school-adjustment issues.

Teacher-Coach

Teacher-coaches offer the same kind of instruction, demonstration, practice, and feedback to their students that athletic coaches and student activity advisers have modeled in the most successful of their programs. The needs of today's students are quite different from those of their counterparts two or three generations ago. The world has experienced several social revolutions and a knowledge explosion that makes it almost impossible to "cover" more than a small part of what students need to know for a reasonably successful life. Cognitive and problem-solving skills, what some call metacognitive skills, are more important today than any particular piece of knowledge. The teacher-coach in the school environment must be a facilitator of learning, a learning guide who helps students find appropriate resources and engage in suitable learning activities.

Members of the Learning Environments Consortium International (Georgiades et al., 1979) describe such a teacher as "not so much educational broadcaster as academic troubleshooter. He devotes fewer hours to lecturing in front of a class and more to working with students individually and in small groups. He spends a good deal of time preparing basic instructional objectives, analyzing the specific strengths and weaknesses of individual students in relation to those objectives, and investigating and making available a wide range of learning activities and methods that will facilitate student success. He recognizes that each student is a unique human being with his own personal learning needs and style, and he knows that what works well for one may not work at all for another."

In this vein, Perkins (1992) proposed "Theory One," a simple theory of teaching and learning that proclaims: "People learn much of what they have a reasonable opportunity and motivation to learn." Theory One frowns on much of contemporary educational practice. It encourages good didactic instruction (direct explanation) when needed but also coaching for skills training, practice, and feedback, and Socratic teaching for open-ended engagement, inquiry, and reflective conversation. Theory One strongly supports a "learning paradigm."

Barr and Tagg (1995) and Lasley (1998) argued that two paradigms exist within American classrooms: an instructional paradigm and a learning paradigm. The instructional paradigm is concerned primarily with what teachers do; the learning paradigm is concerned primarily with how students learn. The instructional paradigm concentrates on teacher behavior, how a teacher lectures or conducts a small group. The learning paradigm is focused on whether, how, and what students learn, on the environment and the facilitation of learning. "Learning paradigm teachers get outside themselves and get inside the minds of students" (Lasley, 1998). They participate in the learning process with their students, in its planning, and its organization. They are concerned with the learning climate, the atmosphere of learning, and how students approach learning and are motivated to learn. Learning paradigm teachers are strong proponents of a Theory One approach to teaching and learning.

The teacher-coach must be a presenter of information when other useful sources are not available, a skills coach (of reading, writing, speaking, listening, seeing, measuring, estimating, or calculating), and a convener and facilitator of small group dialogue. Sizer (1984) highlighted the critical role of coaching. "I, the teacher, can tell you rules for writing—grammar, forms of felicitous phrasing, types of argument. I can show you examples of good and bad writing, and with the aid of an overhead projector I can demonstrate for you how to analyze a piece of work. However, until *you* write and I criticize *your* writing, your expository skills and the thinking behind lie latent. You may know in the abstract how to write, but you don't know in practice how to do it, at least not very well."

Coaching requires *time* to interact with students, to connect with them, to understand their needs, to provide needed information, advice, and feedback about targeted skills, ideas, or issues. Coaching is about problem solving. In fact, Bransford and Vye (1989) conceptualized coaching in terms of problem solving, in these ways:

- Coaches monitor and supervise student attempts at problem solving both to give them experience in real problem solving and to keep them from going too far into flawed solutions
- Coaches help students reflect on their own problem solving, encouraging them to think out loud or even modeling strategies for them
- Coaches identify what students can already do by letting them solve problems and by providing feedback
- Coaches help students experience new ways of thinking as guides to their own thinking, to compare and contrast their own ideas with other possibilities
- Coaches help students comprehend and construct meaning in their experiences using resources related to their needs and interests (not unrelated exercises)
- Coaches use whatever resources are useful to engage students in learning—presentation, discussion, learning packages, computer-based learning systems, personal tutoring, and so on

The teacher-coach role requires flexibility, excellent academic preparation, and good pedagogical skills. The role defines a new kind of teacher for the new century.

Teacher-Adviser

Teacher-advisers are the first line of offense and defense in a school guidance program geared to student success. Advisement is the other facet of the new teacher job description—a helping role. Teachers and other qualified adults join professional counselors in helping students plan and achieve appropriate career and personal-social goals. In advisement, teachers, counselors, and other adults work as a team to promote student adjustment and success in school. Professional counselors serve as advisers to a group of teacher-advisers and help them to learn their role and its functions.

The first formal teacher-adviser program was established at New Trier High School in Winnetka, Illinois, in 1924. The Adviser-Personnel Plan, as it was called, was "designed to provide educational, vocational, social, moral, and ethical guidance and counsel to all students of the school" (Clerk, 1928). Over the years, advisement programs have been called expanded homeroom, advisory period, home base, advisory base, student assistance, teacher-adviser, adviser-advisee, and personal adult advocate. The programs have varied from place to place, but generally call for a teacher to assume school guidance functions that are narrowly limited to:

- Academic program planning
- Career/college information
- School adjustment issues
- Personal-social guidance

In middle schools, many adviser programs take on the character of group guidance, but this arrangement is usually limited in scope and often in success. The most successful advisement programs emphasize personal contact between students and advisers and continuing support of the student in his or her academic program and personal adjustment to school. The teacher-adviser role was integral to the NASSP Model Schools Project (1969–1974) and to Individually Guided Education (IGE). It is a major component of the Learning Environments Consortium model and the NASSP *Breaking Ranks* (1996) recommendations, and is present in many Coalition of Essential Schools' implementations. The *Breaking Ranks* report specifically mentions the role of the Personal Adult Advocate in helping the student *personalize* the education experience.

Teacher-adviser or personal adult advocate programs share a number of common features (Keefe, 1983):

- Virtually all teachers and administrators are responsible for a group of 10 to 20 students. Teacher-advisers (TAs) or personal adult advocates (PAAs) plan group activities, work with individual students in schedule planning, and counsel students on academic and school adjustment problems.

- TAs generally retain the same group of advisees throughout their upper-primary, middle, or high school years. Each student chooses or is assigned an adviser upon entering the school (both methods of selection are successful).
- TAs collect information about each advisee and provide information as needed on personal and school adjustment, school scheduling or activities, and careers or college. TAs maintain personal folders on each advisee.
- TAs help students recognize their personal aptitudes and interests. They meet with them and their parents regularly to discuss student goals, behavior, and academic progress. They serve as a "friend-in-court" for students experiencing adjustment problems.
- TAs function as homeroom or home-base teachers and chief in-school contact for all persons and agencies concerned with the student. They talk to parents, community persons, prospective employers, and college and career counselors on behalf of their advisees.

Shoreham-Wading River Middle School was cited in the Carnegie Corporation Report, *Turning Points* (1989), as an effective advisement program at the middle level of schooling. This program, in operation since 1971, utilizes small advisory groups of 12 students that meet each morning for 12 minutes as a substitute for the traditional homeroom. At lunchtime, advisees meet in the adviser's classroom to have lunch together. On Mondays through Thursdays, advisers have time for 40-minute conferences with individual advisees. Teacher-adviser members of a particular academic team meet each Friday to discuss their students. In the sixth grade, for example, groups of four to five advisers form an advisory *team* for 40 to 50 students, divided into four or five advisory groups. At the end of the sixth grade, these advisers personally place their students in seventh-grade advisory groups. Seventh-grade advisers do the same for their advisees moving to eighth grade. Shoreham-Wading TAs get to know their students very well, plan group activities, hold discussions, talk to parents, prepare report cards, and mediate in case of student behavior problems.

The adviser program at Wilde Lake High School, Columbia, Maryland, originally organized by John Jenkins, is a model of the kind of advisement advocated by the National Association of Secondary School Principals. Wilde Lake, a former member of NASSP's Model Schools Project, stressed a collaborative effort among all members of the school community. Most teachers, except first-year novices, served as advisers to about 20 students. TAs worked with an administrator, a professional counselor, and an adviser coordinator in providing students with support, information, and advice. Students selected their own adviser and had individual conferences at least once a quarter. Wilde Lake provided 20 to 25 minutes each day for advisers to work with advisee groups. Adviser group time was devoted to conferencing and problem solving four days each week. The group participated on the fifth day in a group activity developed by the adviser, which focused on academics, school awareness, group or self-awareness, or school problems. Advisers monitored their advisees' schedules and academic progress. In general, they served as advocates for their students and adult friends in time of need.

The dual role of teacher as coach and adviser is fundamental to the personalization of instruction in a school. The teacher-coach/adviser gets to know students much better than is the norm in conventional schools. As a result, the teacher is able to help youngsters make wiser decisions about learning options and ultimately about life goals. Indeed, many students simply cannot achieve a competent level of self-directed and motivated activity unless the teacher plays a truly caring role.

DIAGNOSIS OF STUDENT LEARNING CHARACTERISTICS

Personalized instruction must begin with knowledge of the learner if the goal is to build a learning environment suited to the aptitudes, needs, and interests of each student. The foundation of any personalized instruction approach is some form of *diagnosis*—determining what are the learning-related characteristics of individual learners.

Many teachers spend a good deal of time *observing students* to find out where they are in the learning process, in checking student progress, and in prescribing learning resources and interventions for more successful performance. This kind of direct feedback and various types of diagnostic assessment are among the principal tools of instruction viewed as coaching, mentoring, facilitating, and advising. Diagnosis is concerned with discovering such student learning traits as developmental level, learning style, and learning history.

Developmental Characteristics

Developmental characteristics are those specific stages in individual maturation when certain capacities for learned behavior appear (e.g., visual perception, language pronunciation, and cognitive thinking skills). These characteristics tell us *when* a student is *developmentally* ready to learn something. They describe individual readiness for learning. Some traits, such as taste in food or clothing, are primarily the result of environmental influences; others, such as the rate of physical development and brain growth, are subject mostly to heredity. When a child grows, increases in weight and height, and develops primary or secondary sexual characteristics, heredity is at work, and an increasing physical maturity is the result. Certain capabilities appear only after the appropriate stage of individual development occurs. If not exercised then, the capacities are not likely to develop later (e.g., skills in athletics, peer relations, language learning, etc.).

If teachers are to personalize student instruction, they must have a good understanding of learner developmental traits. Clark (1991) believes that teachers need to acquire developmental information about the physiological, psychological, and sociological characteristics of their students:

- *Physical development and maturation* can affect student self-concept and self-esteem. Physical size and personality influence the ways individuals perceive their personal competence. Teachers must be sensitive to early and late maturing students and to those who are frail or obese. Advisement and group guidance, as well as recognition programs, can assist teachers in this aspect of diagnosis.
- *Psychological development* is concerned with learning readiness and student self-esteem. Preadolescents and adolescents, in particular, face many challenges to their intellectual growth and sense of self-worth. The period of late childhood and preadolescence is a time that youngsters progress from the stage of concrete thinking to for-

mal thinking. The sequence and organization of subject matter and the choice of instructional strategies must match students' level of cognitive development during this period. Also, self-concept becomes more complex as youngsters develop. Low self-esteem has many undesirable consequences. Teachers must be able to recognize these levels of cognitive growth and self-esteem.

- *Sociological development* relates to peer group membership, student feelings of anonymity and victimization, and individual perceptions of concern and responsibility. Teachers must be on the alert for evidence of student delinquency, and sensitive to student peer group relationships. Teachers can monitor these influences through careful observation, and can build classroom and school climate through such strategies as small group work, cooperative learning, and forms of advisement.

Darling-Hammond (1997) called for "developmentally attentive schools," starting with the presumption that schools should be user-friendly. School organization and student work must build on student developmental considerations. Learning activities should be based on student needs and legitimate interests rather than, arbitrarily, on generic curriculum guides or the contents of approved textbooks. Activities should alternate between relatively short whole-group instruction (when needed) and more extended time for group work and independent reading and study. Particularly in the lower grades, students need hands-on learning with active and concrete learning activities. Nor should developmental attentiveness end with primary schooling. Braddock and McPartland (1993) argued that many problems that teenagers have in school are a result of the notable mismatch between their developmental needs and the learning environments of most junior and senior high schools. When teenagers need close relationships, they get large, impersonal schools. When they need to experience autonomy, they get rigid rules, curricular tracking, and large doses of memorization.

Diagnosing student developmental characteristics and observing the demands of developmental attentiveness are neglected in many schools. Their importance in program planning and instruction can hardly be overstated. If personalization is to grow in schools, teachers must make this kind of attentiveness a priority.

Student Learning Style

Student learning style is the second broad diagnostic element. Learning style encompasses information-processing habits, attitudinal tendencies, and biologically based responses that are typical of the ways a given student learns and prefers to learn. There are three broad categories of learning style characteristics:

1. *Cognitive styles* are preferred ways of perception, organization, and retention. Messick and others (1976) discusses more than 20 dimensions of cognitive control. For example, *perceptual modality preferences*—whether a student prefers visual, auditory, or psychomotor learning—are basic to cognitive style diagnosis. Other significant cognitive styles are *field independence versus field dependence*, representing analytical versus global ways of perceiving; *conceptual tempo*, concerned with impulsive or reflective approaches to concept formation; and *leveling versus sharpening*, assessing variations in memory processing.
2. *Affective styles* include those dimensions of the learning personality having to do with attention, emotion, and valuing. Each learner has a personal motivational approach deriving from his or her cultural environment, from parental and peer pressures, from school influences and, of course, from personality factors. Not every student is motivated to learn in every learning environment.
3. *Physiological styles* are individual traits deriving from a person's gender, health and nutrition, and reaction to the physical surroundings. Important school-related physiological styles are *brain hemispheric dominance, body biorhythms*, and preferences for levels of light, sound, and temperature in the learning environment.

Learning styles, then, are characteristic cognitive, affective, and physiological behaviors that serve as relatively stable indicators of how students perceive, interact with, and respond to the learning environment. They can be measured by a variety of assessment techniques. Learning style is a gestalt that tells us *how* a student learns and prefers to learn.

The *Learning Style Profile* developed by NASSP, for example, assesses 24 independent scales representing four factors: perceptual responses, cognitive styles, study preferences, and instructional preferences. Seven cognitive skills are profiled, including sequential and simultaneous processing skills. The *Learning Style Profile* (now available from Cambridge Educational Services) and other comprehensive style instruments help teachers identify student style strengths and weaknesses and organize instruction more efficiently and effectively. Some learners require highly responsive instructional environments. Most individualized teaching approaches reflect this point of view. Other learners need help to function successfully in *any* learning environment. Their cognitive skills can be modified with careful training. Style assessment makes all of this possible. Learning style diagnosis is a key element in any attempt to make instruction more personalized.

Student Learning History

"Student learning history" is a term utilized by Benjamin Bloom and his colleagues in mastery learning research to describe the aggregate of personal learning that each student brings to a particular course, class, or school program. A learner's "history" characterizes his or her *instructional* readiness or "entering behavior." Learning history is the third broad area of diagnosis. In fact, existing student knowledge and skills define the fertile ground for student success in subsequent learning. Whether a school or teacher is designing instruction for a traditional classroom or for a completely personalized program, it is critical to know what learning has taken place and what still needs to be learned. Bloom (1976, p. 69) discussed learning history in these terms:

> What happens to the learner at one point in his learning career has consequences, positive or negative, for subsequent stages in his learning career. The learning that takes place prior to entry into formal schooling has consequences for learning in the early years of school. These early years of school determine his cognitive entry characteristics for later years of school, and the cognitive entry characteristics produced in these later years of school have consequences for even later years of school. . . . Affective entry characteristics are relatively weak and unformed early in the individual's learning career, but become more structured and effective as the individual accumulates a history of learning.

Learning history, then, tells us what a student knows at a given point in his or her learning career—the knowledge and skills the student possesses before beginning a new learning experience. Diagnosis of learning history involves the determination of what *has occurred* as a basis for what *should occur*. Observation, surveys, inventories, and curriculum-referenced tests (rather than the traditional standardized tests) best assess these knowledge or skill levels. Some of the more important learning history characteristics are:

- Home and socioeconomic factors
- Aptitudes and skills
- Subject area competence (achievement)
- Preparation in and motivation for a particular subject
- Study habits, including the ability to work in groups and independently

The concept that learning involves the assimilation of new content into existing cognitive structures has been the object of much research. Anderson (1977), Voss (1979), Clement (1979), Champagne, Klopfer, and Gunstone (1982), and other researchers have found that student performance improves when prior knowledge and/or skills are stronger. Information about student learning history is available to teachers in cumulative record folders, in teacher and counselor reports, and from student questionnaires, inventories, and various diagnostic tests.

CULTURE OF COLLEGIALITY

Another essential ingredient of personalized instruction is a school culture of collaboration where teachers and students work together in a co-operative social environment to develop meaningful learning activities for all students. Choice theory (Glasser, 1986) proposes that all behavior is an attempt to satisfy basic needs hardwired into our genetic structure. *We always choose to do what is most satisfying to us at the time.* Glasser tells us that "if what is being taught does not satisfy the needs about which a student is currently most concerned, it will make little difference how brilliantly the teacher teaches—the student will not work to learn . . . . Teachers are well aware that hungry students think of food, lonely students look for friends, and powerless students seek attention far more that they look for knowledge." John Goodlad (1984) in his landmark work, *A Place Called School,* which studied more than 27,000 students in American schools, observed: "I wonder about the flat, neutral emotional ambience of most of the classes we studied. Boredom is a disease of epidemic proportions."

A 1990 NASSP shadow study of 162 eighth graders (Lounsbury & Clark, 1990) found students sitting passively in class, listening to lectures, and doing seatwork. The climate of the school was largely "nice" or "pleasant," but teacher-student relationships were "perfunctory" or "cordial but antiseptic." Students, of course, took every opportunity to talk to one another. They were very social, but had little opportunity to actively participate in their schoolwork. Despite their need for sociability and independence, most of the schools made these eighth graders passive recipients of teacher actions and decisions. Some exceptions did exist, of course, especially when schools used cross-disciplinary studies, team teaching, and cooperative learning. Wolk (2007) commented that "Passive schooling creates passive people. If we want people to think, learn, and care about the many dimensions of life, if we want neighbors who accept responsibility of tending to the world and making it a better place, then we need schools and curricula that are actually about life and the world."

Almost all students try hard when they first enter school. When first graders start school, they all want to learn to read. Their parents and others they love and trust have told them that it is important to read. They believe that they will get love and attention if they learn to read. But unfortunately, some first graders are too immature neurologically or psychologically to master reading no matter how hard they try. They fall behind, frustrating their parents and teachers. They learn only to hate school. Reading is neither possible nor meaningful for them at that time. They are like the students in the NASSP shadow study above who were forced to just sit and listen. Little learning occurred because student needs were not being met. In a personalized environment, students can pursue work that is meaningful to them; they can satisfy their needs. A constructivist environment and collaborative learning arrangements characterize a collegial culture.

Constructivist Environment

Many educators today have adopted a constructivist view of schooling. Educational constructivism borrows from various movements in other disciplines: *social construction of reality* in sociology, *phenomenology* in philosophy, and *constructivism* in psychology. O'Neil (1992) characterizes educational constructivism in this way:

> The key tenet of constructivist theory, experts say, is that people learn by actively constructing knowledge, weighing new information against their previous understanding, thinking about and working through discrepancies (on their own and with others), and coming to a new understanding. In a classroom faithful to constructivist views, students are afforded numerous opportunities to explore phenomena or ideas, to conjecture, to share hypotheses with others, and to revise their original thinking.

Constructivism holds that *individual learners construct knowledge by giving meaning to their current experiences in the light of their prior knowledge*. Learners can make meaning of what they are learning, and they construct that meaning quite naturally. If the learning environment is appropriately organized, the process of making meaning is supported and understanding deepens. Time and opportunity for reflective dialogue are critical elements of such a learning environment. Constructivist teachers build instruction on student styles and skills, and encourage students to seek out personal knowledge of a topic. These teachers involve students in self-directed learning and in collaborative approaches like cooperative learning, reciprocal teaching, and topic study. Students work with their teacher-coaches to improve their cognitive skills and to expand their current experience through reflection, seminars, and long-term projects.

Perkins (1992) provides several examples of what constructivist practice might look like:

- One might encourage students in puzzling over and experimenting with what makes some things sink in water while others float. With artful coaching, they may recreate the principle of displacement.
- One might ask young students just learning arithmetic to invent their own ways of adding and subtracting, without teaching the standard algorithms. This actually works!

- One might ask students to build better, more empowering conceptions of themselves as writers by keeping a writer's diary. What things work for them? What things don't? When their writing does well or not, what seem to be the causes?

Constructivist teachers look for opportunities to encourage student reflection, problem solving, and initiative.

Collaborative Learning Arrangements

The task of personalized instruction is to create learning communities in which students can confront important ideas and apply these ideas to real-world experiences that they can understand and use. Collaborative learning arrangements provide an opportunity for students and teachers to work together to verbalize their ideas, to sharpen their thinking, to capitalize on differences. Considerable evidence exists, for example, that students learn better in cooperative groups than when alone (Slavin, 1991, 1995). Cooperative small groups encourage collaboration that is more useful and better socialization than traditional classrooms, yet produce solid achievement gains. Cooperative learning calls for positive interdependence among learners, face-to-face interaction, individual responsibility for mastering the target material, and interpersonal skills fostering collaboration and affective working relationships. Students at all levels of school achievement can work together toward common goals. In Jigsaw, for example, students are assigned to six-member teams to work on subject matter broken down into five sections (two students share one section). Each student studies his or her section, meets with members of other teams in "expert groups" on the same section, and then teaches his or her own teammates about the section.

Glasser (1986) believes that small learning teams offer a good chance of motivating almost all students, for several reasons:

- Students gain a sense of *belonging* by working in teams of two to five students.
- Belonging provides the *initial motivator* for students to do the work. As they achieve some success, they will want to work even harder.

- *Stronger students* find it need-fulfilling to help weaker students toward a high performing team effort.
- *Weaker students* find it need-fulfilling to contribute to the team effort. Alone they are able to do little.
- Students do not depend only on the teacher, but also on the *team* and their own creativity.
- Learning teams provide *needed structure* to avoid superficiality and support in-depth learning.
- Teams have *flexibility* in the kinds of evidence they present about the knowledge learned or skills achieved.
- Teams can be changed to give all students a chance to work together and to serve on high-scoring teams.

Collaborative learning arrangements are a requisite for a personalized learning environment. These arrangements promote interaction, dialogue, and thoughtful reflection. Together with an enhanced teacher role and a strong diagnostic component, a culture of collegiality sets the stage for the practice of personalized pedagogy. In the next chapter, these contextual elements of personalization are detailed.

3

BASIC ELEMENTS
OF PERSONALIZED
INSTRUCTION: CONTEXT

Not everyone agrees that personalized instruction is a good thing. National organizations, regional coalitions, districts, schools, and individuals have proposed models with elements of personalization or attempted to develop wholly restructured schools, in many cases, without notable success. Teachers are often ambivalent about the process. Too much work with only minimal change! Too many iterations—new projects and new programs overlapping, year after year! And disagreements over such basic issues as how to begin reform and how or to what degree to use such strategies as basic skills, interdisciplinary curricula, standardized tests, and professional staff development (Hatch, 1998).

Add to those difficulties the fact that many educators, and very likely most of the general public, believe that education should be HARD, difficult, even burdensome, if it is to be GOOD. The current popular image of "real school" that we discussed earlier is anything but personalized. For example, the recommendations of the National Commission on Excellence in Education, *Nation at Risk* (1983), called for a *longer* school year, *more* homework, and *more* emphasis on science, math, and writing. Most parents, too, can recall personal school experiences that were trying, difficult, and usually boring. There is little reason to question that "real school" for most adults is a place that should be difficult, boring, and certainly not personalized.

William Glasser (1986) asserted that "when we talk about our secondary schools, we are really talking about two very different systems within each school. In the first, both teachers and students are functioning well and filling good colleges with qualified applicants. In the second, the students, many of whom drop out well before the twelfth grade, are nonfunctioning, and the teachers, despite hard work and the best intentions, are able to do little more that serve as custodians." These nonfunctioning students stop working usually by middle school, and many even fail to learn to read. This "second system" is an expensive waste of human and fiscal capital because so little comes of it. If these students do not cause any trouble, they are usually given "mercy passes" to the next grade. To keep them in their underachieving places, many schools "track" them and largely ignore them.

Glasser goes on to point out that elementary schools have fewer students not working because younger children are more concerned with the needs of love and belonging, which can be satisfied in self-contained classrooms with caring teachers. As students move through the grades, however, they rely more on their friends than their parents and teachers for those needs. If their friends are "second system" members, too, dislike of school and typical instruction is simply reinforced. They come to hate school even more. Glasser's "choice theory" holds that nothing outside ourselves, including school, can satisfy our needs for us. We can only do this for ourselves because we are continually constructing our own reality. In this light, Glasser (1986) maintained that "a good school could be defined as a place where almost all students believe that if they do some work, they will be able to satisfy their needs enough so that it makes sense to keep working." Schools have to find ways to become satisfying to "second system" students. In the process, of course, they will become better places for all students. The most important ingredients in this process are personal contact and collaboration between adults and students, freely chosen and meaningful learning, and achievement based on real performance. We like to think of this pattern of interactive learning environments, thoughtful content, flexible scheduling and pacing, and authentic assessment as the *context* of personalized instruction and learning.

INTERACTIVE LEARNING ENVIRONMENTS

Interactive learning environments are designed to foster collaborative learning and reflective conversation. Interactive learning structures include smaller schools, cooperative work, and student-parent-teacher participation. Recent studies have found that high schools restructured to provide interactive learning arrangements produce higher student achievement gains that are also more equitably distributed among socioeconomic subgroups (Lee & Smith, 1995). These studies found that collective responsibility for student learning, an academic emphasis, and high morale are important features of a successful school learning community. Successful practices included smaller school-within-school units, interdisciplinary teaching teams, common teacher planning time, staff participation in problem solving, keeping students in the same homeroom or advisement group throughout their entire school career, cooperative learning teams, and parental involvement. Interactive learning environments are characterized by small school or group size, thoughtful classrooms, active learning experiences, and authentic student achievement. Let us explore these characteristics.

School or Group Size

Large schools may foster anomie and even dehumanization. Students may feel like numbers in a game rather than persons known as individuals. Large schools have some advantages, of course, in range of courses offered, but this flexibility is more than offset by the disadvantages of great size. Darling-Hammond (1997) reported that more than 30 years of studies on school organization "have consistently found that small schools (with enrollments of roughly 300 to 600) promote higher student achievement, higher attendance, lower dropout rates, greater participation in school activities, more positive feelings toward self and school, more positive behavior, less violence and vandalism and greater post school success. . . . These outcomes are also found in settings where students have close sustained relationships with a smaller than average number of teachers throughout their school careers." (See also Howley, 1989, and Gottfredson & Daiger, 1979.)

The Lee and Smith (1995) studies uncovered even more interesting findings on school size for gains in mathematics. When math scores are graphed against school size, a *curvilinear* relationship appears. Achievement rises as school size rises to about 600 students, remains level until about 900 students, and then falls off. Moreover, gains for the highest achieving *largest* schools (more than 2,000 students) are much less than for the lowest achieving *smaller* schools in the 600 to 900 student range. Clearly, this is a strong argument for smaller schools as well as for school-within-school and other subunit organizational plans that strive for personalization but guard against social stratification.

Recent studies on class size in Tennessee (Pate-Bain et al., 1992) reveal similar findings. Project STAR (student/teacher achievement ratio) followed students from kindergarten through third grade in three types of classes: small (13 to 17 students per teacher), regular (22 to 25 per teacher), and regular with aide. Students in the small classes scored statistically and educationally higher on standardized and basic skills tests in all four years and in all locales (inner city, urban, suburban, and rural). The largest gains occurred in small inner-city classes. Moreover, instruction in small classes was completed more quickly, in more depth, and used more concrete materials, enrichment activities, and learning center strategies.

Unfortunately, earlier studies on class size are inconclusive or at least debatable. Smaller class size is invariably the better choice when the group is 20 or fewer, but in the range from 20 to 40 students, class size makes little or no difference (Educational Research Service, 1978; Glass & Smith, 1978). Class size studies are difficult to conduct because so many other socioeconomic, organizational, and instructional variables can intervene. The issue becomes moot, however, when one approaches the issue of class or group size from the learner's point of view. The issue, then, is how can the client best be served? What kind of grouping (large, medium, small) best serves the target content or the activity? A choir or a band usually benefits from a larger size. Activities such as assemblies, performances, or guest lectures lend themselves to very large group size. Skill learning, discussion, and reflective conversation demand small groups. Research and reading are often best done alone. *The size of the group should be a function of its purpose.* Having said this, however, we should reiterate that most school-based learning benefits from smaller-sized groups because they encourage collaboration, interaction, and shared satisfaction.

Thoughtful Environments

Smaller schools and small group size can better support thoughtful conversation, learning by doing, apprenticeship experiences, and authentic student achievement. Schrag (1992) argued for more "thoughtfulness" in classrooms. Researchers at the University of Wisconsin National Center on Effective Secondary Schools developed a set of rating scales for "thoughtful lessons" in social studies based on Schrag's conception of good thinking. The University of Wisconsin research found that social studies classes in 16 schools evidenced more thoughtfulness when school principals and department chairs promoted thinking as a central goal, supported curriculum development aimed at that goal, and encouraged a collegial climate for teachers to examine their own teaching practices.

Daniel Bisaccio, a teacher of natural science in the 1990s at Thayer Junior/Senior High School in Winchester, New Hampshire, unmistakably exemplifies the strategies of thoughtful instruction. Bisaccio employed Socratic techniques, brainstorming, field experiences, and research methods to involve his students in his natural science classes. Bisaccio had 60 minutes on Mondays and Fridays and 90 minutes on Tuesdays through Thursdays. A typical Monday found him planning midweek trips to a "land lab." The conversation went like the following (Wood, 1992, pp. 146–147, 149):

> "What things would you look for if you wanted to really know what was in or on a piece of land?" Sipping from his coffee cup, Dan opens the day with, as usual, a question.
>
> "You mean like what is growing there?" questions Craig, taking the bait.
>
> "Well, what about what is growing there?" responds Dan, with yet another question.

"Do you mean make a list?" Craig isn't answering so much as trying to find out where Dan is going.

"Try this. What would you expect to find growing on a piece of land in the land lab?" asks Dan, with his favorite type of question: "What would you expect?"

"Trees and grasses," Stephanie jumps in.

"Good. Now what if you told someone that the land you were exploring had trees and grasses on it? How might they respond?"

"Big deal," sings out Bruce, in the back. "I mean, they say so what, anybody can tell you that."

"Good. So, what else could we tell them given what you already know?"

A 40-minute brainstorming session followed in which class members developed questions about the environment that Bisaccio wrote on the board. The questions covered these areas:

- Trees: How many, types, size (width and height), distance apart, health of
- Other plants: Types, number of, concentration, and location
- Animals: Tracks, damage to trees, sightings, homes
- Soil: Type, wet or dry, runoff

The entire class discussed these topics to make sure everyone understood what must be done, when to measure and when to estimate, including how to turn a sample count into a general estimate:

"Mr. B, do we have to get all these things for all of the land lab?" asks a bewildered Stephanie as the size of the task slowly dawns on her.

"That's a good question. Who wants to help Steph out on this? Obviously, we can't all check for everything out there."

"Could we divide it up, like in sections or something, and each take a piece?" replies Jenny, who hasn't said much this morning, and who seems ready to go get this right now.

"We could. But what might we miss if we did that?"

"We might miss some of the best stuff," Nicole replied, this time.

"Well, what's the best stuff?"

"You know, the stuff you always say to watch out for. The places where things change and where you find the things you don't expect to find."

"So what do you think, Steph, how can we do this?" He sends it back to the initial questioner.

"I don't know, Mr. B, that's why I asked."

Bisaccio then recommended that the class accept the implications of Nicole's comment and form into teams of two students each to decide on particularly interesting areas to study. He suggested that they start with trees. They came to school the next day dressed warmly for a potential cold and rainy day in the land lab. They went out to the area equipped with field books, tape measure, and notebooks. The land lab is a section of the school property that extends to bordering properties (to which the owners also give students access).

Students quickly chose the most interesting spots—a swamp near a hillside and the top of the hill with mainly grassy fields. Each team marked out a 10-x-10 plot, recorded measurements and other notes, and collected fallen leaves of trees that could not be identified. Bisaccio moved from group to group, answering questions and clarifying unknowns. He particularly directed their attention to a group of small beech trees in the woods and asked them what they might have expected to find (older or larger trees) and why newer growth predominated. One student discovered that beavers were the reason.

When all groups were back in the classroom, they wrote a summary report and produced a catalog of the area plots from their samples, notes, and the field guide. Bisaccio visited each group, pointing out what they missed, suggesting better ways to graph comparisons of tree size and species, and challenging assumptions and conclusions. After one circuit, he turned everyone's attention to the front of the room:

"I noticed that a lot of you were having trouble working out how to determine dominant species, especially when you have nearly equal numbers of trees. What is another way to figure out dominance aside from just counting?"

"How about looking for the oldest trees?" Steve suggests.

"But if they are older it doesn't mean they are dominant. I mean they could be dying out with no replacements," counters Sara.

"Good, that's what you two found in your area, isn't it?" replies Dan, inviting Sara to continue.

"Yeah, we found some large beeches, but all the saplings are oak," she explains.

"And who remembers one of the best indicators of tree age?"

"Within a species, and given the same conditions, size is usually the best predictor," sings out Karen.

"Right, bigger usually, but not always, means older," Dan responds.

"Mr. B," Stephanie calls out, "does that means that the older you get the fatter you are?"

The class dissolved in laughter and Dan dismissed the group. During the remainder of the year, the class continued to investigate the land lab and to pose and answer questions about the physical world. They also took longer field trips to Walden Pond and to a fossil dig.[1]

Dan Bisaccio's instruction is quintessentially thoughtful because it focuses on a few important topics with coherence and continuity, provides plenty of time for investigation and interactive dialogue, raises challenging issues that require students to produce new knowledge, and stresses the quality of supporting explanations and reasons over the need for "right" answers.

Beyer (1992, pp. 94–95) argues that at least four elements must be present for a thoughtful learning environment:

1. *A classroom layout that invites thinking*—not in traditional rows, but students facing each other in groups, working in learning centers or in meaningful clusters
2. *Classroom interactions that involve information processing, rather than information receiving or repeating*—posing and solving problems, seeking out evidence, and judging the quality of supporting reasons
3. *The use of precise, thoughtful language rather than vague terminology or generalizations*—hypothesizing, sifting evidence, questioning inferences and assumptions, making predictions, and drawing conclusions
4. *The organization of classroom study and courses around thoughtful questions*—inquiry built on questions of real interest to students themselves

At Central Park East Secondary School in New York City, all of the classes in the 1990s were organized in seminar style. The objective was to encourage an interactive and more active learning environment. Central Park East students spent their classroom time "building replicas, writing books, transcribing interviews, constructing mathematical models, creating dramas, developing photos, writing lab reports, or debating a class decision" (Wood, 1992). In the field, they spent their time "collecting samples, interviewing contacts, sketching and drawing, looking for tracks, measuring, recording, searching, or just asking why. The point is that they are learning through doing, through genuine experience" (Wood, 1992). Teachers concerned about personalizing the learning process believe in teaching through genuine experiences and thoughtful reflection.

Active Learning Experiences

Kovalik and Olsen (1998) stated that prior learning experiences are critical to the success of active forms of learning. All learning is heavily dependent on pattern recognition, and pattern detection depends on prior experience. "Matching previously recognized patterns—patterns that already have an established post office address—to incoming input is much easier, less time-consuming, and much less frustrating than trying to figure out what the new 'it' is, then picking up on its relevant patterns and attributes." The human brain continuously searches for patterns in incoming information as it attempts to find meaning in the data. *The more active the learning experience, the more likely that the input will be rich in meaning.*

Kovalik and Olsen (1998) suggested two rules of thumb for enhancing learning:

1. Provide real-life richness and context in all learning situations. The less the input, the harder the learner will struggle to find meaning. Breaking learning into small, manageable tasks may actually *obfuscate* any real-life patterns that the learner can detect.

2. Curriculum and instruction must try to utilize all of a learner's prior experience and to maximize the amount of sensory input during learning. Human learning is rarely linear or neat or orderly or typically logical, but rather multilinear, multisensory, and seemingly illogical until the learner perceives clear patterns in the information that are personally meaningful.

The Kovalik Integrated Thematic Instruction Model (cf. Ross & Olsen, 1993) describes six levels of sensory input that teachers must consider in planning instruction. Content and skills only make sense to learners who have adequate prior experiences of the topic or activity. Meaningful learning begins for many students only with new high levels of sensory input and pattern identification that enable real learning to occur. Kovalik taxonomy has six levels of input: being there, immersion, hands-on the real thing, hands-on with representations, secondhand input, and symbolic forms of input.

1. *Being there*—studying things in their real-world context, in the community, in the home, in a business setting, at a mall or a lake, in the country. These experiences provide a richer variety of input, making it more likely that each student will recognize patterns that are personally meaningful and can begin to build personal understanding.
2. *Immersion*—replication of the real-world setting in the classroom or learning environment. Language learning pioneered this approach, but virtually any real-life learning experience can be simulated in the classroom. Kovalik and Olsen (1998) cite an example of a classroom set up to simulate a pond setting. The room has as many real plants and animals as possible, with models, replicas, and pictures of the natural setting and at least 100 books and other print and nonprint resources. The room is decorated to resemble a pond.
3. *Hands-on the real thing*—handling the "real thing" but without the real-world context. Many science demonstrations and laboratory experiences fit this level, as well as some rehearsal/practice experiences in the arts and athletics. The lack of real-life context usually limits the range of sensory input and pattern detection and recognition.
4. *Hands-on with representations*—the use of models, manipulatives, and some forms of computer modeling to represent the real thing. Again, a lack of real-world context usually limits the range of sensory input and student ability to recognize meaningful patterns as a basis for personal understanding.

5. *Secondhand input*—the use of books, ordinary computer pro-grams, media, and other resources that essentially stimulate only sight, hearing, or the imagination. Kovalik and Olsen (1998) argue that "such limited input makes pattern-seeking difficult and pro-vides no opportunities for using or acting upon what is being learned." Much of traditional schooling operates no higher than this level of input.

6. *Symbolic forms of input*—the most difficult level of sensory input for most students to comprehend; for example, the parts of speech, grammar, mathematical formulas, the laws of biology, chemistry, and physics, music theory, charts and graphs, and so forth. Using sym-bolic input successfully requires good verbal and spatial skills and ap-propriate levels of prior experience. Kovalik and Olsen assert that less than 20 percent of students can learn well from symbolic input alone.

Students learn better and more readily when they study things in a real-world context or when they are directly engaged with the object of their learning. Moreover, students need to be actually involved in *do-ing* something, not just listening or reacting. Reading and writing, for example, are *skills* to be acquired and perfected. They are exercised most effectively by *use*. Social studies is best understood by involve-ment in the activities of school or community citizenship. Languages are best learned in the native context or by immersion in the tongue and culture of the target lands. Mathematics can best be acquired by what some educators term a "workshop approach," calling for students to construct their own mathematics. Science and the scientific method can best be understood by using science to explore the real world.

Too many teachers believe that students can learn uninteresting or difficult subject matter if they simply try hard enough, even when the students are neither interested in the content nor understand it. Noth-ing could be further from the truth. We can learn only from activities that are personally meaningful—interesting and comprehensible—to us. If an activity is not interesting or enjoyable to a student, even if the content is memorized, it will not be learned and soon will be lost. Such "learning" is a waste of time and effort for both students and teachers. And, of course, it is not real learning.

Darling-Hammond (1997) praised Wheeler Elementary School in Louisville, Kentucky, for the ways that, after six years of restructuring, children are actively engaged in their learning. "They run a daily school news show, author and illustrate their own books and reports, maintain journals of their learning, engage in science investigations, play chess, use CD-ROMs, and debate current events and mathematical problems." Wheeler teachers developed activities in each of Howard Gardner's eight original areas of intelligence and are engaged in team teaching, shared planning time, and shared management committee work. Student failures have been eliminated at Wheeler and achievement has improved. Students are satisfied and actively learning.

The mathematics standards adopted by the National Council of Teachers of Mathematics (NCTM) also call for classrooms that emphasize active learning. These standards and similar ones from other disciplines advocate changing classrooms from passive and boring places to active and meaningful ones where more students learn regularly from *doing*. The NCTM standards, for example, recommend making classrooms more interactive at all levels (K–4, 5–8, 9–12), with students actively engaged in solving mathematical problems, and with less time given to drill, rote practice, and memorization. Lindquist, Dossey, and Mullis (1995), in their progress report on the mathematics standards, urged that "more time should be spent working with concrete materials and activities that will help students visualize and actually see mathematics. Elementary classrooms need to be equipped with a wide variety of physical material, including counters, blocks, tiles, rulers, and spinners. Simple household objects such as buttons, dried beans, shells, and egg cartons can also be used. . . . Especially by grades 9–12, when students are preparing for higher education or to enter the workforce, their role in the learning process should shift to one of greater responsibility. They should work individually and in groups to conduct mathematical projects and investigations."

For any active learning to be successful, the learning environment must be structured as a knowledge-work organization, with students as workers and learning apprentices, and teachers as designers of high quality work and collaborative problem-solving opportunities. The environment must be rich in sensory input and organized to build on students' prior experiences. The objective is to develop concepts and skills by using them regularly. (See Chapter 6 for additional vignettes exemplifying action learning.)

Authentic Student Achievement

Personalized instruction must also be authentic. Instruction is authentic when it focuses on the kind of mastery found in successful adults. Authentic *human* achievement is concerned with what is significant, worthwhile, and meaningful in the lives of successful adults from all walks of life—from artists and electricians to laborers and scientists. Authentic *academic* achievement, then, must be concerned with accomplishments that are significant, worthwhile, and meaningful for learners preparing for adulthood (Keefe & Jenkins, 1997).

The Center on Organization and Restructuring of Schools (CORS) at the University of Wisconsin-Madison devoted five years of research to the formulation and study of criteria and standards for authentic academic achievement, authentic instruction, authentic assessment tasks, and authentic performance (Newmann, Secada, & Wehlage, 1995). The center characterized authentic academic achievement in terms of three criteria: (1) construction of knowledge, (2) disciplined inquiry, and (3) value beyond school.

1. *Construction of knowledge*—Traditional education generally asks students to *reproduce* knowledge, to label and identify things, rather than to *produce* something. However, adults in many fields must actually produce something—new knowledge and processes and products. Adult professionals, technicians, or artisans build on knowledge developed by others to generate oral or written discourse (speeches, compositions), to build or fix things (art, architecture, manufacture), and to deliver various performances (music, drama, sports). Students, of course, are not expected to produce at the level of adults, but the process of construction is much the same. Students must build on prior knowledge. They must organize, analyze, synthesize, explain, or evaluate information. They must consider alternatives. They must perfect their skills under expert tutelage.

   Conventional schooling emphasizes identification, recognition, and recall. The important tasks involve memorizing words or formulas, recognizing concepts like nouns and verbs or the elements of the periodic table, recalling the names of authors and their works, or historical figures and their events and dates. Authentic achievement asks students to produce real compositions and presentations, to engage in thoughtful conversation or discussion, to mount significant projects, to use technology, to repair automobiles and other things, to perform in plays and musicals and games. Here we are not talking about a few highly talented students but *all* students. Authentic achievement involves all students in *active* and *meaningful* learning.

2. *Disciplined inquiry*—Academic achievement focuses on fields of knowledge with specific facts, vocabulary, concepts, and theories. Disciplined inquiry is concerned with the use of a prior knowledge base, in-depth understanding of an issue or problem, and complex forms of communication to perform the work and to convey it to others.

   Most work in traditional schools entails the transfer of existing knowledge to students. This is just the starting point for authentic achievement. Disciplined inquiry demands that learners use prior knowledge to understand new problems, not simply to assemble a catalog of facts. Disciplined inquiry stresses the probing process that ties new information to that already stored in long-term memory. The goal is in-depth understanding rather than wide content coverage. Students explore the ideas, relationships, and inconsistencies of limited issues and problems to move beyond superficial awareness. Then, as do engineers, journalists, and many other skilled adults, they express their findings and conclusions in real forms of communication (verbal, visual, and symbolic) rather than in the short-answer tests of traditional schooling.

3. *Value beyond school*—Authentic academic achievement always has personal or utilitarian or aesthetic value beyond school grades or honor rolls or college scholarships. Successful adults write, or speak, or build, or create something, with a practical purpose, not just to affirm their competence. They want their ideas and products to be used by others, to have an impact on others. The tasks of traditional schooling often have little value apart from ranking students or classifying them for other similar tasks. Authentic stu-

dent achievement has value beyond simply measuring success in school.

Not all three criteria of authentic achievement may be present in every instructional setting, but all three are important. A work of literature or a math problem may be intellectually stimulating and require in-depth understanding, and yet have little relevance for the real world of the student, either now or later. Repetitive practice and seatwork may be necessary to build a knowledge base, but will likely fall short on authenticity. (Even memory work can become more authentic with interactive computer programs and more interesting content.) The important issue here is that authentic academic achievement facilitates both engagement and transfer (Newmann, Secada, & Wehlage, 1995). Authentic tasks are more likely to motivate students to undertake and continue the work that real learning requires. Students are more likely to use the real-world knowledge and the skills of higher-order thinking and problem solving that authentic achievement engenders.

Wood (1992) pointed out that much of what students produce in school is artificial, with no purpose or audience and little justification beyond pleasing a teacher or external policy makers. In learning environments that are authentic, however, student tasks and achievement are purposeful and intended for a real audience. Wood (1992) recounts some examples of authentic achievement from the schools he has visited:

- First graders at Amesville Elementary School in Amesville, Ohio, prepared books explaining the classroom and program to next year's students
- Second graders at Hubbard Woods Elementary School in Winnetka, Illinois, wrote, illustrated, and bound books for their classroom library
- Fifth graders at Hubbard Woods developed math games for classroom use
- Sixth-grade students at Fratney Street Elementary School in Milwaukee, Wisconsin, wrote alphabet books for the kindergarten classes

- Thayer Junior/Senior High School Spanish class students in Winchester, New Hampshire, taught Spanish one day each week in the elementary school
- Central Park East Secondary School students in New York City wrote a textbook for children on the American Revolution
- Willowbrook High School students in Villa Park, Illinois, planned, built, and maintained a nature area on school grounds (p. 154)

Human cognition is complex, but the need for "authenticity" in learning is straightforward. All learners need to feel competent and capable to understand and accomplish real-world tasks. Newmann, Secada, and Wehlage (1995) argue that "the kind of mastery required for students to earn school credits, grades, and high scores on tests is often considered trivial, contrived, and meaningless—by both students and adults. This absence of meaning breeds low engagement in schoolwork and inhibits transfer of school learning to issues and problems faced outside the school." Engagement here is the key word. Without engagement, much of schooling is meaningless and unproductive. Engaged learning, on the other hand, is more likely to lead to authentic student achievement and to real accomplishments. It is difficult to envision a personalized instructional environment without the element of authenticity.

FLEXIBLE SCHEDULING AND PACING

The schedule of a school makes the educational philosophy of the school evident and visible. If the philosophy is traditional, the schedule will likely be very structured, even rigid. If the philosophy is constructivist or learner-centered, the schedule will almost necessarily be personalized or at least very flexible. Traverso (1996), in one of the few books devoted exclusively to secondary school scheduling, defines school scheduling as "a program and time design bringing students, teachers, curriculum, materials, and space into a systematic arrangement for the purpose of creating an optimal learning climate." The purpose of a schedule is to structure and facilitate the school program. In a program committed to personalization, the schedule must facilitate personalized pacing and instruction. An old saying has it: "Show me what people admire and I will tell you everything about them that matters." If a school community admires control and structure, it will want to constrain the educational process. If it admires personal freedom or creativity or the optimization of personal potential, it will demand a school schedule that makes variation in content and pacing possible.

Past Alternatives

Typically, a school schedule has been defined as six or seven periods of equal lengths of time with additional time for passing and lunch. The traditional school schedule is a product of the factory model, and the traditional school year reflects an agrarian mind-set. Many alternatives have been proposed and tried in the past 50 to 60 years. The 1960s, in particular, produced many new ideas (Keefe & Jenkins, 1997). Innovations such as open education, nongraded schools, and continuous progress education were introduced. A search began for school schedules that offered more options for students and teachers. There was much interest in flexible scheduling. Modular-flexible schedules were attempted in many secondary schools to provide different time frames for different activities. Some activities seemed to require longer than the typical 50- to 55-minute period while some required less time. The six-period day was reconceptualized in these schools to one with 15 to 30 short modules. Modules of 15, 20, 25, and 30 minutes replaced the conventional class period. Teachers requested "mods" depending on the activities planned. A chemistry lab might require 2 hours (eight 15-minute mods), while a chemistry lecture only needed 30 to 60 minutes. Courses were scheduled for different lengths of time on different days of the week.

Many types of "block of time" schedules were also tried. The "Pontoon Transitional Design" (Georgiades, 1969)—so called because it emphasized the function of the schedule as a bridge to greater individualization—integrated two or more subjects from related or unrelated disciplines in 100- to 150-minute blocks to encourage team teaching and instructional flexibility. The "Fluid Block Schedule" (Ubben, 1976) gave much scheduling responsibility to teachers. The teaching team helped each assigned student plan a program for up to three hours of blocked time each day in language arts, social studies, and various electives. The remainder of the day was scheduled more traditionally or, for vocational-technical students, given over to a three-hour vo-tech block.

Continuous progress schedules were a further refinement of the 1960s that supported individualization of instruction. Curricula were sequenced from basic to more sophisticated concepts and skills. Learning packages were developed by teachers for each concept and/or skill. Students were placed in the continuum based on a pretest and previous achievement in the subject. Their progress was individual and largely under their own control. Science, for example, might be organized by concepts rather than the traditional sequence of physical science, biology, chemistry, and physics. In Nova High School, Davie, Florida, science contained 50 sequences that students completed at their own pace. When students had completed all 50 sequences, they were encouraged to enroll in more advanced work. A modified flexible-modular schedule was the typical vehicle for continuous progress. Many of the schools in the NASSP Model Schools Project (1969–1974) utilized this approach. Student schedules were easy to change because of teacher-adviser involvement.

Several important considerations were embedded in the scheduling efforts of the 1960s. Time was primarily seen as a variable and not a constant. Time only measured contact, not student achievement. The length of time that students were scheduled for a learning activity was based on what seemed necessary to complete the activity. Uniform time periods were rare and replaced by approaches that fitted time and place to the learning task. Additionally, teachers and students took part in the scheduling process. In some cases, arena scheduling was implemented to give students an opportunity to select their teachers and meeting days and times. Likewise, teachers accepted or rejected students based on optimal class size, achievement, and perceived motivation. Bell schedules were frequently eliminated except to announce the beginning and the end of the school day. The individual student was paramount. Student needs were instrumental in determining appropriate curricula, appropriate time arrangement, and appropriate instructional strategies.

Current Approaches

Contemporary efforts to restructure schools have generated a renewed interest in changing the school schedule (Keefe & Jenkins, 1997). The most popular approach is the block schedule in which students take fewer courses for longer periods of time. This notion was also popular in the 1960s, but primarily in junior high schools and middle schools (the latter were just getting started then). The block schedule may combine instruction in two or more subjects that support each other. In this configuration, the teaching team reschedules students within the block based on common instructional planning and subject demands.

Today, block scheduling can be found in many secondary schools. The Northwest Regional Educational Laboratory, as well as other scholars (see Cobb, Abate, & Baker, 1999), has identified several popular approaches to block scheduling:

- The Parallel Block Schedule: Used primarily at the elementary school level, this schedule divides student classes into two groups. One group stays with the classroom teacher for academic subjects and the other goes to physical education, arts, or lab classes. Then the two subgroups exchange places.
- The 4 x 4 Schedule (also called the Copernican Plan and the Accelerated Schedule): Students attend four 85 to 100-minute classes each day over the period of one semester, enabling them to complete the equivalent of four year-long courses each semester. Teachers ordinarily teach three courses a semester. Both teachers and students have fewer preparations in the 4 x 4 plan.
- The Alternate Day Schedule (also called the A/B, Day 1/Day 2 or Odd/Even Plan): Students attend three or four 90 to 120-minute classes over two days for the whole year.
- The Trimester Schedule (also called the Intensive Block): Students attend two or three 120-minute core classes for 60 days, paired with two or three year-long traditional courses. Students take two or three additional core courses in the second semester.
- The Extended Time Schedule (also called Reconfiguring the Year): Students are scheduled in three segments, usually two 75-day

blocks and one 30-day block (either positioned between or after the longer segments). Students attend three or four 90 to 120-minute classes during the 75-day blocks and remediation or enrichment activities during the shorter segment.

- The Modified Block Schedule: This approach covers just about everything else at the high school and middle levels. Typical configurations might include 4 x 4 blocks on Monday to Thursday and a traditional 6 to 8-period schedule on Friday; or 2–3 blocks each day coupled with 2–3 traditional class periods.

Can these block scheduling alternatives support a truly personalized instructional environment? And to what degree do the various other scheduling models available today provide a fertile ground for personalization? The following scheduling taxonomy developed initially by Keefe in 1977 for Learning Environments Consortium International schools (and updated for this publication) makes the options somewhat clearer. Personalized instruction can thrive in single classrooms, under team approaches, and especially with client-centered scheduling.

1. Classroom Models—One teacher in a self-contained classroom:
   - *Enrichment/Challenge Areas.* Selected students are allowed to pursue independent work in a convenient place in or nearby the classroom. This approach permits selected students to enrich or accelerate their work on an individual basis while the remainder of the class proceeds in a group-paced fashion.
   - *Learning Centers.* Fifteen to 20 stations are set up within the classroom. Each station has resource materials and directions for carrying out some learning activity in a small group or independent study with minimal teacher direction.
   - *Learning Clusters.* A cluster is an ad hoc or temporary grouping of students engaged in the same level and unit of study. The cluster stays together only as long as the students are working on a common project or materials. Learning clusters demand careful conceptualization of the curriculum, more diversified resources, and flexibility in grouping.

- *Directed Study.* The classroom is organized for maximum flexibility utilizing learning guides, educational contracts, learning centers and clusters, and so forth. The curriculum is structured topically or sequentially and students work in large groups, small groups, or independent study as the objectives dictate. The teacher acts as facilitator, arranging seminar or tutorial groups as needed. Differentiated Instruction is a contemporary version of this plan.

2. Staff Utilization Models—More complex, whole-school arrangements characterized by such strategies as differentiated staffing, variable time patterns, and flexible grouping:

   - *Variable Period (Modular) Schedules.* The school program is conceived in weekly rather than daily terms. Individual teachers or multidisciplinary teams schedule class "mods" of differing length and frequency for large group, small group, and independent learning activities.

   - *General Block Schedules:* Any scheduling format with fewer but longer classes than traditional schedules permit (Jones, 1995). Contemporary variations include the 4 x 4, A/B, and Trimester plans and many variations on these basic approaches. Teachers may or may not share students in these longer blocks of time.

   - *Departmental Block Schedules.* Two or more teachers in the same subject field work with two or more student class groups in 80-minute periods or longer. Pooling of teachers and students in longer periods allows team planning of learning activities, use of paraprofessionals, variable grouping, off-campus experiences, and advisement time. The block may be contrived from two or more conventional periods to allow for coexistence with a traditional schedule.

   - *Transitional Block Schedules.* The transitional block (or "pontoon") is a team teaching, interdisciplinary block schedule incorporating the best of staff utilization concepts and personalized instructional methodology. The classic "pontoon" includes three teachers from differing disciplines, three student class groups, three periods, and preferably, an instructional aide. The pontoon can also coexist with a traditional schedule while providing greater personalization for both student and teacher.

3. Personalized Models—The needs and interests of the individual student are the principal bases for curriculum organization and staffing patterns:

- *School(s) within the School.* An alternative program design that assumes there should be variations in the teaching/learning structures of the school. Alternatives may include a completely traditional approach, variable scheduling arrangements, magnet programs, career and apprentice programs, skill and opportunity centers, and so forth. Each student selects or is given the programs and schedule that best meets his or her needs and interests.

- *Individualized Schedules.* Students working with teacher advisers plan each program of study, use of resources, and amount of time needed for required and personal learning objectives. In theory, the entire day is one large block of time; in practice, students schedule time increments (usually in blocks of time or in 10- to 30- minute mods) for as many days as may be needed to complete each learning sequence. They work in resource centers, the community, or at home, depending on available resources. Schedules are changed as required, usually by teacher-advisers.

- *Open Schedules.* The primary emphasis here is on student needs, interests, learning style, verbal interaction, concrete learning materials and activities, skills development, and teachers acting as learning facilitators and advisers. The school schedule establishes no rigid time divisions nor does it make arbitrary distinctions among subjects and courses. Open schedules stress uniqueness and totally personalized experiences in learning and evaluation. The curriculum may be organized by topics, projects, or workshops; by large or varying blocks of time; by flexible modules, by contract, and/or for continuous progress.

Because the school schedule most directly affects students and teachers, how can a schedule be created that optimally serves both parties? The ideal schedule would adapt to the needs of each student and each teacher. Several of the schedules in the scheduling taxonomy are suggestive of the initial steps in the process. With state-of-the-art computer technology, it is possible to produce a personalized schedule for each student and a professionally satisfying schedule for each teacher.

Client-Driven Schedules

Two ingredients seem to be necessary to the development of a more personalized school schedule. *First, both students and teachers need input into the use of time.* Teachers can accomplish this by making requests through team leaders or department chairs or other representatives. A broad-based scheduling committee might be formed to collect information from teachers and to modify the schedule accordingly. This information would then be communicated to teacher-advisers who would meet with individual students to guide their scheduling decisions and monitor student progress. Obviously, state and local mandates must be acknowledged, such as graduation requirements, length of the school day, and minutes per week. Thankfully, waiver processes are now in effect in many states that permit some latitude in redefining credits and time.

Second, student achievement should be judged on a performance basis. Performance-based learning is a more than viable alternative to existing Carnegie unit, time-based requirements. Placing the emphasis on performance rather than time increases the opportunities for student choices in curriculum and instruction. Flexibility is the key to realizing both of these critical elements of the client-driven schedule.

The client-driven schedule also offers considerably more flexibility for teachers. Working singly or in teams, teachers develop units or topics; create contracts; plan presentations; lead seminars and workshops; arrange for computer use; work with individual students; help students prepare portfolios and exhibitions; advise; analyze assessments of student performance; complete action research projects; and a host of other professional activities. They do not meet with classes of 25 to 30 students in typical classrooms. There is no tracking or ability grouping of students. Project and resource areas replace classroom spaces where students work with a variety of materials on one or more subjects or topics.

Continuous progress scheduling is an approach to performance-based learning that, with appropriate provision for small group interaction and group projects, can personalize the instructional process. In continuous progress schools, general outcomes are identified for each subject in the curriculum, or by courses within subjects. Units of instruction, workshops, or projects are developed around clusters of objectives and materials, permitting students or cohorts to progress at their own pace. Further personalization can take place when instructional options account for different student learning styles and different student interests. Interdisciplinary approaches are possible. When students complete all the units or topics associated with a course and demonstrate mastery of the objectives, they advance to a new sequence or project. In continuous progress programs, students are able to complete unit and course assessments when they are ready to do so. The learning environment is, to a large extent, self-directed and self-pacing.

Contracting is another way to personalize the learning process. Educational contracts can be integrated into a continuous progress system, a modular schedule, or a block schedule; or it can stand alone. In contract-based learning, students design their own learning environments with the help of teachers. A typical contract is a formalized, written document that specifies the objectives, the content, the proposed learning activities, a list of resources, a time line with due dates, and planned ways to assess performance. It also contains a signature section for the students, the teacher, the adviser, and the parents. A completion schedule is developed to facilitate monitoring by both students and teachers. The flexibility of contracting allows individuals or small groups of students to focus on different objectives and content while simultaneously adjusting for learning style. Initially teachers may assume a coaching responsibility for selecting and organizing content, developing activities, and assigning due dates. Gradually students are able to create their own structures. (See Chapter 4 for further discussion of contract-based learning.)

Scheduling for personalization requires flexible use of time and the kind of teachers who can assume the dual role of subject matter coaches and academic advisers. Both continuous progress arrangements and contracting can facilitate personalization, but a schedule that supports a project or cohort approach may be more convenient if much of the activity requires small group work. In this case, a *flexible block or modular schedule* may be the vehicle of choice.

A block or modular schedule can better serve project, topic, apprenticeship, and other more highly interactive instructional approaches. In these, as well as the other scheduling approaches, teachers model student target outcomes or performances and coach their students. In topic study, for example, the process begins with a story or narrative read by the teacher, followed by in-depth analysis in small groups. Activities flow out of the discussion, which may take several weeks when supplementary reading and research are needed. Emphasis is placed on exploration of ideas, hypothesis generation, problem solving, and teaching for comprehension. Students work with the teacher acting as coach and with each other in small groups—or independently with interactive software—to investigate content related to the topic, to develop appropriate skills, and to produce written reports, essays, diaries, poems, stories, and computer programs (Farnham-Diggory, 1992). (See Chapter 4 for more on topic study.)

In his book, *Horace's School: Redesigning the American High School*, Theodore Sizer (1992) proposed a sample high school schedule designed to tailor school practices to the needs of every group of adolescents. Periods 1, 2, and 6 are 105 minutes each. Periods 3, 4, and 5 share 2 hours for lunch, advisory, and tutorials by the teaching team. Team members decide on group and individual activities. Advisers schedule tutorials for individual students. Period 1 has a 10-minute passing period; all others have 5 minutes. Subjects are scheduled on a four-day rotation to provide opportunities for teachers and students to meet at different times of the day. The sample schedule from the Coalition of Essential Schools is as follows (Sizer, 1992, p. 226):

Time	Monday–Friday
7:00–8:00	Activities (band, chorus, etc.)
8:00–9:45	Period 1
9:55–11:45	Period 2
11:45–1:45	Periods 3, 4, and 5: Lunch, Advisory, Tutorials
1:45–3:30	Period 6
3:30–4:00	Team Meetings for the Staff
4:00	Activities (band, chorus, etc.)

A modular schedule is a weekly schedule that divides the school day into 10 to 30-minute modules (mods), enabling the school to offer classes of varying lengths of time and placement during the week. A modular schedule from Wilson High School in Portland, Oregon (Kosanovic, 1994, p. 40) employs mostly 18-minute mods to achieve needed flexibility, as follows:

Mod 1	7:25–7:45
Teachers Report	8:00
Mod 2	7:50–8:10
Warning Bell	8:10
Mod 3	8:15–8:33
Mod 4	8:37–9:03
Mod 5	9:07–9:25
Mod 6	9:29–9:47
Mod 7	9:51–10:09
Mod 8	10:13–10:31
Mod 9	10:35–10:53
Mod 10	10:57–11:15
Mod 11	11:19–11:37
Mod 12	11:41–11:59
Mod 13	12:03–12:21
Mod 14	12:25–12:43
Mod 15	12:47–1:05
Mod 16	1:09–1:27
Mod 17	1:31–1:49
Mod 18	1:53–2:11
Mod 19	2:15–2:33
Mod 20	2:37–2:55
Teacher Checkout	3:30

The schedule is a key ingredient in helping a school staff achieve the school's goals and objectives. These priorities show the relationship of scheduling to the purposes of the school. The longer time periods possible in block or modular schedules allow the school to tailor the available time to the subject matter and permit students to take part in community service and other extended experiences. Teachers also have more time to plan with colleagues, to serve as advisers to a prescribed number of students, to work on curriculum, instruction, and assessment, and to contact parents.

One justification often presented for block or modular scheduling is that it forces teachers to consider other approaches to instruction than traditional lecture, discussion, or direct approaches. Such thinking clearly places the educational cart before the horse. *The schedule should grow out of the philosophical and pedagogical assumptions defined and held by the school itself.* If these assumptions support personalization of instruction, then the schedule should be—must be—personalized.

AUTHENTIC ASSESSMENT

Authentic assessment is the sixth defining element of personalized instruction. Assessment is the process of gathering information about students. The improvement of student learning, not sorting or grading, is the primary purpose of assessment. Assessment is authentic when it focuses on real performance and mastery of a field of knowledge. If instruction is the means by which content, standards, and outcomes are made known to students, then assessment measures the degree to which the standards and outcomes have been achieved. Assessment and testing are often used interchangeably. Tests, however, are only one form of assessment. Assessment goes beyond testing and includes such activities as demonstrations, oral and written presentations, recitals, performances, contests, projects, and individual and group problem solving. Athletic competitions are assessments of how well a team or an individual has prepared for a contest. How a team or individual plays may also reflect the quality of coaching and the talent and motivation of the participants. Similarly, a dramatic performance is an assessment of the cast's talents and readiness. The audience response is a measure of the quality of the performance.

In all cases, the method of assessment should fit the purpose of instruction. If students are expected to learn to write well, the competency can hardly be measured by multiple-choice questions about grammar. Having the students actually write or develop responses to open-ended questions is a more suitable device. Even better is to give them time to write and then revise their writing.

Richard Stiggins (1995) contended that, "assessment literates know the difference between sound and unsound assessment. . . . [They] come to assessment knowing what they are assessing, why they are doing so, how to best assess the achievement of interest, how to generate sound samples of performance, what can go wrong, and how to prevent those problems before they occur." They also never place students in situations where their achievement might be incorrectly measured.

Grant Wiggins (1989) argued that authentic assessments have four common characteristics:

1. Authentic assessments are designed to be representative of performance in the field. Learners actually write rather than take tests about spelling or writing. They engage in science projects using mathematics, statistics, and other disciplines as tools rather than just read or listen to a teacher about them.
2. Authentic assessment criteria are utilized to rate the "essentials of performance" against clear performance standards. These standards are based on explicit school and district goals and are known to students, teachers, parents, and the community as a whole.
3. Authentic assessment attempts to help students learn how to rate their own work against published standards and to revise it as needed. Self-direction, self-motivation, and self-assessment of progress are hallmarks of this characteristic.
4. Authentic assessment often demands a public product. Students are asked to make a public presentation of their work, either orally or by demonstration, to affirm their mastery and to deepen their understanding.

Forms of Authentic Assessment

The various types of authentic assessment can be grouped under naturalistic assessment, performance assessment, and portfolio assessment (Case, 1992). *Naturalistic assessment* is the kind of appraisal that takes place during normal learning activities. Naturalistic assessment involves the teacher as a "participant-observer," a technique long used in anthropology. The teacher systematically collects information about students and records it for later analysis and summation. Of course, all teachers engage in informal naturalistic assessment when they question students about an assignment or check whether work has been done. The difference is in the formality of the process. Naturalistic assessment uses several formal information-gathering strategies. Teachers may develop *anecdotal records* from field notes taken while observing a student constructing a project, engaging in a discussion, or solving a problem. Several weeks or months of notes convey a larger and more composite picture of the student than a simple test. *Checklists* are often used to quickly record such student learning events as books read, homework completed, behavior observed, and so forth. *Student-teacher conferences* offer teachers the opportunity to gather additional information about students to help them with learning problems and study habits. Actual *student work* can be collected over time (as a student would do for a portfolio) and analyzed for successful achievement. Some teachers like to "triangulate" evidence (like anthropologists), basing assessment on anecdotal comments, information from peer and student self-assessments, and actual products of student work. (These procedures also are often associated with qualitative action research.)

Performance assessment is an omnibus term that "refers to evaluating what students can do by examining them in the process of demonstrating some skill, by performing a specified task, or a product that students construct and develop in response to a set of directions" (Ryan & Miyasaka, 1995). The object of this kind of assessment is a student performance or student-developed product. Performance assessment can be directed to such diverse activities as conducting a science experiment; using or programming a computer; debating; delivering a speech; driving a car; engaging in sports; manufacturing or repairing an object; playing a musical instrument; presenting a play; singing a song; speaking a foreign language; typing; and writing a script or story. Some educators call the more formal versions of these performance assessments "exhibitions." These are not typical assignment tasks like doing a mathematics problem, engaging in a classroom discussion, or writing an essay. Rather, exhibitions are comprehensive demonstrations enabling students to present their academic efforts for review and discussion, and to certify their competencies.

Exhibitions are intended to demonstrate broad, even interdisciplinary, competencies, creativity, and initiative. In Essential Schools, for example, exhibitions are demanded in all subject areas and students are expected to "exhibit their work" to earn their diplomas. Exhibitions also can be used as tools in regular classrooms and as summative devices at the end of a period of schooling. At Central Park East Secondary School (Darling-Hammond, Ancess, & Falk, 1995), science students were asked to design and analyze an original and realistic amusement park ride, and to use computer software to analyze the horizontal and vertical velocities of a body in horizontal motion. Both are typical exhibitions used for ordinary assessment. Exhibitions and other forms of performance assessment enable teachers and students to focus on what is important or essential in the content and skills of a discipline and in the totality of a learning experience.

Portfolio assessment has its origins in the practices of artists, architects, and designers who assemble key examples of their work for employment interviews or to affirm their levels of competence. This kind of assessment involves both students and teachers. Students collect and select pieces of their own work over a period of time as evidence of completing their learning objectives or targets. Usually, they also write a rationale to explain why they think the selected pieces are their best work. Student portfolios may include artwork; essays and other writing samples; logs or journals; notes and reflections; observation checklists (student and/or teacher); peer evaluations; photographs related to projects; reading inventories and lists; reports (personal or of group work); self-evaluations; solutions to problems; tests and quizzes; video and audio recordings of presentations and performances; and worksheets (Case, 1992; Ryan & Miyasaka, 1995).

Portfolio assessment engages teachers in the process of developing, reviewing, and evaluating portfolios of student work based on explicit criteria and procedures called "scoring rubrics." The real purpose of portfolio assessment is not sorting or grading, however, but documenting what students know and are able to do. Teachers exercise their advising and mentoring roles in this process, recognizing that when instruction is personalized, only *authentic* forms of assessment can appropriately characterize student performance.

In a personalized learning environment, traditional tests and standardized testing can offer, at best, only an incomplete picture of student knowledge and skills. We discuss assessment types and strategies in detail, along with progress reporting, in Chapter 5.

THE BIG PICTURE

Personalized instruction requires a dual teacher role, the diagnosis of student characteristics, a culture of collegiality, an interactive learning environment, flexible scheduling and pacing, and authentic assessment. A higher-education example may help to illustrate the gestalt of personalized instruction. Uri Treisman struggled to make sense of low achievement among African American and Hispanic students in introductory mathematics courses at the University of California, Berkeley (Treisman, 1992; Singham, 1998). Treisman was puzzled at the lower achievement of these minority-group students despite their having already been through remedial courses and other interventions to help them stay in college. The usual reasons were suggested by his colleagues for lower minority versus Caucasian achievement: that the minority students came from poor or less stable homes with less emphasis on education or that they went to inferior high schools and hence were less prepared or less motivated. What Treisman actually found, however, was that African American students at Berkeley came from good families, many of them middle-class suburban, with a high interest in education. Many students also had attended excellent high schools and were well prepared. Treisman did find wide diversity in the group, with some students from inner-city segregated communities, but the cause of their poor achievement was neither obvious nor stereotypical.

Treisman set out to study the problem by narrowing his investigation to African American students and high-achieving ethnic Chinese students. He discovered that:

- Both African American and Chinese students socialized with students in their own group.
- Chinese students also *studied together*, sharing information about what worked and what didn't work. They traded strategies and tips for success. If one of the group made a mistake, he or she shared it and others were able to avoid the problem.
- African American students studied alone, suffering more mistakes and making slower progress. Typically, they had no idea how well they were doing in relation to the class until they received poor grades. These students thought they were doing all that was expected of them to succeed.

Treisman's ultimate solution was to design *a workshop approach* for his mathematics students. In these workshops, students were organized into groups and worked together, sharing ideas while discussing mathematics problems. The groups were mixed ethnically and in light of previous achievement, so that each group represented a cross-section of learners. Perhaps the most significant characteristic of the workshop approach, however, was that all groups were given demanding problems—much more difficult than they would have experienced in regular classes. This feature ensured that no one regarded the workshops as remedial programs for minorities, and the challenging nature of the problems virtually guaranteed that no stigma was attached if a group failed to solve them. In fact, when students were successful in solving a problem, they were further motivated by mastering something so difficult. And African American students in the workshops improved in achievement by as much as a letter grade.

Perhaps not every aspect of these math workshops is technically authentic, but the methodology is caring, diagnostic, collegial, interactive, and flexible. The rewards are exhilarating. The outcomes are impressive. The approach is highly personalized.

George Wood characterizes the quintessential personalized instructional environment in his description of the learning community at Hubbard Woods Elementary School in Winnetka, Illinois; he writes:

"A community of learners." This is the watchword of the Winnetka school district. It graces the cover of the most recent district curriculum report, appears frequently in newsletters home, and is often referred to by the staff as a guiding principle. It is not mere rhetoric. The notion of the school as a learning community directs virtually all aspects of the school—from the length of the school day, to teaching, to staff relations, to the very layout of the buildings. . . . Most tasks are taken on collaboratively, with students working in teams to solve problems, create large-scale displays, or write plays, for example. Much of this is possible because the curriculum is geared to the developmental needs of children. Rather than workbooks and worksheets which require only the ability to manipulate a pencil and to copy, most classroom tasks involve a hands-on experience. Math games, tools for measuring or counting, costumes for plays, plants and animals all fill the rooms so that students can touch, feel, and experiment as they learn. Such learning does not require that students memorize "correct" answers, compiling enough of them to earn a grade; in fact, letter grades are not given. Rather, students learn through collaboration how to help one another find out, how to ask good questions, in short, how to learn. The notion of competitiveness on abstract tasks only hinders learning, and so these teachers break away from that orientation. Katy Beck, a fourth/fifth-grade teacher, explains it this way: "I found that when I was in school I couldn't wait to get out so I could start learning. I want that type of learning to go on here." (1992, pp. 27–29)

Personalization at Hubbard Woods or at U.C. Berkeley is different only in the details. In the final analysis, personalized instruction is nothing more that a deep concern for learners and the willingness to search for ways to adjust the teaching/learning environment to meet the learning needs of individual students.

In the next chapter, we discuss some of the notable strategies and tactics developed, mostly in recent years, for renewing the grammar of schooling and personalizing the practice of teaching.

NOTE

1. The portion of text describing teacher Daniel Bisaccio's classroom is from *Schools That Work* by George Wood, 1992, and is used with permission by Dutton, a division of Penguin Putnam, Inc.

4

STRATEGIES AND TACTICS FOR PERSONALIZING INSTRUCTION

It is not unusual for educators to believe that there is only one way to personalize instruction. For some, it means getting to know students personally, being their friends, and knowing their names. For others, it means establishing an instructional procedure in which a student progresses at his or her own rate through a predetermined curriculum. In actuality, personalized instruction embraces both of these elements and a good deal more.

Historically, one can recall the image of Mark Hopkins, the teacher, seated on one end of a log and James Garfield, his student, on the other. Probably the first documented example of attempts to personalize instruction in a school setting can be traced to the work of Preston Search, in 1888, in the schools of Pueblo, Colorado. The curriculum was arranged so that students could progress at their own rate in each subject area. Nonpromotion was eliminated, and teachers reported the number of units each student completed rather than a letter grade. Search's work influenced further developments toward a form of personalized instruction at the elementary school affiliated with the San Francisco State Normal School in California. There, "self-instruction bulletins" for each subject were developed and refined to enable students to proceed "at their natural rate, neither retarded by slower children nor hurried by faster ones" (Washburne & Marland, 1963, p. 9). Dr. Frederic Burk, president of San Francisco State Normal School, wrote a monograph, *Remedy for Lock-step Schooling*, describing what they were doing and why. His indictment of the traditional class system is captured in the following passage:

> The class system has been modeled upon the military system. It is constructed upon the assumption that a group of minds can be marshaled and controlled in growth in exactly the same manner that a military officer marshals and directs the bodily movements of a company of soldiers. In solid unbreakable phalanx, the class is supposed to move through the grades, keeping in locked step. This locked step is set by the "average" pupil—an algebraic myth born of inanimate figures and addled pedagogy. (cited in Washburne & Marland, 1963, p. 9)

Given the educational context of the early twentieth century, it is not surprising that rate of learning was the focus of a personalized approach to learning. The speed with which a student could complete a standard scope and sequence was deemed the primary indicator of his or her progress. This standard was a reflection of the growing popularity of translating everyday experiences into measurable units, foreshadowing the advent of behaviorism as the primary theory influencing educational practice.

The work at Pueblo and San Francisco influenced subsequent initiatives in the elementary school at Winnetka, Illinois, and later at nearby New Trier High School. The first superintendent of schools of Winnetka was Carleton Washburne, who became known as "the father of the Winnetka Plan." Prior to going to Winnetka, Dr. Washburne was teacher-principal of an elementary school near Los Angeles. While there, he noted the following:

> I discovered . . . that all children classified as "sixth grade," for example, were not of equal ability or advancement. In arithmetic, there were those who lacked the foundations they should have laid in the fourth grade; others for whom even the sixth grade work was too easy to be challenging. The situation was similar in all subjects and in all five grades.
>
> So, not knowing any better, I planned each child's work to fit his apparent readiness. Usually there were several children, scattered through various

classes, who seemed to be ready for the same assignment in arithmetic—who, for example did not really know the simple facts of multiplication, or who could not read books of the same level of difficulty. I therefore organized the children into small informal groups, without regard to age or grade. In each group, the children worked together and helped each other. The groupings changed from subject to subject and week to week. (Washburne & Marland, 1963)

Interestingly, when one searches the Internet for references to personalized instruction, most of the sites describe programs for "at-risk" students. Usually, the student-teacher ratio is maintained at a figure well below what is found in regular education classes. It is assumed that small classes enable teachers to offer more personalized instruction to students who have not been successful with traditional schooling. But, the smaller classes do not ensure that personalized instructional strategies will necessarily follow. Personalized instruction seems more a matter of the quality of interaction and thoughtfulness between the student and teacher and the student and other resources. It is also contingent upon the teacher's understanding of the principles of contemporary cognitive science.

Instruction is personalized when it: (1) focuses specifically on the needs, talents, cognitive-learning style, interests, and academic background of each learner and (2) when it challenges each learner to grow and advance from where he or she is at a given point in time to a point beyond.

TYPOLOGY OF APPROACHES TO PERSONALIZED INSTRUCTION

English (1994) described a typology as a classification of types. The types of personalized instruction discussed here are by no means exhaustive. They represent a sampling of what seem to be the best current attempts at making instruction more interactive and more thoughtful. They also represent optimism that strategies can be devised to enable more students to succeed with challenging schoolwork. The ideal of personalized instruction suggests that, to the degree that schools can accommodate individual differences effectively, students can be successful in school. The more intense the interaction between the source of the teaching and the student, the more likely students will learn. As students engage thoughtful material at their own level of development, they can advance to more challenging levels, eventually coming to a point where they can solve problems previously not encountered or generate new knowledge in a particular domain, subject, or discipline.

For convenience, we rate personalized instruction approaches on two continua: (1) the responsiveness of the teacher, mentor, materials, and other aspects of the learning environment to differential learner characteristics, and (2) how effectively learners can thoughtfully apply knowledge and skills in a variety of circumstances. Four levels were selected for each type ranging from 1 (the lowest) to 4 (the highest). A critical incident technique was used to define the lowest and highest manifestations of each type. Intervening levels 2 and 3 are interpreted as a step closer to either 1 or 4 (below).

Levels of Interaction

1	2	3	4
Adjustments to differences in learner characteristics are limited.		Adjustments to differences in learner characteristics are frequent and comprehensive.	

Levels of Thoughtfulness

1	2	3	4
Learners acquire basic knowledge and skills to enhance their ability to learn on their own.		Learners apply knowledge and skills to solve real problems and create new knowledge.	

Table 4.1 combines both types of personalized instruction into a two-dimensional matrix and locates each of the selected strategies and tactics in a cell showing our best estimate of where it falls along the continuum for each type. For example, style-based instruction, one of the strategies, is judged to be at level 2 for both interaction and thoughtfulness. Authentic pedagogy is judged to be at level 3 on interaction but level 4 on thoughtfulness.

Table 4.1. Personalized Instruction

Interaction Level	Thoughtfulness Level			
	1	*2*	*3*	*4*
1	Individualized Instruction	Accelerated Learning Mastery Learning Direct Instruction	Independent Study/Quest Montessori Approach	
2	Experiential Learning	Style-Based Instruction	Technology-Assisted Learning	
3		Cognitive Skill Development Inquiry Approaches	Contract Learning Peer Tutoring	Socratic Seminars Authentic Pedagogy
4			Differentiated Instruction Dewey's Project Learning Reciprocal Teaching	Guided Practice Cooperative Learning Cognitive Apprenticeship Topic Study

The 22 strategies and tactics displayed in Table 4.1 were selected because they contain one or more of the basic elements of personalized instruction described in Chapters 2 and 3. Some of the strategies and tactics contain more of the elements and some have fewer. This distinction will be made clear in the descriptions that follow. Additionally, care was taken to select only those strategies and tactics that could be supported by a reasonable body of research. As with the elements of personalized instruction, some of the strategies and tactics have a stronger research base than do others. The interaction level (I) and the thoughtfulness level (T) under discussion are indicated.

Individualized Instruction (I-1, T-1)

This strategy was initially associated with Skinnerian programmed instruction. Students worked through programmed materials at their own rate of speed. Skinnerian forms of programming always follow the same format:

- A question or problem of some sort is displayed.
- The student is required to respond actively by constructing an answer.

- Feedback, either reinforcement or correction of an error, is immediate.
- Errors are minimized through the following procedures:
  Material is presented in small steps that capitalize on what the student already knows.
  Techniques of prompting, fading, shaping and chaining are used.
- Students work at their own pace.

Individualized instruction has been modernized using forms of branching wherein failure to respond correctly to a question directs the student to a remedial segment before going back to the main program. Programmed instructional techniques have been used in some computer-assisted instruction software especially for students with weak basic skills. Computer-assisted instruction frequently provides drill-and-practice and tutorial assistance for individual students.

Individualized instruction can be viewed both as a theory and as a method of organizing instruction. Theoretically, it means *diagnosing* the instructional needs of each student and prescribing appropriate learning activities. As a method of organizing instruction, it can take a variety of forms, but requires that teachers determine the scope of students' needs and the availability of resources to accommodate differences.

Adaptive Instruction and Individually Guided Instruction (IGE) are two applications of individualized instruction. The former was created for students with special needs and resulted in the development of the familiar IEP (Individualized Education Program). Based on an approved set of procedures, school districts and schools assess a student's academic and social characteristics to determine their eligibility for services, usually resulting in placement in special classes. Currently, many students with special needs are placed in regular classes and given help by an additional teacher appropriately certified. IGE as an approach to individualized instruction was developed by /I/D/E/A/, a division of the Kettering Foundation. Student assessments are conducted in various subject areas to determine achievement levels in each. Students are then assigned to instructional groupings or offered individual work based on the results of the assessments. Adaptive instruction and IGE emphasize success for students by adjusting instruction to their academic level of functioning. Both approaches allow for individual progress through predetermined content and permit students to progress at their own rate.

Accelerated Learning (I-1, T-2)

Henry Levin, David Jacks Professor of Higher Education and Economics at Stanford University, formulated a plan for improving the learning of at-risk and low-achieving elementary school students. The plan operates on the principle that these students should have enriched and accelerated instruction rather than traditional approaches to remediation. Levin began his accelerated learning program with two elementary schools in the San Francisco Bay area. The project now claims over 1,000 elementary and middle schools located in 40 states. Accelerated schools are designed to bring all students into the educational mainstream by building on their natural strengths, acknowledging the different experiences that they bring to the school setting, and consistently stressing higher expectations. Levin asserts that at-risk students have the same characteristics as gifted and talented students, but have a different set of experiences than those schools expect for success. One of the project's main features is the use of learning strategies and tactics usually found in programs for gifted and talented students. The goal is to speed up the learning of at-risk students so that they will be able to perform at grade level by the end of elementary school or by the end of middle school.

The approach to instruction is labeled "powerful learning," and includes active learning experiences through independent projects, problem solving, and work with manipulatives (Levin & Hopfenberg, 1991). Members of the school community work together to transform classrooms into "powerful learning" environments, where students are encouraged to think creatively, explore their interests, and achieve at high levels. Because the instructional program is not prescribed, schools determine their own level of interaction between students and teachers, and students and students. The instructional approaches operate on the assumption that at-risk students share strengths that schools often overlook. According to Levin and Hopfenberg (1991), at-risk students bring curiosity to school in oral and artistic expression, the ability to learn through manipulation of appropriate learning materials, and the capacity to delve eagerly into intellectually interesting tasks.

Mastery Learning (I-I, T-2)

In mastery learning, the focus of instruction is on the time required for different students to learn the same material. It is an instructional strategy based on the principle that all students can learn a set of reasonable objectives with appropriate instruction and sufficient time to learn. In a mastery learning environment, the challenge is providing enough time and employing diverse instructional strategies so that all students can attain the same level of learning (Levine, 1985; Bloom, 1984).

The key elements in mastery learning are: (1) clearly specifying what is to be learned and how it will be evaluated, (2) allowing students to learn at their own pace, (3) assessing student progress and providing feedback and remediation, and (4) testing to ensure that the final learning criterion has been achieved.

The approach was developed by Benjamin Bloom at the University of Chicago, based on the work of John B. Carroll, and was the result of many years of research into the factors that seem to have the greatest impact on how students learn well. It was Bloom's belief that if something could be taught, it could be learned by any ordinary person, if enough time and effort could be devoted to both the teaching and the learning. He often cited his findings on learning basic algebra as an example. When time was varied, students were able to master algebraic skills and concepts. In addition to time, Bloom also emphasized the appropriate use of instructional variables, such as cues, participation, feedback, and reinforcement, as elements of mastery learning (Slavin, 1991).

There are two general approaches to mastery learning: (1) "whole class" models (Bloom, 1984), which seek to bring all learners in a classroom up to high levels of learning before proceeding further and (2) models that incorporate continuous progress. Continuous progress programming adjusts instruction to rate of learning. Students advance through a predetermined curriculum *at their own pace*. The curriculum is usually standard for all students enrolled in a grade level or course. A scope and sequence is developed defining what students need to complete and in what order. Teachers, sometimes with student help and feedback, write learning guides or instructional packets. The guides or packets contain a rationale, a pretest, learning objectives, activities, and a posttest. Students take the posttest when they are ready. Successful completion of one learning packet leads to another until the student completes the entire scope and sequence. As students work through the packets, teachers monitor their progress. They review student work, confer on a one-to-one basis, and encourage students to maintain a reasonable time frame. Failure to meet the criteria for passing the posttest results in students being rerouted to sections of the packet in which they exhibited weaknesses.

Instructional modules of this type lend themselves favorably to skill development. They are frequently used in technical and vocational education programs. Some schools use self-paced modules to address specific skills in language arts, mathematics, technology use, and other skill-dependent areas.

With varieties of activities to attain specific objectives, learning packets or modules can provide alternatives to adjust for individual student differences in learning style and/or interests. Scope and sequence can be modified so that student can pursue individual interests through contracts, independent study, or projects. When adjustments like these are made, levels of interaction and thoughtfulness are advanced somewhat. Scope and sequence can be modified for individual differences either by making the sequence less linear initially or by making adjustments for individual students. The list below shows an English I (12 units equals one credit) scope and sequence designed to increase student options.

> *Unit One:* Writing Workshop: This unit aims to improve student writing skills. Emphasis is placed on the ability to organize logically, to use effective supporting detail, and employ proper mechanics and usage.
> *Unit Two:* Learning Guides: Students work through various guides at their own pace. When ready to demonstrate mastery of the objectives for a particular guide, students may request to be tested.
> *Unit Three:* Minigroups: These groups are teacher-paced and may be required of some students, or offered as options to others.
> *Unit Four:* Writing Workshop (see Unit One).
> *Unit Five:* Learning Guides or Minigroups (see Units Two and Three).
> *Unit Six:* Open Unit: Open units are determined jointly by the teacher and the student. The unit may be a learning guide, a minigroup, or a contract.

Unit Seven: Writing Workshop (see Unit One).

Unit Eight: Open Unit (see Unit Six).

Unit Nine: Open Unit (see Unit Six).

Unit Ten: Writing Workshop (see Unit One).

Unit Eleven: Open Unit (see Unit Six).

Unit Twelve: Final Examination: The student's growth over the course is assessed.

Direct Instruction (I-1, T-2)

According to Rosenshine, direct instruction is a summary term for a set of findings in effective teaching. It refers to a systematic method of effective teaching that emphasizes proceeding in small steps, checking for student understanding, and achieving active and successful participation of all students. Direct instruction involves six teaching functions:

1. *Beginning the lesson with review and check of previous work.* Effective teachers begin a lesson by correcting homework and then reviewing salient concepts and skills presented previously.
2. *Presenting new material.* Effective teachers introduce new materials by giving a series of short presentations with detailed instructions and numerous examples. Presentations are followed immediately by having students practice the skills or apply the new material. The teacher asks questions to check for understanding. If understanding appears to be lacking, the teacher repeats the appropriate parts of the presentations.
3. *Guided practice.* After the material has been presented, students work alone or in pairs with guidance from the teacher.
4. *Providing feedback and correctives.* When students make errors during guided practice, the teacher provides correction and help as necessary. Sometimes this involves explaining again the steps to be followed.
5. *Independent practice.* When the majority of the class is able to work alone without error, independent practice begins. This step is facilitated by additional guided practice and helps students achieve competent performance.

6. *Weekly and monthly review.* These reviews and tests provide additional practice that students need to become smooth performers, capable of applying their skills to new areas (Rosenshine 1984, 1991, pp. 75–76).

In a history lesson, for example, a teacher might begin with a quiz over previously presented material. Students would exchange papers for grading, and the teacher would review the correct responses to the questions. The teacher would then present new material, pause to ask questions, and lead a discussion on the key points. Guided practice of the new material would follow (Rosenshine, 1984, 1991).

Direct instruction is typically implemented with a whole class. Thus, it falls to the teacher to account for individual differences and student interests while following the steps of the process. A student's prior knowledge and skill level obviously are important to the level of his or her involvement in the process of direct instruction.

Independent Study/Quest (I-1, T-3)

Independent study/quest is an in-depth inquiry into an area of interest. Students work alone or with other students on projects of interest or on materials predetermined by a teacher. Ostensibly, the most effective independent projects are developed by the students themselves with help from a teacher. Independent study or quest enables students to realize a closer connection between their learning projects and the real-life goal of improving the quality of their lives.

The science fair project is one example of independent study/quest. Students investigate a topic of interest, design an approach to the investigation, and complete it. Results are presented in a written or oral report to a panel of judges and a select audience. The students devote considerable time to completing the project on their own with periodic assistance from a teacher, mentor, or learning preceptor. The notion of the science fair project can be generalized to other subject areas through the process of independent study. The process requires the identification of a topic, the establishment of definite objectives, a listing of resources, a time budget, and a scheme for judging the project's success. Working with a mentor or preceptor proficient in the area of investigation, the student develops and completes the project. The nature and amount of help given depends on the individual learner. In some cases, much structure is needed; in other cases, students are able to create their own structure.

Some schools name a director of independent study/quest to work with students interested in conducting a project outside regular classroom instruction. This person can be a media specialist, a teacher on special assignment, or an administrator. The director assists students on general project design, conducts regular meetings of groups of students pursuing independent study projects, and helps students locate a mentor. Together with the mentor, the director monitors the student's progress and pace.

Rather than think in terms of eligibility for independent study/quest, many schools make the process accessible to all students based on characteristics such as purpose, enthusiasm, viability of ideas, imagination, and curiosity. Independent study/quest can be an option for all students. The crux is adjusting topics and support to the functional level of the students.

Montessori Approach (I-1, T-3)

Dr. Maria Montessori was an Italian physician whose career was dedicated to the study of children. She created what she believed to be the perfect education for a child according to level of development. In the Montessori approach, students learn and apply many unique techniques to construct and apply knowledge and skills. The approach is really a point of view that embraces a child at work on *self-selected* tasks of interest in a prepared environment that features the teacher as programmer and facilitator of the learning process.

There are graded Montessori didactic materials, gymnastics, exercises of practical life, and other individual and social activities designed to achieve such diverse aims as training the senses, enhancing language development, utilizing powers of absorption and concentration, and refining manual skills. The child works for self-mastery through the acquisition of self-discipline and various habits of mind (Orem & Alexander, 1964).

The Montessori approach is designed to accommodate various stages of development in children occurring in roughly three-year cycles. From birth to three years of age, a child absorbs directly from the environment, in a way somewhat analogous to a sponge. It is at this stage that many language and motor skills are acquired without formal instruction. During the second phase from three to six years of age, the child reaches a stage in which repetition and manipulation of the environment are critical to the development of concentration, coordination, independence, and a sense of order. Imagination characterizes the next phase of development, in children aged six to nine. Children increase their awareness of the world and an interest in its wonders. During this phase, the child is presented with the "big picture," an overview of the interrelatedness of things. Concepts are introduced through hands-on materials that encourage and engage the child and assist in understanding the nature of the concepts. As the child enters the next phase, ages 9 to 12, hands-on activities broaden in scope and include practical applications outside the classroom. Projects become more involved and diversified.

Montessori learning occurs in an environment carefully prepared by an educator trained to work with children at a specific developmental level. Children choose their own activities and develop practical and intellectual abilities through individual discovery and exploration of language, mathematics, geography, art, and music. Materials are available for different levels of development to encourage students to become actively engaged in their studies. The materials are often placed in learning centers. For example, a center containing sensory materials allows a student to physically manipulate a tower of cubes, centimeter rods, and trays of geometric designs, each with its own hidden lessons. What begins as casual manipulation of wooden blocks translates into an early understanding of the basics of mathematics.

The Montessori approach prepares students to work independently and in small groups, and to make their own decisions. A major aim is to help students become problem solvers, to make choices, and to manage their time and lives well.

Experiential Learning (I-2, T-1)

The most common form of experiential learning finds students serving as volunteers in the community. Some high schools have a service learning component as a graduation requirement. One state, Maryland, requires students to perform service as a condition for receiving a high school diploma. Students serve as volunteers in elementary schools, day care centers, nursing homes, and centers for handicapped children. The rationale is that when students engage in meaningful tasks in the community, they begin to see a connection between what they are asked to do in school and its practical application. Additionally, students emerge with a respect for the diversity among people and an increase in their ability to interact with others. Alt (1997) distinguishes *service learning* from other types of experiential learning by two factors: (1) participants engage in activity that serves an unmet community need, and (2) it integrates useful service work with intellectual challenge and academic content, often using thematic links between classroom and off-site experience, and ensuring that volunteer work reinforces skills and knowledge learned at school.

Community internships have been part of a nationally sponsored program for a number of years. In many cases, high schools adopt the program and integrate it into their curriculum. In other cases, districts and schools have modified the national program, offering internships in law offices, stockbroker offices, hospitals, medical centers, retail stores, government agencies, and social service agencies. Students learn firsthand about the inside of an organization and what people actually do. They observe "experts" in action on a regular basis and frequently work beside them as novices. The internship offers an opportunity for students to see how knowledge is applied and to gain insights into the kind of schooling necessary to launch a career or a profession.

Field studies also take students into the community for learning. The students observe firsthand what they may read about in their textbooks. The notion of the field *trip*, familiar to all educators, is being replaced by the concept of field *study*. Groups of students accompanied by a teacher visit museums, historical sites, art galleries, courtrooms, the state legislature, nature sites, or any number of other places to give a reality base to the curriculum. What used to be considered a day off by students is now seen as an integral part of instruction. A field study is, as the term implies, an opportunity to study outside the classroom. Students are transported to the field site to observe, investigate, ask questions, gather information, form tentative hypotheses for further investigation, and expand their knowledge base. Upon return from a field study, students discuss the experience, reflect on what they discovered, and devise follow-up steps. In some instances, such as archaeological digs, the field studies extend over a longer period of time. The field study site actually serves as the primary learning environment (Willis, 1997).

Rutter and Newmann (1989) found that reflecting on volunteer experiences and community placements was the key element that helped students increase their sense of civic responsibility. Hamilton and Zeldin (1987) noted that the degree of learning taking place in different public service internship programs was directly related to how closely the content of follow-up seminars reflected issues involved in the public placement. Hence, two factors seem to be necessary for experiential education to succeed at a high level: (1) students must have some prior knowledge of the area of placement and (2) they must have opportunities to reflect on the experiences with teachers or adult mentors.

Style-Based Instruction (I-2, T-2)

Style-based instruction adjusts the learning environment to differences within and among students. Usually a formal assessment is conducted using a generic learning style instrument. Depending on the nature of the instrument, profiles are derived that give information about perceptual modalities, cognitive skills, and instructional and study preferences. Results are confirmed by teachers observing students at work, by personal interviews, or by administering diagnostic assessment instruments. The results are used to plan and implement alternative learning activities.

Differences in perceptual strengths and preferences are usually accommodated by introducing new or difficult information in accordance with the individual student's strongest response mode and reinforcing with secondary and tertiary strengths. For example, a student whose strongest perceptual response is visual might encounter new information initially by reading or viewing. Reinforcement might be approached by listening to an audiotape, a teacher presentation, or by experiencing the information kinesthetically.

Students who prefer an informal learning environment might sit on soft furniture or on a carpeted floor. A standard desk or table and chair would accommodate a preference for a formal setting. Students who need mobility can move about the classroom as they need, as long as they do not bother other students. Introverted students with low verbal risk may be paired with another student or meet with a teacher one-on-one to discuss content or share ideas.

Contract activity packages (CAPs) and other types of individualized learning packets offer students choices of assignments to meet common objectives. These materials replace whole-class instruction. CAPs, for example, are subject-matter outlines for students who respond favorably to a *structured* learning environment or who thrive with choices. CAPs contain a variety of resources: auditory (audiotapes), visual (books, transparencies, videotapes), and kinesthetic (simulations, interactive CD-ROMs, games). These resources provide students with the information they need to meet the CAP objectives. They complete one activity and one reporting experience for each objective. In a haiku poetry CAP, one alternative activity had students tape-record an interview with a fictional haiku poet in which the nine characteristics of haiku poetry were revealed and explained. The students choosing this activity were required to play their tape for two other students and have them critique the content. CAPs also may include several cooperative group activities keyed to specific outcomes.

Comprehensive style-based instructional models also attempt to accommodate cognitive style differences by offering students skill augmentation or enhancement, and by providing supportive learning environments while students work to improve their cognitive skills. (See the cognitive skill development approach in the following text for more on this aspect.)

Usually, style-conscious teachers work with a class group, varying instruction within the total group to accommodate individual differences. What makes a style-based program personalized is the attempt to diagnose and accommodate differences and to enhance varying skills among students.

Technology-Assisted Learning (I-2, T-3)

New technologies can add to the supports that students require in order to understand challenging concepts. Rather than watering down material for students with limited experiences or skills, the efficient use of technologies—like training wheels on bicycles can help students comprehend difficult material. In Salem, Massachusetts, for example, a program called, *Universal Design*, is helping students in special education comprehend the nuances of *Hamlet*. Using a computerized white board, the teacher beams a slide presentation of story bullet points. With specialized cues, she translates Hamlet into symbols at the students' level of understanding. Prepositions like "in" and "through" become simple illustrations. Nouns like "soldier," "ghost," and "imagination" have representative drawings (Galang, 2007). It is a matter of raising expectations by starting where students are and moving forward.

Educators at Washington State University (WSU) in Pullman, Washington, have been helping preservice teachers to begin their practice teaching prior to the formal internship by tutoring and mentoring students in five Washington school districts statewide. The project uses high-end videoconferencing links statewide between college-level students and K–12 students. The project fosters educational interactions between public school students and college student tutors using customized websites and e-mail (Strenge, 2007).

The tutoring project has been expanded to employ PC writing tablets and high-definition cameras to create a virtual social learning environment that captures most of the teaching and learning advantages of one-on-one and small-group tutoring sessions. In collaboration with three classroom teachers, educators and students at WSU undertook a cyber mentoring project with eighth grade students at two different schools. The project centered on a bridge-building simulation that included several exercises to teach fractions, perimeters, ratios, and some basic geometry. The students were instructed to build a bridge spanning two moveable tables using plastic drinking straws, straight pins and masking tape, and capable of supporting the greatest weight suspended by a string from the middle of the bridge. Needless to say, there was much trial and error as the students tested various possibilities (Strenge, 2007).

Fourth grade students in Hawaii used a newly developed device called an "Indigo" to observe and record the behavior of humpback whales. Indigos are wireless handheld computers that are networked to a laptop, which typically is used in a classroom and controlled by the teacher. In Hawaii, the laptop accompanies them to their observation point on the Hawaiian beach. In classroom use, each student has his/her Indigo connected to the teacher's laptop. The teacher can ask an open-

ended question and get a response from all of the students within a reasonable time frame. She can then transmit all the student responses to
all the students, expanding insights and the knowledge base, leading to
further discussion (Olsen, 2007).

A joint project involving Northwestern University and New Trier
High School, Winnetka, Illinois, provides online mentoring for science
students working on long-term projects. Practicing scientists give advice
and criticism to students. Students investigate topics ranging from
earthquakes to avalanches. The online mentor helps them obtain and
analyze data (O'Neill, Wagner, & Gomez, 1996). For example, the Earth
Lab Project employs a local area network (LAN) to enable students to
use technology collaboratively as professional scientists do. Focusing on
earth science, the Earth Lab Project attempts to breaks down the barri-
ers between mathematics, science, and writing. Students are provided
individual and group workplaces on the network so they can easily store
and retrieve information on any computer in the network. They are also
assigned e-mail accounts for enhanced communication. Because the
computers are networked, students can work on their projects any-
where, even at home. The Earth Lab Project has evolved into a "computer minischool" involving multiple classrooms. Students maintain
their workplaces from year to year, and develop a continuing portfolio
for evaluation purposes (Newman, 1992).

By now, the concept of the virtual high school is well established in
most states. Here, students can take classes online and communicate
with the teacher via e-mail. Students can interact with the teacher when
they have questions. Unfortunately, the cyber teacher isn't always available when the student's question arises. Some schools have overcome
this obstacle by teaming an onsite teacher, certified in the subject area,
with the cyber teacher.

Rapid advances in technology will probably result in all of the above
approaches becoming obsolete in the near future. The point, however,
is that technology is and will continue to be an important tool in a
teacher's tool box. Today's students are far more sophisticated in the use
of technology than cohorts from a previous time and even their current
teachers. As teachers become more skillful and as the technology develops further, more effective approaches to personalized instruction can
be brought to fruition.

Cognitive-Skills Development (I-3, T-2)

Learning is a process whereby learners integrate new information with previous knowledge. The process demands that new information add to or modify existing information in long-term memory. The quality with which this process is completed depends on the accuracy of the new information and the accuracy of the categories and hierarchies of information a learner holds in long-term memory. This process is different for each learner because each one has different experiences and different levels of strength in the cognitive skills that control the information processing system. Generally speaking, good students have strong cognitive processing skills; poor students do not.

When students have command of the basic cognitive processing skills, they are able to advance more easily from one level of understanding to another. New information is processed more thoroughly, better understood, and contrasted and compared with existing information. Enhanced processing skills and new understandings slowly change a novice into a more sophisticated learner. We know that learning occurs when a learner's behavior changes. This change is relatively permanent and enables the learner to experience the world at a higher level of meaning. As students construct meaning from experience, their level of understanding increases. Unfortunately for many students, however, the process is not that straightforward. Lack of relative strength in the cognitive skills limits what they learn and how well they learn it. Unless steps are taken to augment weak cognitive skills in students, they will continue to experience the world at less-than-optimal levels.

Different researchers identify different cognitive skills. Messick et al. (1976) identified 20 cognitive controls. Letteri (1985) found that seven of these skills positively impacted the achievement of middle-school students on standardized tests in mathematics. Successful students evidenced strength in at least four of the seven skills. He later applied these findings in clinical settings with students of varying ages to improve their achievement in school. The cognitive skills assessed by the *Learning Style Profile* (LSP)[1] closely parallel the seven identified by Letteri, and include analysis, spatial orientation and visualization, discrimination (focusing), breadth of categorization, and memory. The developers of the LSP added sequential and simultaneous processing.

Whatever model of cognitive skills is adopted, the task is clear: help students strengthen weak skills and learn how to apply them in their quest for knowledge. Cognitive development is accomplished in several ways. It begins with a formal diagnosis using some form of instrumentation or an informal approach based on teacher observation. Either way, weak skills can be strengthened by practice. Teachers grounded in cognitive science and information-processing theory can work with students individually or in small groups (typically for one to two hours per week). Teaching teams can be staffed with one member who serves as a cognitive resource teacher and works with students who exhibit weak skills. The goal is to help all students learn how to apply information to solve problems. The process begins by strengthening cognitive skills.

Students exhibiting weak cognitive controls may be assigned for brief periods to work with a cognitive resource teacher or can be given specific exercises to strengthen their cognitive skills. Cognitive skill development encompasses analysis, spatial skill, focusing (selective attention), categorizing skill, short-term memory, and sequential and simultaneous processing. Weaknesses in any of these controls limit the effectiveness of a student's information processing. Instruction to augment a skill usually

proceeds through a regimen that begins with nonverbal exercises to generic activities to subject-specific activities. For example, as a starter, students with weak analytic skills are given activities such as this: *Draw as many parts of the circle as you can* (see Figure 4.1).

Students proceeding systematically may discover up to 14 subsections.

Figure 4.1

Inquiry Approaches (I-3, T-2)

In the wake of early Soviet successes in the space race with the United States, mathematics and science curricula were developed in the 1960s with an emphasis on the heuristics of the disciplines. Heuristics, a word from the Greek *heuriskein,* which means "to discover," became a popular educational expression. The theory was that by teaching students how to think like a mathematician, a chemist, or a historian, they would emerge with an understanding of the respective disciplines that is seemingly absent in traditional approaches. New math, new science, and new social studies were prominent for a while and then retreated with a reemphasis on basic skills.

Inquiry approaches were aimed at helping students acquire the habits of mind necessary to inquire into the nature of a discipline. When they worked, they were far superior to previous approaches. When they failed, it was largely because teachers did not understand the disciplines themselves. Inquiry learning was not something they had experienced in their university or secondary school education. They were unprepared to implement the new approaches fully.

With our new understandings in cognitive science, it now appears that the aspirations of inquiry educators can become a reality. Inquiry approaches can begin at students' current levels of knowledge and skills, and advance them along a continuum toward mastery. Teaching students the modes of inquiry of different disciplines enables them to gradually become more independent learners. They are better able to confront problems, analyze ideas, examine a range of views, and ultimately resolve controversies. Inquiry instruction begins by asking students, "What do you think?" rather than proclaiming, "This is what it is." The approach applies a developmental model of instruction and often uses a process Sylvia Farnham-Diggory (1994) labels "perturbation." Here, students move along a continuum of understanding from novice to expert. Questions are raised about naive understandings in order to *disturb* students' less productive theories and advance their thinking. As students achieve new levels of understanding, questions that are more penetrating can lead to an even deeper understanding of the material.

Inquiry approaches in schools often stem from a belief that all students can improve their critical thinking skills. Usually, by focusing on "real" problems, students can be prompted to monitor their own thinking, to assess what they know, what they don't know, and what they need to know to solve a problem effectively. Unlike didactic instruction where teachers ask questions with right answers, solutions to authentic problems are typically complex and often fluid. They change as new knowledge is discovered. New knowledge is obviously a relative term and can be applied to a total domain or to an individual learner.

Helping students to monitor their own thinking is a process labeled metacognition, or thinking about their own thinking. It can be applied to reading comprehension, long- and short-term memory, problem solving, and critical thinking. Metacognition seems best taught by initially exposing students to the idea and then providing examples of thinking in action. Teachers model the process by "thinking aloud" as they approach a problem. Like any skill, students need the opportunity to practice metacognition in a variety of situations and can do so individually and in problem-solving teams. Research for Better Schools, in conjunction with the Maryland Center for Thinking Studies, has developed an excellent resource to demonstrate metacognitive instruction in a variety of school settings (see *Metacognitive Teaching: Developing Student Potential*, 1992).

Contract Learning (I-3, T-3)

Contract learning is an approach to instruction whereby a teacher and a student design a learning activity with objectives, activities, a time frame, and assessment. The student then implements the contract on his or her own. The contract does not replace other methods of instruction, but offers an alternative for students who wish to accelerate or study more in-depth or who have a special interest they wish to pursue.

Teachers do monitor student progress on contracts, but students also exercise a good deal of responsibility for their own learning. The relative degree of responsibility or structure depends on the individual student and is usually determined by the teacher. Contracts typically include statements about the content to be included, a statement of learning objectives, a list of agreed-upon activities, resources to be consulted, a time line with due dates, and a description of how the work will be evaluated. Generally, the student, teacher, and frequently a parent sign off on the contract. The signature part of the contract adds reality and nurtures commitment on the part of the student.

Contracts enable the teacher to give attention to individual student needs and interests. The teacher can subtly address pacing, a problem in the typical classroom where students exhibit different levels of readiness for mastering material. The student can assume responsibility for his or her own learning, cooperating with the teacher to assess strengths and weaknesses and to establish learning objectives. Students can develop critical thinking skills and capitalize on individual learning style as they select activities (Daniel, 1991).

Contract teaching is appropriate for students who want to work ahead, students with special problems, students whose native language is not English, and absentees who need a way of catching up in a class-paced program (Daniel, 1991).

Peer Tutoring (I-3, T-3)

Peer tutoring is a familiar practice in schools. An older or abler student acts as mentor to a younger or less advanced student. It can be done on a one-to-one basis or with a small group. The student-tutor usually has a better understanding of the material than the tutee, but frequently lacks the skills to make adjustments for learner differences as the process unfolds. Research has shown, however, that when students tutor students, both the tutee and the tutor benefit—the tutor because he or she is attempting to teach information, thus applying it; the tutee because the tutor can often identify with the student's world more closely than can the professional teacher. A report of the National Diffusion Network (1992) describes successful cross-age tutoring projects where at-risk students tutor younger elementary school students.

Think of a reading or music lesson where the peer tutor introduces something new. He or she may model the performance for the tutee, who then tries it out while the tutor observes. Corrections are made and the student tries again. This process continues throughout the lesson. In preparation for the next scheduled tutorial, the tutee is expected to practice the new material or technique. Sometimes the tutor may suggest that the student tape-record the instructions so that they can be reviewed during the practice sessions at home.

Technology can also serve peer tutoring. The Government of Western Australia has introduced the concept of cyber tutoring in four high schools. Cyber tutors are peer tutors who work with four students every week or two-week period using e-mail. Peer tutors in this program are provided free e-mail accounts and design Web pages that introduce themselves to their tutees.

Authentic Pedagogy (I-3, T-4)

Authentic pedagogy, developed at the University of Wisconsin, establishes a set of standards by which classroom practice can be evaluated to determine its "authenticity." These standards are derived by examining the type of mastery demonstrated by successful adults, such as scientists, musicians, business entrepreneurs, politicians, craftspeople, attorneys, novelists, nurses, and designers (Newmann, Marks, & Gamoran, 1995). What people do in the real world as they solve problems, create new knowledge, and resolve controversies serves as the basis for determining the criteria of authentic academic achievement. The goal of authentic pedagogy, which includes both the daily teaching practices and assessment of student learning, is to realize authentic achievement for all students.

The following three principles of authentic achievement can be used as a template for determining the degree to which teaching and assessment are worthy of the label authentic. First, persons involved in the world construct or produce knowledge. They do not merely reproduce as is done in conventional school settings. Second, achievement is grounded in a field of knowledge or in several fields of knowledge; that is, it is rooted in high standards of intellectual quality and is not simply idiosyncratic to a particular learner. Third, it has personal or utilitarian value beyond documenting that a student has accomplished something. The achievement must influence an audience, result in a product, or communicate ideas in a way that demonstrates a deep understanding of a field. Authentic achievement is similar to what teachers experience when they attempt to teach something to someone else. Authentic assessment is performance oriented and not simply a contrivance to determine whether a student passed or failed (Newmann, Marks, & Gamoran, 1995).

Authentic criteria or standards create a framework for planning and implementing instruction. The approach is based on the notion that all students create their own meaning. Consequently, instruction should be aimed at helping students systematically construct more complex understandings of a subject, a discipline, or a field of study. The depth of student understanding is dependent upon the knowledge and skill they bring to a learning task. The deeper the beginning knowledge and the stronger the cognitive processing skills, the more robust are the meanings that can be generated. The relationship between the beginning knowledge base and current information forms a dialectic of ever-increasing intellectual sophistication.

Teachers who practice authentic pedagogy have respect for students' prior knowledge and establish a means to assess it. They emphasize opportunities for higher-order thinking and in-depth understanding. They offer multiple opportunities for students to express what they know in various forms—writing, speaking, building things, painting, and so forth.

They serve as coaches, mentors, facilitators, and guides in a relationship with students similar to the cognitive apprenticeship (discussed in the following text). Teachers stress collaboration among students and high expectations for intellectual accomplishments. They create learning opportunities to help students develop proficiency in constructing knowledge, in disciplined inquiry, and in addressing problems that have meaning beyond mere success in school (Newmann, Marks, & Gamoran, 1995).

Research findings show that the practice of authentic pedagogy results in higher student performance in mathematics and social studies as measured by tests using items from the National Assessment of Student Progress. The research also shows that authentic pedagogy is equally beneficial for students regardless of gender, race, ethnicity, or socioeconomic status.

Socratic Seminars (I-3, T-4)

The idea of Socratic Seminars as a regular part of instruction can be traced to Mortimer Adler's "Paideia Proposals" (Adler, 1982). Adler identified three instructional methods, each with a distinct purpose or goal. Goal one was the acquisition of knowledge and was deemed best delivered by didactic instruction. The second goal, the development of intellectual skills, was achieved through one-on-one coaching. The third, the understanding of ideas and values, was achieved by Socratic Seminars. A typical school day for a Paideia student involved all three approaches. Adler recommended that Socratic Seminars be held in each subject area once per week for approximately 90 minutes.

The focus of the Socratic Seminar is some type of text, such as a book, a painting, a poem, a film clip, a DVD, a mathematical theorem, a newspaper editorial, or a scientific hypothesis. Typically, a Socratic Seminar begins with an opening question for which there is no single, right answer. The question is purposely designed to elicit conversation for the duration of the seminar. For example, after reading David McCullough's *1776*, a seminar on the American Revolution might begin by asking, "Was George Washington the appropriate choice to serve as the leader of the Continental army? Why or why not?"

Students are seated in Socratic Seminars so that they are able to interact easily—either around a table or with desks circled. The teacher is one of the participants and not the "sage on the stage." But the teacher is not passive; he or she moderates, guides, corrects, leads, and argues with students (Adler, 1982, p. 54). The key concept here is to maintain a discussion that delves more deeply into a topic and expands a student's understanding. Socratic Seminars acknowledge that each student brings some understanding of a topic to the seminar, and as a result of the discussion, whether or not he or she says anything, will enlarge that understanding.

Several critical thinking skills can be identified in the typical seminar: analysis of text, synthesis of ideas, evaluation of concepts and values, and inferential reasoning. Over time, these skills become stronger along with a deeper understanding of ideas and values. Even shy or reticent students begin to participate more when the frequency and variety of seminars are increased in the school setting. Some teachers ask students to maintain journals reflecting on the value of the seminar to their intellectual growth.

Conducting successful Socratic Seminars requires training. One approach is to have the principal—the principal-teacher—conduct seminars as part of faculty meetings or professional development community groups.

Socrates wandered about Athens asking questions of all people in an endeavor to help them and help him achieve excellence. Choosing Socrates as the guiding spirit of Socratic Seminars is to emphasize that philosophy and thoughtful discussion are not the sole property of higher academic institutions.

Differentiated Instruction (I-4, T-3)

This approach to personalizing instruction has been popularized recently by the work of Carol Tomlinson (1999, 2006) at the University of Virginia. As a form of instruction, it is solidly based on the venerable one-room schoolhouse. In that earlier era, the teacher was challenged to find ways to teach students of different ages and differing needs. It was not unusual to have elementary and high school students in the same classroom. The contemporary approach draws heavily on best practices employed in special education and gifted education, as well as research in learning styles, multiple intelligences, and authentic assessment.

Tomlinson (2006) stated that differentiated instruction is not a recipe for teaching, nor is it an instructional strategy. Rather, it is a way of thinking about teaching and learning based on beliefs of students' readiness to learn, their styles of learning, and their life circumstances. Good teaching is a matter of connecting content with students. In a differentiated class-room, the teacher typically offers two to four learning options for students or may even give the students opportunities to choose their own options.

In a high school pre-calculus class using differentiated instruction, for example, students select from among a group of activity folders to en-hance their understandings and skills. Students work independently or in small groups on an activity folder. Teachers work with individuals or small groups, assisting them with problems, checking their progress, and challenging them with questions geared to their level of understanding. Although the teacher uses a fair amount of whole-group instruction, most of the class is organized into small groups of three to four students. Students are assigned to specific groups based on their levels of readi-ness for the material being studied. Students work collaboratively, help-ing each other to understand and correct their work while the teacher monitors the activities.

Working with students from economically disadvantaged backgrounds, Tomlinson and Jarvis (2006) found that when teachers focused on student strengths as opposed to deficits, student achievement improved dramati-cally. This study screened primary grade children using assessments based on five of Howard Gardner's multiple intelligence areas, and adjusted content to the identified strengths of individual children. The researchers and the children's teachers worked together to find ways to effectively make these adjustments. For example, one child with spatial and kines-thetic strengths was encouraged to write about the structures he built rather than from a scripted text or some other standard source of content.

In many ways, differentiated instruction resembles a grouping strategy called "directed study" used in the National Association of Secondary School Principals Model Schools Project (1969–1974) to introduce enter-ing students to the skills and practices of continuous progress learning. In this sense, differentiated instruction may well be a useful transitional strategy for schools as they move toward school-wide personalization.

Dewey's Project Learning (I-4, T-3)

In 1896, the philosopher John Dewey established the University of Chicago Laboratory School. Dewey's belief in the centrality of the individual student permeated the school. He saw all life as interdependent, and children as the center of their own universe. All experience is thus integrated from the standpoint of the individual. For convenience sake, humans segment experience into compartments, departments, units, concepts, and things in order to manage what William James labeled "a booming, buzzing confusion." Unfortunately, what was instituted as a convenience is mistaken for reality. Dewey's notions of education were aimed at combating this phenomenon.

The project method started with the world of the student, gradually evolving from direct experience to formal studies to integrated studies. The curriculum for younger children focused on familiar occupations. Starting with the children's own perceptions, the teacher led them to investigate each occupation in greater detail. They often began their group inquiry by going to nature or into the community directly. By skillfully asking questions and drawing the children's attention to aspects of the environment, teachers encouraged further study. Pupils expressed their understanding through writing, oral expression, constructing replicas, building models, and dictating to the teacher.

According to Dewey, a focus on occupations permitted children to learn in ways that were natural and interesting to them. Dewey listed four ways in which this was true: (1) occupations involve motor skills and "hands-on" learning; (2) occupations involve the use of the scientific method (investigating, observing, analyzing, quantifying, and predicting); (3) occupations involve other people; and (4) occupations involve the exchange of ideas (Farnham-Diggory, 1992).

As children progressed through the school, they moved from group inquiry to group and individual projects. They gradually developed sophisticated skills in conducting inquiries. They discovered the conditions that gave rise to subject matter and individual disciplines. They experienced their own need to read, write, spell, and compute before they were introduced to formal instruction in these areas. Learning was direct and meaningful. Abstract interpretations *followed* an understanding of the human aspects of knowledge. An accumulation of experience provided students with the background to grasp the origins of knowledge, skills, and procedures, and the historical antecedents of their present circumstances.

Secondary students pursued methods of experimental research rather than informal projects. Emphasis was placed on higher-order thinking and personal synthesis. Each student was encouraged to formulate a philosophy of learning. Mayhew and Edwards, teachers at the laboratory school, described their students, aged 12 to 15, as follows:

> These children of the present followed the fast moving life-stream of the past. Through the power of imaginative thinking, each child became . . . one of the currents and was swept into and carried on to a more sympathetic understanding of the dynamic story of the race. Little by little, the idea was born that the use of thinking is to manage experience. This idea . . . grew into a consciously formulated principle. . . . Each child began to see the value of reviews, of summaries, of the analysis of a problem or a situation, of the classification of facts into their categories and the logical arrangement of knowledge to facilitate its further use in any field of activity (Farnham-Diggory, 1992, p. 532).

One can readily see from these descriptions that Dewey's project approach to learning was not frivolous, as some of his critics contend. Rather, project learning probed deeply into the nature of the world and its knowledge. Beginning with a basic unit, students were led to see the reason for separations of knowledge and then led back to see the interdependence of all life.

Reciprocal Teaching (I-4, T-3)

This innovative instructional activity takes the form of a dialogue between teachers and students regarding segments of text. It was originally developed to increase the reading comprehension of students with learning disabilities, but has been demonstrated as being effective for a variety of students, including those who are learning a second language. The strategy is useful for any task that requires reading comprehension; for example, reading to gain information from a social studies text, a science text, or a reference book.

The teacher models each of four reciprocal teaching steps and then asks students to practice in pairs in a guided reading situation before they are asked to use the teaching steps alone. The four steps are: *summarizing, question generating, clarifying,* and *predicting.*

In reciprocal teaching, the teacher and the student take turns assuming the role of teacher. Students use each of the reciprocal steps on a portion of new material (e.g., a paragraph of text). The teacher takes on a passive role, monitoring progress and providing feedback. Other students are encouraged to interact with the student/teacher as he or she carries out the step. The ultimate goal is to have the student internalize the use of the strategies and to be able to apply them independently (Jones et al., 1987).

Teachers provide encouragement and temporary supports that are adjustable for each student. The supports are gradually removed as learners become more autonomous. Reciprocal teaching actively engages students in the construction of meaning through the development and use of the four steps, which are considered life skills.

Palinscar and Brown (1984) reported on middle school students who were extremely poor readers. Students were instructed how to ask each other questions about what they were reading, to summarize the text, and to make predictions about what would be said in the next section of text. After several weeks of using this approach, the students scored markedly higher on tests of reading comprehension than matched control-group students who engaged in intensive reading practice without reciprocal teaching.

Reciprocal teaching is customarily introduced to students with some discussion about the reasons why text material may be difficult to understand, why it is important to have a strategic approach to reading and studying, and why this procedure will help them understand and monitor their understanding as they read.

Students are then given an overall description of the procedure, which emphasizes that reciprocal teaching takes the form of a dialogue or discussion about the text and that everyone takes a turn assuming the role of teacher in the discussion. Typically, the person who is assuming the role of teacher first asks a question that he or she thinks covers important information that has been read. The other members of the group answer the question and suggest other relevant questions. The "teacher" then summarizes the information read, points out anything that may have been unclear, leads the group in clarifying, and, finally, predicts the upcoming content.

Guided Practice (I-4, T-4)

Guided student learning appears in several forms. The approach is widely used in the arts and in athletics; and music teachers and athletic coaches readily spring to mind in this form of pedagogy. In fact, many successful coaches are excellent teachers. In coaching, a low ratio of coaches to players is maintained in order to provide more personal attention. Coaches work with small groups or one-to-one. They demonstrate what they want the players to do and then watch them carefully as they attempt to do it. The player's performance becomes the assessment, which is evaluated in terms of an optimal performance. Corrections are made, the assessment repeated, and the performance evaluated again. This process is repeated until the player's skill approaches a predetermined standard.

Joyce and Showers identify five major functions of coaching. Coaching makes provision for:

1. *Companionship*—interchange with another human being over a difficult process
2. *Technical feedback*—perfecting skills, polishing them, and working through problem areas
3. *Analysis of application*—deciding when to use a particular strategy or tactic
4. *Adaptation to players (students)*—adjusting the approach to fit the needs, skill level, and background of particular players (students)
5. *Personal facilitation*—helping players (students) feel good about their efforts as they practice new skills (1982, pp. 3–4)

When asked, "How do you get incoming freshman football players to 'know' what the skill is?" Coach Rich Brooks of the University of Kentucky responded, "We tell them, show them, demonstrate with people and with film, show them films of themselves, and have them practice with the mechanical dummy. We have them practice each move separately, then put the moves together; first one, then two, then three—how their knees should be bent, where their arms should come up, where they should strike, what all the muscles should be doing" (Joyce & Showers, 1982).

The translation of the coaching strategy to teaching involves students practicing the target behavior under the supervision of the teacher-coach. By asking appropriate questions during and following the process, teachers gain insight to optimize the behavior. They may even ask students to verbalize the steps they are using. This feedback is really formative assessment that may lead the teacher-coach to suggest subsequent steps. In some cases, students may be encouraged to perform a skill or solve a problem as completely as possible so that the teacher-coach can determine the point at which intervention is appropriate. Coaches identify what students can do by letting them go ahead on their own and then providing appropriate assistance. The coaching model is highly personal and involves teachers working with small numbers of students and individuals wherever possible.

Teacher-coaches provide various kinds of supports to students by additional instruction, modeling, or asking pertinent questions. The supports that coaches provide are adjusted in accordance with learning characteristics, the nature of the task, and the nature of the material. Scaffolding is a commonly used support. Scaffolding has been described as a "process that enables a child or a novice to solve a problem, carry out a task, or achieve a goal which would be beyond his unassisted efforts" (Wood, Bruner, & Ross, 1976). Just as a scaffold in the construction industry is used to extend the reach of the worker, a scaffold in learning "is a temporary support . . . to help students bridge the gap between their current abilities and the goal" (Rosenshine & Guenther, 1992). As students move toward the goal and become more self-sufficient, the scaffold is gradually removed ("fading"). Some students may need little more than prompting, while others may require demonstration or modeling. Scaffolds may also take the form of visual prompts, such as cards picturing the steps of a strategy or a graphic representation of text (Jones et al., 1987).

Cooperative Learning (I-4, T-4)

This important approach to personalization can stand on its own or be included in such other models as cognitive and style-based instruction and inquiry or authentic pedagogy. Some educators recommend that a preponderance of classroom instruction be devoted to cooperative learning (see Glasser, 1986). Cooperative learning groups are small groups in which students work together to accomplish an academic task. Each student is accountable for both the academic task and the working relationships and procedures of the group. The teacher's role is to set the task, to establish the procedure, to encourage a clear interdependency among group members, to provide resources and content as needed, and to monitor the social skills in group participation.

Four elements are essential for small-group learning to be cooperative: (1) Positive interdependence among learners, (2) face-to-face interaction, (3) individual accountability, and (4) interpersonal/small-group skills. The most frequently used cooperative learning strategies have been developed at the University of Minnesota by David and Roger Johnson and at Johns Hopkins University by Robert Slavin. These strategies include:

- *Student Teams-Achievement Divisions (STAD)*—Students are heterogeneously grouped in four- or five-member teams. The teacher introduces new materials by lecture or discussion. Students use worksheets and help one another in pairs. Individual tests contribute to team scores.
- *Teams, Games, and Tournaments (TGT)*—This strategy uses the same teams, instructional format, and worksheets as STAD. Students participate in weekly academic tournaments to show their mastery of subject matter. Competition is organized among equally achieving individuals from different teams with scores contributing to team totals.
- *Jigsaw*—Students are assigned to six-member teams to work on subject matter divided into five sections (two students share one of the sections). Each student studies his or her section, meets with members of other teams in "expert groups" on the same section, and teaches his or her own teammates about the section. Individual tests are administered over the material.
- *Group Investigation*—Two- to six-member groups use inquiry methods and group discussion to develop cooperative projects. Teams choose subtopics from a unit being studied by the entire class, break their subtopics into individual tasks, and prepare a group report for presentation to the class.

The following example of the Jigsaw approach was taken from a high school American history class.

Objective: To become knowledgeable about key events and key people during the Civil War period.

Step One: Assemble in six-person teams.

Step Two: Each team member chooses one of the following subtopics (except one topic in each group will be investigated by two students):

- Decisive battles of the Civil War.
- Important military and political leaders for the North and South.
- Comparisons of relative strength of the North and South in terms of (a) military, (b) economy, (c) transportation, (d) capital, and (e) morale.
- The Emancipation Proclamation: What was it? Why was it written? What is its relationship to the 13th Amendment to the Constitution?
- Lincoln's *Gettysburg Address*: The events surrounding the address, where and why it was given, some comments on the content.

Step Three: After consulting a variety of resources, each team member prepares a one-page summary of his or her topic.

Step Four: Members of different teams with the same subtopic meet in "expert groups" to discuss their findings and to help each other improve their one-page summaries.

Step Five: Members reconvene in original groups for the purpose of teaching each other the information about the different subtopics. Individual team members may teach their subtopics in different ways. (For example, present a radio interview with Lincoln defending his decision about the Emancipation Proclamation.)

Step Six: Successfully complete an examination on the five subtopics.

Cognitive Apprenticeship (I-4, T-4)

This contemporary strategy blends Dewey-type principles with concepts drawn from the world of craft apprenticeship (Farnham-Diggory, 1992). In craft apprenticeships, procedures and strategies usually can be demonstrated nonverbally. In cognitive apprenticeships, however, they often must be displayed verbally. The cognitive apprenticeship requires the mentor to describe what he or she is doing as the student listens and observes. Students work side-by-side with mentors who are experts in a given field. A novice student learns through the process of acculturation from observing, practicing with, and interacting with an expert mentor to master new knowledge and skills. In many ways, the apprenticeship is a logical extension of independent study or quest but with more intensity and for a longer period of time. It is also similar to an executive internship where students work under the watchful eye of an informed supervisor. Teachers familiar with action research will recognize the similarity of the cognitive apprenticeship to the process they followed in learning action research from an experienced colleague or a university professor in a school setting. The journey from novice researcher to expert takes time, effort, and much practice.

The cognitive apprenticeship may include situated learning as described above, but also may be incorporated in a school learning environment. Collins, Brown, and Newman (1989) developed a comprehensive framework for the cognitive apprenticeship. Their framework for establishing an apprenticeship includes four main categories with a variety of subsets. Category one, *content,* includes domain knowledge, problem-solving strategies, control strategies, and learning strategies. The second category describes *methods* for helping students learn on their own. In modeling, the expert carries out a task so that students can observe and build a conceptual model of the processes required to accomplish the task. *Sequence* is the third category with three approaches: seeing the big picture before practicing the subskills, increasing complexity, and learning how to apply one's learning in different contexts. The final category, *sociology,* defines the environments in which cognitive apprenticeships are situated.

Cognitive apprenticeships also assume intrinsic motivation on the part of the learner. Csikszentmihalyi (1990) described the true learning experience as one that emanates from an individual's desire to extend his or her knowledge and skills. It is intrinsic to the task and idiosyncratic to the individual learner. And finally, in a cognitive apprenticeship, students are not in competition with one another. They work together toward a common end. When competition does arise, it focuses on the different tasks students do, rather than differences in their status (Farnham-Diggory, 1992).

The cognitive apprenticeship incorporates many of the strategies already described. Teacher-mentors employ coaching, scaffolding and fading, projects, reciprocal teaching, cooperative learning, and technology to enable students to master knowledge and skills in a given area of study. A good example is the Expeditionary Outward Bound Program organized around a series of learning expeditions—long-term, in-depth studies of a single theme or topic that usually involves field work. Two illustrative expeditions are a long-term investigation of a pond, producing a field guide, and a class study of World War II, interviewing veterans and then writing, directing, and performing a play about it.

Topic Study/Storyline (I-4, T-4)

Topic study is an application of the cognitive apprenticeship in a group setting. This strategy had its beginnings in Scotland, not in the United States. Sylvia Farnham-Diggory (1992) remarked on the similarity of the two approaches despite the distance between their origins. She believes that because topic study and the cognitive apprenticeship were developed independently, the workability of the approach in a school setting is confirmed. Both approaches involve students in a group inquiry supported by a teacher-mentor.

Fred Rendell, a former radio script writer, developed topic study in Scotland, and is currently associated with the Jordanhill College of Education. It is characterized by several principles: (1) It is grounded in the idea that the world is complex, and that students have their own ideas about how the world works; (2) The studies begin with a story line, establish a place and time, introduce people/animals, and set up problems to deal with; (3) It employs the general strategy of inquiry and discovery; (4) Students learn that ideas are negotiable if they supply evidence to support them; and (5) Students are participating agents in their own learning.

Topic study focuses on a theme and usually requires a full semester or sometimes two to complete. The thematic approach integrates reading, writing, spelling, mathematics, social studies, literature, science, and the expressive arts. *Whale*, for example, is a topic study created for use with upper-elementary and middle-level students. It contains 10 units. Each unit expands the complexity of the inquiry. Students work directly with primary source material and are helped to generate questions, which lead to hypotheses, which lead, in turn, to tentative answers and more questions. Classrooms are transformed into learning laboratories in which students immerse themselves in the content and process of the topic. *Whale* also uses computer technology to broaden the database (Farnham-Diggory, 1992).

The process begins with the teacher reading a narrative and leading the class in an in-depth analysis of the content. The analysis generates questions that lead to more penetrating questions, as students plumb the depths of a topic. Students frequently work in collaborative groups where opportunities to learn from each other abound. Teachers employ various tactics, such as modeling, coaching, and scaffolding, to help students understand complex concepts and posit their own theories. Topic studies are used throughout the Scottish system from elementary to secondary schools. By the time students reach the secondary level, they are well grounded in the principles associated with this comprehensive cognitive apprenticeship.

In the United States, topic study is called "storyline," but it is the same approach. Creswell (1997), an elementary school teacher in Portland, Oregon, described his journey in learning about storyline and applying the general principles to his fifth grade class.

> Storyline is based on the principle that stories help students to understand the world and provide a meaningful context for teaching all aspects of the curriculum. The teacher develops the storyline and captures the students' interests by involving them in choices for their own learning. A storyline on designing a vehicle for space travel might begin with a letter from NASA, written by the teacher, inviting the students to create and test a space vehicle suitable for travel to another planet. After analysis and discussion, the class decides to accept the invitation, and the project is launched. Each student contributes to the final product by joining a team suitable to his/her interests, talents, and skills.

To plan the storyline topic, the teacher's role is to help students articulate what they do not know and what they need to know, to question students to the limit of their prior knowledge, and to provide structure and support for activities associated with the topic. These activities usually involve developing and creating characters, making presentations, creating murals or friezes, investigating areas, and writing reports. Final reports are often assembled in a topic book that tells the story of their project and what they learned in the process. The vehicle in the story of the space vehicle, for example, is placed on exhibit in the school for other students and community members to see. The students serve as guides for the visitors.

PERSPECTIVE FROM THE PRESENT

Any attempt to classify instructional approaches into one category or another must necessarily be tenuous. Placement clearly involves subjective judgment. Some approaches probably cover several levels and depend on the quality of implementation. We postulated four levels primarily to help practitioners gain a sense of the status quo and the scope of developing strategies. Personalized instruction clearly is the direction that schools should take for our new century and beyond if the diverse needs of a diverse student population are to be served. Level-one strategies are the first step; level-four strategies are the current state of the art. The ideal is to develop instructional approaches that acknowledge diversity among students so that each learner can find an appropriate path to mastering challenging subject matter and needed skills.

The key to solving most social and motivational problems in today's schools is to alter the learning environments that cause or occasion them. As W. Edwards Deming observed, "Either everyone wins or everyone loses." There is no happy mean here. Personalizing the learning experience brings us closer to this ideal. In her book, *The Right to Learn*, Linda Darling-Hammond (1997) wrote, "Building a system of schools that can educate people for contemporary society requires two things U.S. schools have never been called upon to do: *to teach for understanding* and *to teach for diversity*" (p. 5). The ingredients presented in this chapter are designed to offer schools a practical way to achieve both goals.

NOTE

1. The Learning Style Profile (LSP) is marketed by Gains Educational Group and available online from Cambridge Publishing.

5

AUTHENTIC ASSESSMENT AND PROGRESS REPORTING

Imagine that you are observing an elementary, middle, or high school class. The elementary school children are working in groups at tables in the middle of the room or with one or two others at learning centers at the periphery of the room. The teacher is circulating throughout the room, taking notes, and marking checklists as she observes the activities and interactions of the mixed aged group of 8-, 9-, and 10-year-olds.

The middle-level group of 12-, 13-, and 14-year-olds is engaged at round tables in various parts of a fairly large room. They are proceeding through the stages of a modified Jigsaw small-group exercise on the origins, meaning, and applications of congressional impeachment. The students have researched and studied some aspect of the topic to become knowledgeable enough to share and discuss with other "experts" of their sub-area, and then will teach their topics to their home group. The teacher with this group is encouraging the students, occasionally clarifying a sticky point, and observing and recording the small-group skills of the learners.

The high school group of mostly juniors and seniors is engaged in independent study, either working through learning guides or selecting their writing samples or other products for their personal portfolios or as the basis for their graduation exhibitions. Teachers are available as mentors or coaches, some circulating, others by appointment. No typical classrooms here; no conventional groupings, and no traditional assessments. In fact, these learning environments are operating at various levels of personalized instruction, with an emphasis on authentic assessment.

In recent years, many educators, and most policy makers, have been more concerned with standards and standardization than with assessment—finding out what *individual* students know and are able to do. Concerns about accountability and rating students against standardized criteria or against each other have dominated the recent debate and practice of education. The more important issues of assessment have taken a back seat, issues such as preinstructional diagnosis, the uses of assessment in instruction, alternatives to traditional testing, and student grade reporting. The No Child Left Behind (NCLB) legislation has had the unfortunate effect in many states of moving the emphasis from learning to instruction, from focus on the individual student to focus on the school, from concern for students understanding the meaning to simply recalling the facts. Wiggins and McTighe (2005) lament,

> For as long as education promotes a cat-and-mouse game whereby students have incentive to both please us and appear to understand what they are supposed to know (irrespective of whether they do or not), the challenge of assessing for real understanding becomes greater. In short, we must be careful. It doesn't matter how we characterize the difference between knowing and understanding as long as we safeguard the difference. . . . If our assessments are too superficial and fact-centered, we may miss the distinction in the evidence we collect. (p. 51)

Peel and McCary (1997) pointed out that "the unintended consequences of standardized testing have become more apparent (e.g., a narrowed curriculum, frozen instructional practices, and a very limited picture of significant outcomes of schooling)" (p. 704). Of course, traditional and standardized testing practices are used primarily for accountability rather than for feedback. Personalized instruction requires the latter. Standards and accountability are important, but student growth is critical. Houston (2007) warns, "One of the greatest dangers posed by NCLB is that we will reach a point where most kids meet an acceptable standard set by the tests, but do so at the expense of a broad and deeper learning experience. Setting standards can be useful, but only if standards do not lead to standardization" (pp. 745–46). Alternatives to traditional testing are needed then, if schools and districts hope to personalize the teaching/learning process.

It is crucial to remember that, as instruction is the medium for curricular delivery, assessment is the clarifying link between curriculum and instruction. Assessment in a personalized school must encourage student learning, as well as illuminate the degree to which curricular standards and instructional objectives have been achieved. The chief purpose of contemporary alternative assessment is to support instruction and to certify student competence. Most alternative assessments show clearly what students know and are able to do.

ATTRIBUTES OF AUTHENTIC ASSESSMENT

Case (1992) insisted that assessments are authentic only when they are: (1) valid, (2) fair, and (3) supportive of learning. In classical measurement theory, *validity* determines whether a test or assessment actually measures what it is purported to measure. Does a math test, for example, actually measure the actual universe of math skills that it claims to assess? By *valid* and *authentic* assessment, Case means that an assessment measures "the real, actual, or genuine thing as opposed to measuring a poor substitute." A valid authentic assessment of writing calls for real writing (and rewriting) rather than multiple-choice items on grammar or spelling, or even on writing samples. Planning a camping trip, for instance, is a valid and authentic measure of such skills as reading maps, arranging for a trip, and evaluating alternative courses of action. A valid *authentic* assessment is virtually ensured to be valid in the psychometric sense of the word.

Of course, most standardized tests are not true measures of student knowledge and skills, but classroom assessment also may be deficient even if it uses so-called "authentic assessments." A student portfolio filled with worksheets and various learning exercises is unlikely to be authentic. Proponents of authentic assessment suggest two solutions to this problem—either that we make our assessment tasks more like regular classroom tasks or, alternatively, more like the real challenges that adults must cope with as citizens, parents, professionals, and workers. The first of these approaches can work if the classroom tasks are authentic representations of the goals that we value and that adults seek to achieve. In fact, however, classroom tasks rarely rise to this level. The second approach holds more promise if we can agree on what we really value that our schools should attempt to do or, again alternatively, if schools can offer enough variety in the educational experience to make various options truly feasible.

In addition to these philosophical considerations, to be valid, authentic assessments must gather enough evidence to avoid the "one-shot" criticisms that are so often aimed at standardized and other traditional tests. No single observation or performance task can provide sufficient evidence of valid and authentic student achievement. Multiple assessments are needed, like those in well-constructed student portfolios, graduation exhibitions, and teacher longitudinal anecdotal records. Moreover, the tasks themselves must be valid measures of the targeted skill or performance. Case (1992) cited an example of a flawed performance task that required eighth graders to demonstrate understanding of an assigned reading by drawing a picture of the *location* of the story—hardly an exact or equitable assessment of reading comprehension.

Case's (1992) second attribute of assessment authenticity is *fairness*. Authenticity and fairness are veritable synonyms. Because tests and assessments are regularly used to make important and life-changing decisions about students, they must be fair. Decisions about promotion, graduation, college entrance, and employment require evenhandedness and consistency. Surprise tests, timed tests, tests without published standards, and many other unfair practices in the traditional testing lexicon work against many students. Any assessment that demands all students to perform the same task in the same way is certain to be unfair. Timed tests penalize the reflective. Written tests advantage the more verbal; creative assessments advantage the imaginative. To be fair, assessments must not only be culture-neutral (if that is possible), but they also must be flexible enough to characterize the knowledge and skills of a widely diverse student body. Only personalized assessments can meet this criterion.

The final characteristic of assessment authenticity (Case, 1992) is that it must *enhance student learning*. Authentic assessment must promote real understanding and student proficiency. Traditional standardized and classroom assessments seek only "single right answers" and tend to discourage real understanding in favor of rote learning and memorization. Authentic assessment attempts to capture what society really values, the goals and objectives of adult life. And it attempts to achieve a close integration of instruction and assessment. D. Monty Neill (1997) of the National Center for Fair and Open Testing (Fair Test) and the National Forum on Assessment wrote:

> Imagine an assessment system in which teachers had a wide repertoire of classroom-based, culturally sensitive assessment practices and tools to use in helping each and every child learn to high standards; in which educators collaboratively used assessment information to continuously improve schools; in which important decisions about a student, such as readiness to graduate from high school, were based on the work done over the years by the student; in which schools in networks held one another accountable for student learning; and in which public evidence of student achievement consisted primarily of samples from students' actual schoolwork rather than just reports of results from one-shot examinations. (p. 34)

Assessment that enhances learning permits—even encourages—students to use various ways to demonstrate their knowledge and skills. Students must first of all learn how to evaluate their own work, to work closely with their teachers and teacher-advisers in tracking their progress, and come to understand what good work, quality work, really looks like. Teachers, in turn, must learn to use assessment at the front end of instruction for gathering information about the learning skills, habits, and preferences of students. They must learn to record observations and make anecdotal records of their learning activities, to help students develop portfolios of representative work samples, and to support them in extended projects and performance assessments. But above all else, because assessment that enhances learning is interactive and integrated into instruction, teachers and students must talk regularly about learning goals, problems, and accomplishments. Teachers must continuously ask themselves and their students how instruction and assessment can help the learners surmount the most difficult learning tasks and gain greater facility in learning.

Case's criteria for authentic assessment do not address the psychometric *reliability* of these emerging forms. Reliability is a measure of test consistency or stability, the extent to which any assessment provides much the same results for the same group on repeated administrations. This is a critical characteristic in all group testing, particularly for standardized measures, to ensure that successive groups of students are being evaluated fairly and equitably. Do the results of a test given to group A mean virtually the same for groups B, C, and so on? How to standardize scoring rubrics and performance criteria for high-stakes assessments is an ongoing issue for psychometricians. Progress is being made. Reliability for this type of testing is less of an issue, however, when assessment is tailored to the activities of individual learners. In this case, validity—that the assessment really measures what the learning activity hopes to achieve—is more relevant and can be established with reasonable effort and concern for the authenticity of the assessment tasks themselves.

The American Psychological Association (APA) published a set of learner-centered psychological principles in 1993 as guidelines for school redesign and reform. A section of the report on the implications of the 12 principles provides examples in the areas of instruction, curriculum, assessment, and instructional management. The report suggests that effective assessment must be authentic; integrated with instruction; performance-oriented; based on collaborative learning goals and appropriate standards; must measure student growth and success; and promote student self-assessment. "A central assumption is that to improve educational outcomes for all learners, one has to create a learner-centered assessment system that requires *high* standards for each student for each goal, individually negotiated by the student and the teacher" (APA, 1993, p. 15). The difference between this kind of system and typical initiatives is that by involving students in setting the goals, the system gains credibility and the potential for authenticity and personalization. Such assessment starts with students and the goals that are relevant to the students. It leans toward authenticity in that it measures the knowledge and skills that are valued in real life. Of course, it must be personalized because the needs of individual students are its starting point and the learning performance of those same students is its end point. The following sections present "best-practice" examples of authentic assessment intended to enhance learning and to improve instruction.

AUTHENTIC ASSESSMENT PRACTICES

In Chapter 3, we grouped authentic assessments under three categories: naturalistic, performance, and portfolio. These categories are not entirely discrete, but represent a continuum of analysis beginning with the observation of everyday learning activities, to the demonstration of student competence through performance or the creation of a product, and finally to the collection of student work samples over time. Recall that authentic assessments are designed to represent real-life activities, that they are based on clear performance standards, that they attempt to help students rate and improve their own efforts, and that they often require a public performance or product. These characteristics assume that learning is a social process and demands a social manifestation. They also presuppose that the methods of assessment should be aligned with the purposes of instruction. Instruction that aims at personalization must employ assessment strategies that are sound, meaningful, and facilitative. Some examples will make this clearer.

Naturalistic Assessment

Naturalistic assessment, a type of formative assessment, examines the day-to-day tasks of the school learning environment. Some educators refer to it as curriculum-based assessment or progress monitoring; Stiggins (2007) calls it "assessment for learning" (not "assessment of learning," which is summative or evaluative) (p. 22). Much of this appraisal takes place during typical classroom activities, with the teacher (or student) as participant-observer. The evaluator, whether teacher or student, gathers information about the learning process and records it in various ways for subsequent analysis. The strategies of naturalistic assessment are more formal than typical (informal) classroom assessment, but the substance of the process remains the same. The evaluator looks for evidence of learning and for signs of learning problems, records the evidence, and shares it by way of feedback with the student.

Smith (1998) pointed out that "we don't need to test all or any of the children in a classroom to discover whether learning is taking place. We just have to look at what is going on in that classroom. If the students are engaged in activities involving mathematics or science or engineering, and they don't look bored or confused, we know they are learning about mathematics, science, and engineering." It may not be quite that simple, but finding out what is going on does not require traditional tests. These tests often are poor measures of learning that involves analysis and problem solving and application of academic principles to real-life issues. "Finding out" is the essence of naturalistic assessment. Checklists, logs, reports, records, and conferences are common strategies. The following examples represent some of the best of these.

Student Self-Evaluation and Student-Kept Records. Many continuous progress programs encourage students to engage in self-testing as a diagnostic tool and facilitator of learning. These self-tests can be simple previews or reviews of new subject matter, the rehearsal (or practice) of performance routines, or "scaffolds" that guide practice and application.

A *scaffold*, for example, is a temporary cognitive support developed by a teacher or student to bridge the gap between a student's present knowledge or skill and a learning goal. A scaffold can be anything from an introductory teacher presentation, a demonstration, cue cards available for guided practice, or checklists used for feedback and student self-evaluation. The example in the following text is a typical scaffold. In the context of self-evaluation, students could used it as a cue card or checklist at any stage of the learning process to "bridge" from prior learning to new knowledge or skill. The scaffold to summarize a paragraph is as follows:

1. Identify the topic.
2. Write two or three words that reflect the topic.
3. Use these words as a prompt to figure out the main idea of the paragraph.
4. Select two details that elaborate on the main idea and are important to remember.
5. Write two or three sentences that best incorporate these important ideas (Rosenshine and Guenther, 1992, p. 38).

Learning Environments Consortium International (LEC) and Canadian Coalition of Self-Directed Learning (CCSDL) schools encourage students to use *self-tests* in their pursuit of continuous progress learning objectives. These diagnostic assessments are prepared by teachers or students to assist learners in grasping the principal concepts or in acquiring the needed skills of a learning task. Self-assessment may lead to further study and research, to conferences with subject-matter teachers or teacher-advisers, or to completion of the learning unit. Self-tests can take many forms, from constructed-response quizzes and short essays, to student logs and journals that record progress on a specific skill task or a more protracted project. Some schools even use student-kept logs or journals in unit or course portfolios as a basis for granting credit.

Student-kept records are a particularly useful self-evaluation strategy. At the Bronx New School in New York City, for example, students keep personal records of their own reading and writing, their interdisciplinary projects, and their responses to teacher conferences (Darling-Hammond et al., 1995). Student *reading* logs enable students to record their accomplishments and their teachers to chart the type, difficulty, and pace of student reading interest and progress. *Math journals* are used by some teachers to monitor student work on three or four more demanding problems assigned at the beginning of a week. Students record their work in the journals and share them at week's end. Some also keep *math notebooks* to record "student-invented math problems or teacher-designed individualized problems." *Project folders* are used to record project work, with the attendant questions, answers, and products.

Primary Language Record. The Primary Language Record (PLR) is an authentic instrument for observing and recording young children's language development in talking and listening, and reading and writing. The PLR, developed by British educators in 1985 (Barrs, et al., 1988), is a framework for measuring children's growth in literacy. It allows teachers to systematically assemble anecdotal records on students' learning activities and to collect work samples and other evidence about their learning strategies and styles. It makes provision for focused interviews with students, parents, and other teachers.

The PLR contains these sections (Barrs et al., 1988):

- Record of a discussion between the child's parents and a class teacher, and record of a language/literacy conference with the child (Autumn Term)

- Comments on the child's development and progress as a language user, in talking and listening, reading and writing (Spring Term)
- Comments by parents on the record and comments on the language/literacy conference with the child, plus information for the receiving teacher (Summer Term)
- Observations and samples—diaries of observations in talking and listening, reading and writing, and writing samples in English and/or other community languages

The PLR is a classic example of authentic, naturalistic measurement. It reflects a contemporary assessment philosophy that believes language acquisition and development must be grounded in meaningful activities that both embrace a diversity of context and span the curriculum. Falk (1998) asserts that "the Primary Language Record represents a shift in thinking about the purposes and uses of assessment. . . . Rather than measuring student performance in deconceptualized snapshot-like testing situations, it captures authentic demonstrations of learning in natural contexts over time" (p. 42). The PLR assumes that good teaching is personalized instruction that requires teachers to know curriculum, teaching methods, *and individual students*.

In New York City, more than 50 public elementary schools have collaborated since 1990 with local districts and the New York City Office for Research, Evaluation, and Assessment to develop alternatives to standardized testing in the early grades. Teachers affiliated with the New York Assessment Network have worked with the authors of the PLR to create their own version. Teachers observe learners in different contexts across the curriculum to understand the details of their learning processes and to define the kinds of learning environments and instructional strategies that will help individual learners. California educators have collaborated with British educators to extend the PLR to the arts, mathematics, science, and social studies. Together, these educators have developed a method of "moderating" the PLR results to boost the reliability of teacher ratings and to make this form of assessment more suitable as an alternative or adjunct to state and district norm-referenced tests. California also has adapted the PLR concept to create a high school scale and employs an alternative version prepared by the British to rate bilingual children's development in English.

Teachers report that the PLR enriches the way they view their students and their students' families. It encourages a communication-rich learning environment with much more flexible scheduling arrangements, varied learning materials and experiences, and greater integration of subject-matter learning across disciplines.

Descriptive Review of a Child.   The Descriptive Review, which was developed by Patricia Carini and her colleagues at the Prospect Center in Bennington, Vermont, takes naturalistic, authentic assessment to the next logical step. The Review helps teachers look more closely and collaboratively at students and their work—in particular, at one learner (or one piece of work). The developers characterize the Review in these terms:

> The primary purpose of the Descriptive Review of a Child is to bring together varied perspectives, in a collaborative process, in order to describe a child's experience within the school setting. An underlying assumption of the Process is that each child is active in seeking to make sense of her or his experiences. By describing the child as fully, and in as balanced a way as possible, we begin to gain access to the child's modes of thinking and learning and to see their world from their point of view: what catches their attention; what arouses their wonder and curiosity; what sustains their interest and purpose. To have access to that understanding of a child or children, offers a guide to the education of the child's fullest potential. Recommendations can be made which draw upon and support the child's strengths, interests, and power to make and do things.
>
> The perspectives through which the child is described are multiple, to ensure a balanced portrayal of the person, that neither overemphasizes some current "problem" nor minimizes an ongoing difficulty. The description of the child addresses the following facets of the person as these characteristics are expressed within the classroom setting at the present time:

> - The child's physical presence and gesture
> - The child's disposition
> - The child's relationships with other children and adults
> - The child's activities and interests
> - The child's approach to formal learning
> - The child's strengths and vulnerabilities

> (Prospect Center, 1986, pp. 26–27)

The Philadelphia Teachers Learning Cooperative (TLC), an informal consortium of mostly public elementary school teachers, has utilized the work of the Prospect Center since the early 1970s to introduce the descriptive processes into their schools. The TLC Descriptive Review protocol has six parts:

1. The chairperson presents the child's pseudonym, age, and the teacher's guiding question.
2. The presenting teacher describes the child under five categories: (i) physical presence and gesture (characteristic bodily expressions, energy level, and pace), (ii) disposition (characteristic temperament and its expressions), (iii) relationship with children and adults (friends, day-to-day contacts, adult ties), (iv) activities and interests (strong preferences and abiding interests), and (v) modes of formal thinking and learning (cognitive styles, preferred modes of learning, thinking skills).
3. The chairperson summarizes the teacher's dominant themes as the chair perceives them.
4. Other participants describe their work with or observations of the child and ask questions to clarify the descriptions or the content.
5. The chairperson summarizes any new information, restates the guiding question, and asks for recommendations that can support the child.
6. Participants make recommendations that relate directly to the presenting teacher's original question; the chairperson pulls together and critiques the Review, summarizing the themes of the recommendations and any follow-up ideas

(Featherstone, 1998; Cushman, 1996).

The Descriptive Review is usually presented by the student's classroom teacher or teacher team. The chair is preselected (often by rotation) and defines a "focusing issue or question" with the presenter(s) before the session. In an opening presentation, the chair usually presents a brief history of the child relevant to the focusing issue, and reminds the participants of the purpose of the protocol. No rumor or innuendo, no prejudice or prejudgment is allowed—only information and discussion to support the growth and strengths of the child. The presenter prepares a display of the child's work for the Review and a note-taker documents the process for the school's permanent records.

The Descriptive Review is authentic assessment and personalized instruction at its best. The process demands that schools be responsive to individual students, their needs and differences, rather than view them as problems to be endured or warehoused. In the Descriptive Review, schools, teachers, and parents take responsibility for each student. Through observation, documentation, presentation, and follow-up, educators discover the details and nuances of a child's learning development, how to direct school resources and support where they are most needed, and, in the process, how to build a learning community in the school.

Performance Assessment

Performance assessments are skill tests that students complete in the context of instruction. They measure a student's ability to perform such tasks as essays, speeches, playing a musical instrument, driving a car, or conducting a science experiment. Anyone who ever participated in scouting will remember the procedures for earning a merit badge. The required outcome was described in the merit badge book. When the scout was ready to be tested, he or she performed the required behavior. For example, if a scout wanted to earn a merit badge in international Morse code, he or she learned the code and then practiced until the required skill level was reached. This is performance-based learning. The final performance is described at the beginning of instruction so that learners know what is expected of them. Instruction is varied to meet the learning needs of different students. Time is varied and under the control of the student and the teacher(s). Students decide when they are ready to complete the final assessment. The final assessment rates the successful completion of the outcome, or provides data for recycling the students until the outcome is mastered. The evaluation of a performance outcome requires valid and reliable rating criteria. Criteria are established as scoring rubrics and applied to students' work. These scoring rubrics are reviewed when we discuss portfolio assessment.

Common Types of Performance Assessment. Performance assessment should be continuous to tie together evidence of instructional effectiveness and instructional planning. Gathering salient information on an ongoing basis enables teachers to make adjustments in the instructional process. Feuer and Fulton list a number of common forms of performance assessment, which are discussed here (with several others) in order of increasing complexity:

- *Constructed-response items* require that students devise their own answers to questions rather than just respond to the alternatives of a multiple-choice item. These items may range from filling in a blank and completing a statement to solving mathematical problems or describing the results of an experiment.
- *Oral discourse* can be one of the simplest and yet one of the most penetrating forms of performance assessment. Teachers typically use interactive questioning and interviews to evaluate the work of very young children or the mentally disabled when the learner's writing skills are immature. Foreign language instruction and some of the arts rely on oral assessment. Oral interviews are also integral to the most advanced forms of assessment, such as graduation portfolios and university-level graduate examinations.
- *Writing skill* is most commonly assessed by real performance. A student needs to write frequently to learn to write skillfully. The best way to assess the level of writing skill is to have students write a short piece that demonstrates competence in composition, language use, grammar, and syntax.
- *Essays* require even more reflection and development of ideas. Some subject areas like literature and social sciences have long relied on essays to assess student understanding and ability to relate information in a coherent whole. The essay may range from one or two paragraphs to an extended treatment.
- *Experiments* are to the sciences and technology what essays are to the humanities. Experiments enable the teacher to assess student knowledge and skill in the scientific method, from developing hypotheses, to carrying out experiments and related measurements, to writing up the findings and applying the concepts.
- *Performances* provide the proof of skill in such practical disciplines as athletics, art, dance, drama, and music. Students demonstrate their ability to play a team sport or to perform an individual athletic

skill such as track and field, skating, or skiing. They paint or draw pictures, present a play, ballet, or concert. A performance is the logical test of any applied skill.

- *Products* carry experiments a step farther. Products are the final stage of the processes of design, invention, or manufacture. Many subject areas urge students to do original work, to use interdisciplinary skills to make something, to design computer hardware or software, to write or bind a book, to construct a nature study area, to develop a math game, or to devise any kind of project. Products are the performances of applied technology.

- *Exhibitions* are the ultimate performance assessment. Exhibitions are *comprehensive* demonstrations of student competence, through the presentation of a performance or the creation of a product. Exhibitions require initiative, persistence, creativity, and interdisciplinary skills. We discuss exhibitions in greater detail below (1993, p. 478).

Performance Dimensions.   Student performance can vary in several ways. Linn and Gronlund (1994) distinguish between restricted-response and extended-response tasks. Restricted-response tasks are designed for specific or narrow skills. They ordinarily elicit a narrow range of student response and usually are easy to score. Extended-response tasks, on the other hand, require greater understanding and coordination of skills. They usually elicit a wider range of response and are harder to score.

Davey and Rindone (1990) suggested a more comprehensive matrix for analyzing student performance tasks. All of the types of performance assessment above can be analyzed and categorized according to this schema. Ryan and Miyasaka (1995, p. 4) summarized the five dimensions of the framework:

1. Length
   - Short: One class period or less.
   - Long: More than one class period; might be done over a month or more (mostly outside).
2. Amount of Structure (Information) Provided
   - High structure: The problem or task is carefully defined; guidance and direction are provided, especially on how to get started; relatively few alternative pathways to solving the prob-

lem exist; there is a correct answer to the problem or single correct model for the performance or product.

- Low structure: Students have wide latitude in selecting or defining the problem or task; no guidance or directions for getting started are provided; there are many ways to approach the problem; there is no one correct answer or correct model for the performance or product.

3. Task Participation
- Individual: Students work alone through all phases of the task.
- Group: Students work as part of a group in all phases of the task.
- Mixed: Students work alone on some parts of the task and in groups for other parts.

4. Evaluation Focus
- Process: Students' actions and behaviors (i.e., actual performance) are observed and rated.
- Product: The concrete product of the performance is observed and rated (i.e., paper, report, a model, apparatus, proposed answer).

5. Performance Model(s)
- Single: Only one performance mode or product is evaluated.
- Multiple: Students must perform in a variety of modes (e.g., written report, oral report, graph or chart, log, etc).

The different choices within the dimensions can be variously combined to produce different performance assessments ranging from very simple restricted-response tasks to very demanding and extended exhibitions. In reviewing these dimensions, keep in mind that no particular approach is right or necessarily recommended for any or all assessment tasks. The needs of the students and the purposes of instruction must be the guiding norms. Remember also, real performance requires an integration of competencies, not just knowledge of unconnected facts or skills.

Case (1992) recalled trying to teach his seventh-grade students how to plan a picnic lunch for a field trip. He had the students practice word problems costing-out picnic needs and expenses for groups of students. Yet, despite their success in solving these problems, students could not figure out how much money each one would need for their own field-trip lunch. They made no connections between the theoretical problems and the practical challenge. (Psychologists call this transfer of learning.) They still could not find the answer even when the connection was specifically explained to them. They just could not integrate the needed competencies. A simple performance assessment showed that the students needed to be taught *how* to cost their own field-trip lunches. Case (1992) observed, "If we do not assess beyond isolated competencies in artificial situations, we are unlikely to know of, and less likely to promote, our students' abilities to use their knowledge in significant ways" (p. 17).

Exhibitions.   Exhibitions are more comprehensive performance assessments. Schools of the Coalition of Essential Schools and many other schools with strong commitment to personalized instruction and authentic assessment require students to exhibit their work, even to establish competence for graduation by a comprehensive and public exhibition. Exhibitions consist of presentations of student's actual products and performances followed by peer and teacher or public discussion.

Good exhibitions spring from good instruction. Sizer (1996) wrote, "All sorts of provocations can work as exhibitions, from Socrates' questions in his ancient garden to some of the better brain-teasers in puzzle books. Each probes the depth of a student's understanding of ideas, and each tests that student's ability to express herself. Most require dialogue. One rarely plumbs a student's understanding well without probing for clarification and affirmation" (p. 83).

Students are always challenged by exhibitions because they must know the content well, be able to exhibit work samples that display their knowledge or present a performance that exhibits real skill, and be able to explain their conclusions or choice of repertoire. (The record of their exhibited work over a period of time is called a *portfolio* by many. We discuss portfolios in the next section.)

Exhibitions have been employed widely and for many years in such subject fields as art, music, physical education, and science. It is difficult to imagine an art course without displays of student work. Professional artists build their careers on periodic exhibitions and portfolios of their collected works. All kinds of music activities assume that performance is the goal. A band or chorus that does not perform is inconceivable. The marching band or the athletic team is judged primarily on the totality of the live performance, not just on audio or video recordings of performance excerpts. The science fair is a staple in many schools and districts. Exhibits are judged on their creativity, presentation, and potential contribution to the field. Public performance and critique are powerful incentives for improvement and excellence.

Coalition of Essential Schools' participants employ exhibitions in all subjects and in all coursework. Teachers and students work together to ensure that learning targets are clear and that the products of learning are "exhibitable." Teachers must make sure that what is expected is precisely understood and that students and their parents agree that the required work is worth the effort. The consequences of strong or weak effort are apparent to everyone. Busy work and activities just to get a grade have no place here.

Sizer (1996) put it this way:

> Going public brings sloppy work to light. It can also lead educators to discover that many students who have been labeled "superior" or "incompetent" in fact are at neither extreme. We have learned how distressingly weak many students—perhaps most students—are, even in the advanced section at high schools. They may be able to tell us things, but too often they are not able to explain why those things are so or to use what they have learned in a new context. The clarity of the Exhibition process is both illuminating and sobering. . . . It is demanding work. However, those Essential schools that have been using Exhibitions long enough to see the effects clearly strongly attest to their importance. Exhibitions concentrate a school's priorities in the right place. (p. 86)

Anzar High School, a member of the Bay Area Coalition for Equitable Schools (BayCES) near Monterey, California, has established an interesting and systematic plan for graduation by exhibition. Anzar students complete multiple exhibitions during their junior and senior years. The exhibitions are presented six times each year during three-day sessions before a jury of teachers, students, and community members. Scoring criteria are based on the Essential School "habits of mind" that guide curricular and instructional strategy in the school: evidence, perspective, extension, relevance, and reflection. The scoring criteria rate students on the following elements (Cushman, 1997, p. 5):

- Presents biases of self, others, and the research used
- Indicates understanding of alternative points of view and experiences
- Presents sufficient evidence, including multiple choices available, clearly and convincingly

- Presents an analysis of the deeper implications, including how the student's conclusions might affect the future, what might happen if something changed, and identification of any patterns or connections to other ideas
- Shows a deep understanding of the topic's relevance to self and community
- Includes reflection on what the student learned and what other questions the project brought up
- If appropriate to the topic, shows empathy and explains how doing the project changed the student's thinking

Anzar students are not allowed to present until they show sufficient readiness. Occasionally, a presenter is required to make revisions or to do additional work before being passed.

Students consolidate several disciplines in a major graduation project that enables them to synthesize everything they have learned during their high school experience (Joy, 2007). Cushman (1997, p. 5) summarizes the six categories of the Anzar graduation exhibition:

1. *The postgraduate plan,* which includes an employment or college portfolio, a physical challenge portfolio, and a self-reflection piece
2. *The history-social studies written and oral exhibition,* in which students choose a complex topic of personal interest, draw conclusions, and make connections about it based on research, and project patterns from it into the future
3. *The language arts written and oral exhibition,* in which students draw on material they have read and written, taking and defending a position that considers many sides of a complex issue
4. *The science exhibition,* in which students create, conduct, document, and defend an experiment related to a complex topic and carried out using the scientific method, including written and oral explanations and analysis
5. *The mathematics exhibition,* in which students complete a pure or applied project exploring a key mathematical question or conjecture, and provide an in-depth, clear, and correct explanation using at least two different approaches

6. *The service learning exhibition,* in which students present their service experiences over the course of high school, reflect on their value, describe plans for future service, and reflect on their responsibilities to society

Students may combine exhibitions if it seems appropriate. A Spanish (or another world) language component and an arts component are also required. The student must present orally in the second language as a meaningful part of one of the six exhibitions listed above. In addition, he or she must create, and include in at least one of the six exhibitions, an original work in dance, music, or the visual arts.

The Collaborative Assessment Conference and Tuning Protocol. These are two other facilitated discussion techniques designed to look more closely at student work and especially at student exhibitions. The Collaborative Assessment Conference, developed by Seidel (1991) and his colleagues at Harvard University's Project Zero, asks teachers to look closely at student work for the meaning and insight beyond the parameters of the particular assignment. The Tuning Protocol was developed by McDonald and Allen (1995) for the Coalition of Essential Schools to assist schools in determining the readiness of students to graduate according to a school's standards or criteria. Several versions of the Tuning Protocol have been devised, but the variations generally include: (1) an introduction, (2) teacher presentation of student work, (3) clarifying questions, (4) participant reflection on the type of feedback to be given, (5) warm and cool feedback, (6) presenter reflection and response, and (7) debriefing (open discussion). For more information on these and other related strategies, consult Allen (1998).

Portfolio Assessment

A portfolio is a collection of student work put together over some period of time by the student with the help and supervision of teachers. Students select samples of their work to serve as evidence that they have completed the school's learning objectives and major outcomes required for graduation. Teachers provide guidance and help students keep their portfolios properly focused and manageable.

Portfolio assessment emphasizes problem solving, reasoning, effective written communication, and research skills while still allowing the assessment of knowledge, facts, concepts, and procedures. It seeks a comprehensive assessment of student knowledge and skills. Portfolios are more than open folders into which selected samples of student work are filed for future reference. They are structured to contain specific kinds of samples consistent with curriculum goals and instructional objectives. A well-crafted portfolio includes a table of contents, five to seven pieces of student work germane to the subject or topic, and written justification from the student for selecting each piece of work. A portfolio concurrently assesses student performance and helps the student internalize standards of quality.

Quality is a topic that is rarely discussed with students. Most teachers seem to think that students know what quality work is. Unfortunately, this is usually not the case. If the adage "students get good at what they spend time doing" is correct, then ample time must be devoted to helping them understand the concept of quality. Teachers should begin the process by talking about quality in a general way. The general discussion might focus on the things in the students' world that they judge to be of quality and why. For example, teachers might begin by asking students to look for quality in how they dress, how they wear their hair, their music, and the movies they attend. The discussions do not have to be long, just frequent. Subsequently, teachers can engage students in discussions about the meaning of quality applied to the subjects or topics under study and then to the nature of their own work.

Scoring Rubrics. Portfolio (as well as exhibition) quality is assessed through scoring rubrics. The key step in portfolio assessment is "establishing and communicating explicit procedures and criteria that will be used to evaluate the quality of the materials contained in the portfolio. . . . Students' work and performance must be judged against a criterion or set of criteria of quality to have assessment. The criteria of quality are established through the development of scoring rubrics, and the application of scoring rubrics to students' work forms the basis for all effective assessment systems" (Ryan & Miyasaka, 1995). Educators have developed four types of scoring rubrics: holistic, modified or focused holistic, analytic, and modified analytic. Table 5.1 summarizes these four approaches to rating and scoring.

Table 5.1.   Four Approaches to Rating and Scoring: Example of a Scoring Rubric for Writing

Description of Scoring Approach	Assessment and Instructional Information
Holistic	
Overall judgment with no criteria. A student's performance is compared to a series of ordered or graded models (e.g., 1, 2, 3, and 4), and is assigned a "holistic" score based on which model it most closely matches.	Provides general information about student performance. Provides no instructional information about dimensions of learning exhibited by the student's performance.
Modified or Focused Holistic	
Holistic scoring with embedded criteria. A total or "holistic" score is assigned based on a scorer's judgment about the student's performance. Each score point on the holistic scale is defined by levels of student performance related to features of important learning dimensions.	Provides general information about the performance as a whole and indicates some instructional information about the level of a student's performance related to the learning dimensions.
Modified Analytic	
Analytic scoring with a total score. A "partial" score is assigned based on the scorer's judgments of specific learning dimensions underlying the student's performance. For each learning dimension, features of particular levels of performance and the number of points to be awarded are defined. A procedure for combining the scores is specified. Thus, the overall or total score is the sum of the dimension scores.	Provides general information about the performance as a whole and indicates specific instructional information about the level of a student's performance related to the learning dimensions.
Analytic	
Judgments of specific dimensions or characteristics. A partial score is assigned based on scorer's judgments of specific dimensions. For each learning dimension, features of particular levels of performance and the number of points to be awarded are defined. There is no total score, only several partial, analytic scores.	Provides more detailed instructional feedback about specific dimensions of learning. Since there is no total score, there is no information about the performance as a whole.

Source: Data from Ryan, J. M., and Miyasaka, J. R. 1995. Current practice in testing and assessment: What is driving the changes? *NASSP Bulletin* 79: 8.

Ryan and Miyasaka (1995) point out that scoring rubrics are not as difficult to develop as it may at first seem. Experienced teachers usually have an implicit or explicit set of scoring criteria that they have used to rate student work. This can be a good starting point. Rubrics then can be developed gradually, perhaps as a function of the ongoing professional development program of the district or school.

The Francis W. Parker Charter School Standards. The Parker School is an example of a school that has formulated criteria for excellence, school standards, and scoring rubrics for three school divisions, with the academic disciplines integrated under "domains": Arts and Humanities (AH), Mathematics, Science, and Technology (MST), Spanish, and Wellness (W) (for more information, visit their website at: http://www.parker.org).The typical criteria for excellence are the same across the three divisions (grades 7–12), but the school expects that as students move up levels, their tasks will become more complex, their work will display more autonomy and initiative, and their awareness of their own and others' work will increase. The holistic rubrics for each division describe how student work looks in each division (a two-year cycle) when it: (1) is just beginning to meet, (2) approaches, or (3) meets (or exceeds) Parker's expectations at that level (Cushman and Rogers, 1997). The list below shows the Parker rubrics for the technology area. The draft rubrics are brief in this category, but those in reading, math, and the other major domains are much more descriptive, reflecting their more advanced stage of development.

Parker School Standards for Technology

Criteria for Excellence remain the same across the Division levels. In each Division, students strive for understanding progressively more complex concepts and skills with progressively more initiative, autonomy, and awareness.

Criteria for Excellence

- You can touch type on a standard keyboard.
- You can use a word processing program to produce a written document.

- You can use an electronic card catalogue.
- You can load, run, and use a database program on the computer.
- You can use a graphics or drawing program on the computer to create graphs, charts, or other visual aids.
- You can use and create a spreadsheet.
- You can use and create computer simulations to model the behavior of systems over time.
- You can acquire information for specific purposes using online sources such as the World Wide Web.
- You can exchange information on the Internet using electronic mail.
- You can use manuals and onscreen help to learn how to use software programs.
- You can troubleshoot problems in operating computer equipment and software.

Draft Division I Standards

- You can touch type on a standard keyboard at least 15 words per minute with 100 percent accuracy.
- You can access and use a word processing program to produce a written document.
- You can use an electronic card catalogue.
- You can acquire information for specific purposes using online sources such as the World Wide Web.
- You can exchange information on the Internet using electronic mail.
- You can use a computer spreadsheet.
- You can use a graphic or drawing program on the computer to create graphs, charts, or other visual aids.
- You can use a computer simulation to model the behavior of systems over time.

Draft Division II Standards

In addition to meeting Division I standards,

- You can touch type on a standard keyboard at least 30 words per minute with 100 percent accuracy.

- You can load, run, and use a database program on the computer.
- You can create a computer spreadsheet.
- You can create a simple computer simulation to model the behavior of systems over time.
- You can use manuals and on-screen help to learn how to use software programs.

Draft Division III Standards

In addition to meeting Division I and II standards,

- You can troubleshoot problems in operating computer equipment and software.

Oakland Aviation High School Portfolios.   Aviation High School (OAHS) is a comprehensive charter high school located at the Oakland, California, International Airport. Aviation prepares students for college or a career in aviation or business. The school is representative of the new vocational education available in California. It offers a college-prep program, but also career-prep, especially for students with academic problems. OAHS has small classes (20 or fewer students) and an advisory program. Students select one of three major areas of concentration: (1) aviation maintenance technology, (2) business or international trade, or (3) a personalized business internship. OAHS prides itself on a school culture that is "collaborative, performance-based and data-driven. . . . At every step, data is used to measure how well teachers are teaching and students are learning. . . . The cycle begins with formative assessments that measure the current abilities of students in comparison to the California state standards and the school-wide benchmarks. . . . The assessment cycle forms a feedback loop that allows each member of the community to monitor how well the school is doing at teaching students, and offers multiple opportunities for setting clear objectives and taking an active role in promoting student success" (OAHS Website, 2007).

All OAHS students develop portfolios that demonstrate their progress toward the grade level benchmarks for each course and toward their individual goals. Teachers and students select daily and weekly assignments for inclusion in the portfolios. Students participate in a "portfolio exhibition" twice each year. Portfolios are evaluated by at least three teachers, two peers, and a parent/community member based on a standardized rubric and utilizing grade level benchmarks. Portfolio exhibitions take many forms including, but not limited to oral, written, and musical expressions, and dance or video. Exhibitions take place publicly before fellow students, faculty, parents, and community members. Passing scores are required for promotion and graduation.

The Digital Portfolio. The Digital Portfolio is computer technology created specifically to simplify and enhance portfolio collection. A digital portfolio is a digitized version of the same material found in hardcopy portfolios, but easier to update and to circulate online or by disk. It is a specialized multimedia website.

The Coalition of Essential Schools mounted a research project funded by IBM called the Exhibitions Project (1990–1993) that studied "school-developed performance-assessment systems or 'exhibitions'" (McDonald, 1996). Six schools in Kentucky, New Hampshire, and New York participated in the project. An early version of the portfolio is found in Niguidula (1993). More recent sample portfolios are available on CD-ROM (Niguidula, 1997) from Brown University's Annenberg Institute for School Reform.

The CES Digital Portfolio incorporates three critical design decisions (Niguidula, 1998, p. 185):

- The school vision should be the lens for looking at student work. The Portfolio's "main menu" features the school's goals for students.
- The student work itself must be prominent. The portfolio software shows actual student work, not just grades or teacher comments.
- The student work must be presented in context. Most project schools ask students to cite the original assignment along with student, teacher, and third-party evaluations and comments about the work.

The Digital Portfolio is customized for each school's assessment system. The main menu consists of the school's goals for students (its vision). The initial screen shows the generic goals intended to cover all curricular disciplines. One of the project schools, for example, required that all students develop the skills of "communicator, researcher, and problem solver." The portfolio main menu provides these three buttons and a fourth labeled "individual" for the student to categorize and display work samples and other information that might not fit under the main categories. A second project school listed 19 goals; a third used seven interdisciplinary domains; a middle school listed eight skills; an elementary school defined four "selves" (social, academic, artistic, problem-solving). The Digital Portfolio can accommodate these variations.

Clicking on the main menu buttons takes the reader to a second menu that contains a list of student work entries by each goal. The work can also be sorted by curricular areas. Each entry screen contains several windows of student work. Screens show the actual assignments, audio explanations, math calculations, diagrams, other graphics, video demonstrations of laboratory experiments, and self-reflections. A reader can click on any of these entries to review the actual student work and its context.

The developers of the Digital Portfolio view it as more than a piece of technology for sorting student work samples. They see it as a kind of "provocation for school change" whose "development could raise questions and highlight important areas of a school's work for it to consider" (Niguidula, 1998). Schools are encouraged to look beyond the technology to at least five areas of school design/redesign:

- Articulation of the school's *vision* of what graduates should know and be able to do
- Development of a school *assessment system* based on the vision
- The *logistics* of portfolio assessment, including the time to collect and catalogue the information
- The *infrastructure*—hardware, software, networking, support personnel—for the technology
- A school *culture* of student-as-successful-learner, in which work is regularly critiqued to help students meet school goals

The Digital Portfolio is an exemplar of the intimate connection between authentic assessment and personalized instruction. Unless instruction is personalized, assessment is not likely to be truly authentic. But evaluating personalized learning with anything less than authentic assessment is self-defeating. The two are interdependent.

ASSESSMENT ISSUES AND PITFALLS

The No Child Left Behind (NCLB) legislation has complicated an emerging trend in assessment: that its purpose should be to support and enhance learning. Without intending to be an obstacle, NCLB has nevertheless diverted attention to the mechanics of large-scale testing and to a focus on the school rather than the child. It has moved assessment 360 degrees away from personalization. The result is somewhat of a stalemate. The current view among scholars and many practitioners is that school curriculum and instruction should better reflect the needs and goals of a twenty-first-century world. One of these changing views considers what students should know and be able to do as citizens of the information age. The view includes a new perception of the interdependent relationships among curriculum, instruction, and assessment. Assessment has a new place of honor in this educational pantheon, not so much for its own sake, but for what it portrays of a more meaningful curriculum and a more personalized instruction. Assessment in this view changes from being a sorting tool to being a catalyst for more authentic teaching and learning.

Yet, in addition to the NCLB stalemate, some other pitfalls do exist. Worthen (1993) highlights several critical issues facing forms of alternative assessment. These are the most noteworthy:

- *Conceptual clarity.* Too much variation still exists in the concepts and language of authentic assessment. More coherence is needed.
- *Technical quality and truthfulness.* The issues here are the validity, reliability, and other technical specifications of alternative assessments. Can more authentic forms of assessment actually portray student knowledge and skills accurately, consistently, and in a cost-effective way?
- *Standardization of performance.* Is it possible (or useful) to standardize levels of student performance, rating criteria, and scoring rubrics without losing the authentic, real-world orientation of the new forms?
- *Acceptability to educators and stakeholders.* Will a majority of teachers and school administrators use the new techniques? Will

schools of education provide more sophisticated instruction in assessment practices than is now the norm? Will the public accept a new form of accountability for schools, districts, and states? Will parents be satisfied with alternative forms of progress reporting?

- *High-stakes assessment.* Can high-stakes decisions, such as graduation, college entrance, and job recommendations, be based with sufficient comfort on authentic assessments? Will minorities and the educationally disadvantaged score as well or even better on authentic assessments? Will legal challenges pose an obstacle?

No easy answers exist for these and the other questions that accompany a movement toward more authentic forms of assessment. Although some see standardization as inimical to personalization and a throwback to the factory model of education, the educational establishment points to 50 years of collected data as a useful benchmark for any analysis of future progress. Perhaps some traditional assessment will be needed, at least for a time, until the issues and pitfalls of authentic assessment are suitably mined.

Authentic assessment can be a tool of enormous value, but it is not a panacea. Nor does the use of naturalistic, performance, or portfolio assessment in itself ensure authenticity. Madaus and O'Dwyer (1999) remind us that, "historically performance testing has been as easy to corrupt through coaching and other means of focused teaching as has the multiple-choice mode of assessing, which conversely can measure some very complex higher-order thinking." Assessment is authentic only when it is a valid portrayal of a real-world task, when it is fair in its intent and mode of assessment, and, most important of all, when it enhances student learning.

PROGRESS REPORTING

In our earlier examination of the broad characteristics of personalized instruction, we indicated that student progress reporting in a personalized system would be based on absolute performance standards and defensible rating criteria, and feature such authentic assessments as exhibitions and portfolios. We have discussed authentic assessment strategies and pitfalls at some length. It remains now to consider the ways such information should be rated and communicated.

Assessment practices have undergone considerable scrutiny in recent years and many districts and schools have undertaken major changes. Grading and progress reporting have received much less attention, however, and few real changes have occurred in the ways schools rate and report student performance. Teachers rarely discuss the "teach, test, and grade" model that still dominates much of educational pedagogy. And yet, most scholars and practitioners agree that student evaluation must be more than the traditional labeling and sorting.

Traditional grades may be the major culprit. O'Connor (1995) explained, "Grades are convenient shorthand that have come to have a general acceptance in schools in North America. They serve many purposes—administrative, instructional, motivational, control, and communication. Herein lies probably the most serious problem with grades—as they serve so many functions, many ingredients (achievement, attitude, effort, behavior, participation, attendance, and so on) have been packed into grades so that they have become meaningless for what should be their main purpose—communication." O'Connor suggested that "achievement should be the only basis for grades (not poor effort or misbehavior)." Unfortunately, the problem is more complicated than that; any solutions (as O'Connor himself mentions) must move beyond simple tinkering with existing practices.

Glasser (1998, p. 109) said that school grades have two major purposes:

1. To give information to students, their parents, and others who may be interested, like colleges, in how well the student is doing
2. To serve as a substitute for pay

Grades and other forms of progress reporting must, first and foremost, provide useful information to all interested parties. Information stokes the engine of student and school improvement. Grades can also act as rewards if they are high enough. In a personalized school, low grades are an anachronism, perhaps even an oxymoron, certainly a contradiction. A school committed to personalized instruction and to quality student performance cannot permit a student to be satisfied with a low grade. Glasser (1998) says,

> In a quality school, there are no bad grades. . . . High grades are a reward for quality work and are very satisfying to students' need for power. In a quality school, however, permanent low grades would be eliminated. A low grade would be treated as a temporary difficulty, a problem to be solved by the student and the teacher working together, with the hope that the student would come to the conclusion that it is worth expending more effort. . . . Grades, like pay, should always be tied to increased productivity." (p. 107)

Reporting student progress may be accomplished with or without grades, depending on the school's vision for students, its degree of personalization, and its approach to assessment. Most schools currently use a *relative* system of grading, with the achievement of other students as the frame of reference. But only an *absolute* or criterion grade reporting system can support a personalized program since it applies the same standards equally to virtually all students, based on predefined criteria. It is true that a school must set appropriate standards of performance for an absolute system, and teachers must be creative to organize instruction for individual student differences in ability, style, and motivation. But an absolute or criterion grading model, when properly constituted, can convey both objective and truly useful information to students, schools, and the public about what students actually know and are able to do. No relative reporting system does that.

In practice, student progress reporting systems tend to be idiosyncratic. Typical systems are local hybrids of one or more of these grading schemes (Keefe, 1991a):

- *Percentages*—Students are graded on a 100-point scale with a minimum percentage (usually 50 to 70) set as passing.
- *Alpha grading*—Students are rated on a 5-point scale with the grades of A, B, C, D, and F receiving grade points of 4, 3, 2, 1, and 0, respectively.
- *Two or three level systems*—Some schools award grades on a pass/fail, credit/no credit, or excellent/satisfactory/unsatisfactory basis in an attempt to avoid the most misleading features of the

percentage or alpha approaches. These systems are most often used for elective courses.

- *Anecdotal or descriptive reports*—Teachers write comments or develop an extended narrative about student attitudes, goals, motivation, study habits, and performance. Descriptive reports can be combined with performance grading to serve as the foundation of a more comprehensive system of authentic assessment in a school.
- *Performance grading: Exhibitions and portfolios*—School-wide or district-wide criteria are established for rating student work or skilled performance. Students exhibit actual samples of their work and demonstrate their competence, by performance or product, before review committees composed of faculty members, other students, and community members. Assessment is always conducted on an absolute basis. Some of these programs assign two- or three-level grades, such as credit/no credit or exceeds criteria/meets criteria/ approaches criteria. Some use a modified alpha system, with A, B, and "in-progress" the most common designations.

Reporting systems seem to vary from school to school largely based on the level of personalization present. In Chapter 4, we proposed a typology of approaches to personalized instruction based on the levels of interaction and thoughtfulness exhibited by programs. Approaches at the lower levels of this typology, such as individualized instruction, experiential learning, and direct instruction, tend to retain traditional grading practices. Even programs that stress greater levels of thoughtfulness, such as independent research, technology-assisted learning, and those with higher levels of interaction (such as style-based instruction, cognitive skill development, and inquiry approaches), usually rely on alpha grading or modified alpha approaches. Programs at the highest level of the typology tend to use descriptive or performance rating and reporting. Indeed, it is difficult to conceive of effective guided practice, topic study, or cognitive apprenticeship programs without an absolute criterion model of progress reporting.

Thomas Haney Secondary Centre, a grade 8–12 public school in Maple Ridge (Vancouver), British Columbia, has evolved a collaborative and interactive approach to student grading and progress reporting for its self-paced continuous progress program. Thomas Haney likes to say that it has worked to "mark smarter" and more authentically. Former Haney principal Ian Strachan (personal communication, June 1999) succinctly described his school assessment system for its learning guide–based curriculum:

> We did extensive inservice on criterion-based assessment and adopted it as a model throughout the school. We use either a 4-, 5-, or 6-point scale (depending on departments), and examples have been identified and displayed by the departments so that students know what is expected of them. Often the mark is assigned after a learning dialogue has taken place between the teacher-marker and the student, with both parties having input into the mark assigned. This short discussion between the marker and the student reinforces our position that a self-paced school is not a distance education model where students work independently without much teacher input, but is, in fact, a partnership, which requires the student and the marker to work in tandem. Much of this form of assessment is based on discussion and demonstration to the point that both parties feel that the mastery of the material has been achieved. This has eliminated a lot of pencil-and-paper testing, but in no way has prevented our students from continuing to achieve above the district and provincial averages in our government exams.
>
> Our first reporting conference of the year is a three-way conference between the teacher adviser, the student, and the parent(s). Students present their portfolios of exemplars and their goals and objectives for the year. This is usually signed off by the parent, student, and the teacher-adviser at the conclusion of the conference.
>
> Our recent acquisition and implementation of an excellent electronic mark book and tracking system allows us to generate regular (normally monthly, but in many cases even weekly) "snapshot" updates to teacher advisers on students' rate of progress. This allows constant feedback to students and parents to show where the student is in a self-paced environment.

Several assessment scholars (Guskey, 1996; Stiggins, 1997; Wiggins, 1998; and Marzano, 2006) have expressed serious concern about the present grading and reporting system of single grades and little descriptive information on student learning progress. Wiggins (1998, pp. 256–257) proposed "five complementary approaches, based on the criteria of honesty, fairness, thoroughness, and usefulness" to remedy this problem:

1. *Report many more subscores of performance in summarizing performance data.* Reporting should be organized by goals and performance standards to differentiate complex performance.

2. *Distinguish explicitly between achievement data and expectation-based evaluation, symbolized as scores and grades, respectively.* Scores would represent performance against objective standards; grades would represent teacher judgments about performance.

3. *Report both kinds of expectation-referenced grades.* Expectations measured for a student's cohort by age, class, etc., (termed *normed*) would be separated from expectations measured by teacher judgment about expected growth versus actual growth (termed *individual growth*).

4. *Analyze students' academic achievements through three kinds of data: level of achievement, quality of work, and progress against standards.* The first is achievement against exit-level standards. Quality captures the value of a presentation, performance, or product at any given level of difficulty. Progress refers to "absolute gains toward exit-standards . . . charted along multi-year continua or rubrics."

5. *Evaluate the student's intellectual character—habits of mind and work—based on established patterns over long periods of time in performance or product.* Reporting should carry teacher judgments about such qualities as persistence and other study habits needed for college or employment success.

Wiggins cites several school districts that have already implemented one or more of these approaches in their progress reporting systems (West Windsor-Plainsboro and South Brunswick in New Jersey; Round Rock Independent in Texas; Cherry Creek in Colorado; Rialto Unified in California).

Assessment in a personalized system of instruction must document what society, schools, and students themselves consider most worthwhile. Most contemporary measures of accountability developed by states and districts are incomplete measures of student accomplishments (and surely inauthentic); they are not cost-effective (indeed they are very expensive), and they are politically difficult to sustain over any period of time.

Peel and McCary (1997) proposed that districts rethink assessment and reporting as real feedback systems to stakeholders. If we really want to focus our efforts on fostering the development of significant competencies in students, grading everything and averaging the results must stop. Grading all the steps in a complex process, such as writing or using numbers, is akin to throwing a nonswimmer into the water and telling him that how he does on this first attempt will significantly determine our judgment of whether he can swim on the final day of instruction. To combat the problems of confusing practice with final performance and of inhibiting risk-taking, we need to reexamine the circumstances under which students have the opportunity to demonstrate their mastery of essential skills and knowledge.

Assessment is the link between curriculum and instruction, and progress reporting is the mirror of student performance. Accountability is the stamp of quality control. All of these elements require new and serious attention in any system of personalized instruction.

The following chapter discusses various ways to personalize the academic disciplines.

6

PERSONALIZING THE DISCIPLINES

This chapter describes specific strategies for personalizing instruction in several domains of knowledge. For purposes of organization, it is divided into three broad headings: the humanities, the sciences, and the arts. The humanities include English/language arts, history, and foreign languages. The sciences highlight biology, chemistry, the physical sciences, and mathematics. The arts encompass the fine arts and the practical arts.

Robert Barr and John Tagg (1995) identified two paradigms, as pointed out earlier, that dominate American classrooms: the instructional paradigm and the learning paradigm. The instructional paradigm focuses on what teachers do, on the presentation of content material with little attempt to connect to the lives of the students. The learning paradigm focuses on how students learn and how students respond to various situations. Learning paradigm teachers get outside themselves and into the minds of the students. They are constantly "reading" the students to determine how to create a better atmosphere for student growth (Lasley, 1998). Personalized instruction aligns with the learning paradigm, which favors an interactive learning environment and active learning.

Depictions of the learning paradigm are found in such films as *Stand and Deliver, Mr. Holland's Opus, Dangerous Minds, The Dead Poets Society*, and *Freedom Writers*. In each case, the teacher begins by struggling to reach students with an instructional approach and gradually awakens to the need to begin where students are and proceed accordingly. By connecting to the world of the students, these teachers were able to lead students to a world beyond their present existence. Escalante (*Stand and Deliver*) offered special tutoring, Saturday school, and summer workshops to give students the background to tackle higher mathematics. Lou Ann Johnson (*Dangerous Minds*) used karate and a variety of powerful messages to connect students with ideas. Mr. Holland linked contemporary music with the classics. In the *Dead Poets Society*, Robin Williams helped students examine poetry from their own perspective and to write their own "life poems" (Lasley, 1998). Erin Gruwell, a white, first-year teacher at Woodrow Wilson High School in Long Beach, California, confronted racism and violence in the lives of the students in her freshman English class in the film *Freedom Writers*. Erin's strategy will be described more fully in the English/Language Arts section of this chapter.

Although Hollywood depictions of teaching are often idealized, these five reach out to audiences because they are responsive to the needs of the students. All five teachers overcame the restrictions of a school culture where the instructional paradigm reigns supreme. All five fought passionately for their students. The word education comes from the Latin *educere*, meaning "to lead out." We might add to this definition the phrase "from one's self." These teachers were real leaders.

The following examples from the humanities, the sciences, and the arts suggest the exceptional range of personalized instruction that can be found in varied learning environments.

THE HUMANITIES

English/Language Arts

Socratic Seminars and Reading Comprehension.   Margaret Metzger (1998), a teacher of English at Brookline High School, Brookline, Massachusetts, uses Socratic-style group inquiry to move her classes toward a deeper understanding of literature. The students are given a short passage, usually less than one page, and are asked to read it and take notes before coming to class. In class, they divide into an inner and outer circle.

The inner circle holds a discussion while the outer circle observes. The discussion is prompted by open-ended questions developed by the teacher to which even she does not know the answer. Members of the inner group read the passage aloud two or three times. The first discussion lasts 10 minutes. The outer circle then gives 10 minutes of feedback, after which the groups change places. The new inner circle holds a 10-minute discussion and then receives feedback from the outer circle for 10 minutes. The teacher serves as the facilitator of the discussion.

As one might suspect, the students' skills improve with practice. Early seminars focus on the process itself. Students learn how to interact civilly, listen, and use each other's comments to inquire in-depth. Observers learn about what to note in the discussions, how to discern key points, and how to help discussants avoid one-upmanship in favor of group inquiry. The teacher models collaborative behaviors for both groups and often interrupts a discussion to focus on a key question or an important observation. Initially, progress is slow, but if group inquiry is used regularly throughout the school year, students begin to improve their skills.

When the students have a reasonably good grasp of the group process, the teacher shifts their focus to comprehension techniques. Ms. Metzger used readings from *Their Eyes Were Watching God*, *The Great Gatsby*, and *Ozymandias*, to help the students learn from each other how to attack written materials in ways that will enrich understanding. Her two classes of freshman English discovered 15 different techniques for interpreting *Their Eyes Were Watching God*. They then applied these 15 techniques to the ending of *The Great Gatsby*. They checked out vocabulary, followed key words from paragraph to paragraph, focused on metaphors, paraphrased sentences, worked on verb tenses, and asked whether Fitzgerald was telling the truth. Working through the intermediary steps enabled the students to do the difficult task of abstracting, generalizing, and concluding.

Students kept lists of reading techniques that emerged during the Socratic seminars. Many strategies focused on close reading of individual words; other strategies were broader, paying attention to point of view, the bias of the writer, the cultural context, or flaws in logic. The students' comprehension improved markedly when they discovered that how material is presented is a matter of the author's choice. "The awareness that writing is crafted allowed the students to imagine different choices, thereby considering the author's reasoning and purposes" (Metzger, 1998).

Topic Study or Storyline at the High School Level.   Erin Gruwell was a student teacher and then a first-year teacher at Wilson High School in Long Beach, California. The time period was 1994 in the wake of the Rodney King riots in Los Angeles. Her freshman English classes were composed of a mix of historically low-achieving African American, Latinos, Asian, and Caucasian students. Gangs were prevalent in the community and their animosity toward each other did not cease at the school's front door.

After intercepting a racist note with a caricature of one of the African-American students, she decided that her predetermined lesson plans should be scrapped in favor of focusing on the topic of *tolerance*. Tolerance toward others became the storyline for the students' exploration of literature, writing, and oral expression. Gruwell was probably unaware of topic study or storyline when she invoked the principle of *The Teacher's Rope*, a key to the storyline approach. This principle refers to the critical partnership between the teacher and the students in exploring a storyline topic. The story is the link between teacher control and student control. The teacher holds the rope while allowing for twists and bends based on the interests and experiences of the students (Creswell, 1997, pp. 9–10). In Gruwell's case, the students knew far more about disruption, violence, and even death than she did.

She began the story by asking the students, "How many of you have heard of the Holocaust?" No one raised a hand. She followed with, "How many of you have been shot at?" Most students raised their hands. Her cursory diagnosis of the students' prior knowledge led her to discuss what she judged to be the "worst gang in the history of the world," the Nazis. She gave examples of how they terrorized, imprisoned, and killed people who did not conform to their ideas of what acceptable people should be like. Jews especially were the target of this hatred (Gruwell, 1999).

She distributed notebooks, which she bought, and asked the students to keep a journal or diary of their experiences. Her only assignment was to write what you want to write in the manner in which you want to write. She told them that if they wanted her to read them, they should place them in the locked cabinet to which only she had access. As she read the diaries, she became more aware of each student's experiences, characteristics, interests, and writing level (Gruwell, 1999).

Next, she prepared students to read *The Diary of Anne Frank* by bringing in guest speakers who had survived the Holocaust and by taking field trips to visit the Museum of Tolerance and Juvenile Detention Centers, and to see the film *Schindler's List*. She presented information about Miep Gies, the Dutch woman who, at great risk, sheltered Anne Frank. The students were asked to read the *Diary of Anne Frank* and *Zlata's Diary: A Child's Life in Sarajevo*, both books by people their own age (Little Dust Productions, 2007). They read voraciously.

The enthusiasm for their new-found interests induced them to invite Miep Gies to come to Wilson High School. They engaged in several fund-raising activities to pay her expenses, not the least of which was a sponsored Read-a-thon. During Gies' visit, she told them that the ghettos where the students live were America's war zones and praised them as heroes. Later, one of the local businessmen in Long Beach sponsored a trip to Europe for 60 students accompanied by Erin Gruwell. They visited Auschwitz, Sarajevo, and Anne Frank's attic (Little Dust Productions, 2007).

The writing in their diaries continued and displayed growth in understanding, knowledge, and skill. Their enthusiasm for reading and writing expanded. The concept of the Freedom Riders, who during the 1960s integrated buses in America, became a metaphor for the diaries created by the students. They became the Freedom Writers, symbolizing the freedom that Erin Gruwell gave them to overcome their failures, to begin anew, and to take responsibility for their own learning.

The *Freedom Writer's Diary* was published in 1999 by Broadway Books, a subsidiary of Random House. It contains the writing of 150 students whose lives were changed by a teacher who believed that her role was to model, coach, support, and guide students to discover talents of which they were previously unaware. In the words of Theodore Sizer, "We don't know the half of what kids can do," and maybe they don't, either.

History

Students as Historians: A Project Approach.   A team of 10 students at Homer-Center High School in Homer, Pennsylvania, wrote an original history of their 84-year-old high school. In the process, they learned about primary source materials, interviewing, analyzing, decision making, prioritizing, marketing, and the continuity of community life. The students began by leafing through old yearbooks and perusing old school newspapers. After getting an overview of the changes experienced during the school's history, they created a 15-step plan, as follows:

1. Survey the available materials.
2. Construct an outline of categories to be included.
3. Develop a research plan.
4. Schedule regular meetings for research updates.
5. Gather photographs, school memorabilia, and anecdotes.
6. Organize material and select photos.
7. Write.
8. Edit.
9. Contact printers for samples of their work and bids.
10. Select a printer and send materials to him or her.
11. If the publication is to be sold, prepare brochures and media announcements for presales.
12. Proof galleys.
13. Check the layout and design.
14. Print.
15. Market and distribute (Fazio, 1992, p. 65).

In formulating the plan, the students investigated sources on the establishment and development of the high school. They read more than 80 years worth of records: school board minutes, student newspapers, yearbooks, and student handbooks. They located articles about the school in regional newspapers. When materials they needed were missing, they ran ads in the local newspaper requesting assistance from former graduates and community members. They consulted microfilmed issues of the local newspaper on file at nearby Indiana University of Pennsylvania.

Community residents provided anecdotes and photographs. Collecting the anecdotes gave students the opportunity to practice their interviewing skills. Among those interviewed was one of the 12 students to graduate in the Class of 1918. Her story gave the students an opportunity to compare their experiences at the school with hers. She graduated at the age of 15. At the time, the high school had only three grades with one teacher for each grade (Fazio, 1992).

Students learned that during World War II, it was not uncommon for high school students to enlist in the armed forces. The shortage of male students left the school with an insufficient number to field a football team. Students learned that things change over time and that these changes are sometimes precipitated by outside forces. They also became aware of new information sources, including such government documents as Reports of the Superintendents of Schools. They had the occasion to handle fragile artifacts from the early twentieth century. More important, they became producers of new knowledge rather than simply consumers.

An Inquiry Approach to the American Revolution. The social studies department of Aragon High School, San Mateo, California, has developed an approach that places thoughtful exploration of an issue or problem at the heart of learning (Onosko, 1992). The main features of the model include a central question, an introductory grabber, rich detail, and a culminating activity—an approach much like topic study.

Each unit is constructed around a *central question*. The central question forces teachers to limit their content coverage and to avoid superficial treatment of information and ideas. The central question focuses student inquiry and places the student in the role of problem solver. Some typical central questions are: Were the colonists justified in declaring their independence from England? Is the United States today more like Athens or Sparta? Whose presidency was more democratic—Jefferson's or Jackson's?

An introductory grabber draws the students into the material and foreshadows the unit's central question. It can be a film clip, primary source material, a short story, a poem, a political cartoon, a guest speaker, or a brief simulation. The assumption behind the grabber is that poor student performance in history is due primarily to lack of engagement and motivation, not deficiencies in students' mental capacities, abilities, or prior knowledge (Onosko, 1992).

Rich detail is defined in relation to the customary "nondetailed" textbook. It implies that students explore material in greater depth if meaningful learning is to occur. Rich detail includes readings, eyewitness accounts, definitions and examples of concepts, detailed and competing arguments, vivid images and pictures, and various forms of evidence and counterevidence.

The culminating activity gives students an opportunity to share their findings with an audience. Usually the audience is the class itself, but can be extended to include other students, teachers, and community members. The scope of a culminating activity is limited only by the creativity of the student and the time and resources available. It could be a skit, a play, a television newscast, a radio talk show, a debate, a speech, a newspaper publication, or small group presentation. In essence, it is a report of how a student or a group of students answered the central question. The example below presents a sample lesson from a high school unit on the American Revolution (Onosko, 1992, p. 194):

Sample Lesson from a Unit on the American Revolution

Central Question: How Were the Colonists Able to Win the American Revolutionary War?

Lesson One

- Introductory Grabber: Show a 10-minute excerpt from the film *Revolution*, starring Al Pacino and Natassia Kinski. The excerpt shows one of the first battles of the revolution and clearly illustrates the differences between the British army (organized, uniformed, machine-like precision) and the colonists (chaotic, rag-tag, inadequately equipped). After viewing, ask the students for their initial impressions. What did they see? What are the differences between the British army and the Colonial army? Make a list of observations on the board or overhead or computerized display. What overarching conclusions can we draw from the apparent differences between the two sides?
- Introduce the Central Question (How in the world did the colonists win?): If students wish to suggest answers, write their ideas on the board or overhead as hypotheses. Continue brainstorming other ideas that might help explain the American victory and write them on the board or overhead (e.g., military power, strategy, leadership, economic resources, supplies, ability to transport supplies, public support, participation, morale, political orga-

nization, allies, propaganda efforts, knowledge of geography, moral justification). Once the list is complete, ask the students to categorize their ideas and hypotheses. Limit the number of categories to four or five (e.g., military, public support, resources, political organization).

- Explaining the Unit: The class goal for the next few days is to collect enough information so that each student can make an informed decision about how the Americans won the Revolution. In small groups, the students will be responsible for finding information about the hypotheses within a given category and sharing research with the rest of the class. In preparation for the next day's data gathering, students are to read the textbook chapter with the central question in mind.

Subsequent lessons involve small group investigations into the various hypotheses. The culminating activity reshapes the groups so that experts from each of the original research teams have a chance to meet and share their findings. Each new group is composed of experts on the different hypotheses for colonial success. They debate and outline a detailed answer to the central question. Each group then shares its conclusions with the class. As a final evaluation, students are required to write an in-class essay (40 minutes) answering the question, "How did the Americans win the American Revolution?" (Onosko, 1992). Notice that this approach utilizes a modified jigsaw-cooperative-small-group methodology.

Foreign Languages

Immersion: A Form of Cognitive Apprenticeship. Immersion is a method of foreign language instruction in which the regular school curriculum or a major school activity is taught in another language. Immersion programs are generally total or partial. In total immersion, teachers conduct the entire school day, from the very first day of school, in the foreign language. In partial immersion, approximately half the school day is taught in English and the remainder in the foreign language. Peace Corps trainees are often placed in a total immersion program to learn the language of their area of assignment. It is common for them to devote six to eight weeks in an environment where only the new language is spoken.

At the Francis W. Parker Essential School, Devens, Massachusetts, students begin their study of Spanish upon entering grade 7 and continue each year until they graduate from the upper division (grade 12). Learning Spanish well is a school-wide goal in which both adults and students participate. Everyday objects throughout the school are labeled with their Spanish names (Francis W. Parker Charter, 2005–2006). Each Wednesday morning, a gathering of the entire student body is held. Every four weeks the gathering is conducted totally in Spanish (personal communication with Deb Merriam, Academic Dean, May 16, 2007).

Experiences in which students speak only the target language are really cognitive apprenticeships. Students begin to understand the context in which different forms of the language are appropriate and how their specific knowledge and skills relate to it.

Constructing Meaning in German. Susan Ferguson, teacher of German and foreign languages department chair at Hinsdale High School, Hinsdale, Illinois, was concerned that her students were not comprehending text, but "merely transferring vocabulary from the text to their answers" (Ferguson, 2005, p.63). She assigned her students to read the novel *Three Men in the Snow* (*Drei Manner im Schnee*) by Erich Kasner, a well-known German author.

Initially, she assigned writing prompts keyed to the plot. Students were expected to reply to each prompt in their journals in German. The prompts were: (1) What is friendship? (2) How do you know when someone is a true friend? (3) What are the five most important things in your life? and (4) What is something important that money cannot buy? Next, the students shared their journal entries with a partner and then in cooperative learning groups. Finally, the results of the discussions were shared with the whole class (Ferguson, 2005).

Ms. Ferguson told the students to be prepared to interview in German a mystery guest who was coming to the class. The mystery guest was the teacher dressed as Tobler, the main character in the book. The students asked their questions. The teacher answered in character. The time period for the book (1932) prompted the students to ask "Tobler" what he thought of Adolph Hitler and of developments in the German economy. They also asked more personal questions about residence, family, and occupation (Ferguson, 2005).

The teacher then queried the students about friendship, revealing that Tobler, a lonely millionaire, never knew whether people liked him for himself or because of his wealth. "Tobler" then enlisted the students' help to fashion a plan for him to go to a hotel in Switzerland dressed as a poor man, as he does in the novel.

The tactics developed by Ms. Ferguson provided the students with an idea of the plot of the novel and captured their enthusiasm for reading the book. At key points during the reading, she introduced strategies to help the students monitor their comprehension, summarize what they read, and apply what they learned. One strategy was the use of graphic organizers to map Tobler's character, supporting their descriptions with evidence from the novel using accurate German words (Ferguson, 2005). This approach to reading validated the activity for the students who reported that for the first time reading in German became an enjoyable and informative activity. In the teacher's words, "They accessed prior knowledge, set a purpose for reading, actively constructed meaning and synthesized, summarized, and applied what they had learned" (Ferguson 2005, p. 65).

THE SCIENCES

Problem-Based Science Learning: A Form of Authentic Pedagogy

Problem-based learning focuses on a learning paradigm rather than the teaching paradigm of teach, learn, and apply. Students are presented with a real-life problem and asked to solve it. As in real life, the problem is often messy and ill-structured. Sources for the problems are local newspapers, community members, and colleagues. In choosing a problem, teachers consider the prior knowledge and needs of the learners. Hopefully, the students will perceive the problem as meaningful and will assume the role of stakeholders for the situation. Teachers work to create a learning environment in which they coach student thinking and guide student learning, facilitating deeper levels of understanding"

(Torp & Sage, 1998, p. 14). In this regard, problem-based learning is both a curriculum organizer and an instructional strategy aimed at helping students develop habits of investigation that they can apply to situations beyond school.

- *At the Elementary Level:* Students in grades 1–5 at the Westgate Elementary School in Arlington Heights, Illinois, investigated the problem the principal was having in maintaining a healthy and productive flower garden at home. Try as she might, she was unable to get the flowers to grow. So, she asked the teachers for advice. They suggested that the students be challenged to solve her problem. Students examined soil and plant samples from her garden, read about how to grow healthy plants, searched the Internet, contacted local experts, and conducted experiments on growing plants under different conditions (Torp & Sage, 1998). Students learned about persistence and better questioning strategies when, on several occasions, adults whom they contacted did not take them seriously.

  As a result of their inquiry, students in turn solved their problem and helped the principal become a more effective gardener. In the process they learned much about plants, the need to read directions carefully, where to plant flowers to get the right amount of sunlight and shade, and the importance of regular watering.

  Students completed a pre- and posttest in which they were asked to develop instructions on how to grow plants successfully. The pretests contained drawings of seeds, sun, and rain with little or no information. The posttests enumerated necessary components for healthy plant growth that included soil, seeds, water, fertilizer, sun, rain, carbon dioxide, chlorophyll, and space to grow.

- *At the Middle Level:* Seventh grade students at Waldo Middle School in Salem, Oregon, dedicate eight weeks to the problem of endangered species. Each student selected one animal from a list of 25 and completed an individual investigation on that animal. The individual investigation used a variety of resources: CDs on animals, conservation and nature journals, the Internet, personal contacts with experts, and visits to wildlife parks and zoos. The individual report stressed concepts rather than copying facts and definitions from reference materials. To help with the process, the teacher arranged a "Safari Day," in which local zoo experts visited the school and talked about animals and their habitats (Kushman, 2001).

During the second phase of their investigations, students self-selected a small group of three to five students to develop a recovery plan for their endangered animal. The students were challenged to develop plans that truly addressed the nature of the problem. Some students opted for a habitat theme park or developed a captive breeding program in an existing zoo. Others chose to create an educational program in support of the animal remaining in the natural habitat.

Teachers guided the groups, planned a time line for their work, and created a division of labor. Designs for theme parks were required to include cost, available land, and real-life constraints. They were given the unit price for concrete, fencing material, trees, and other materials so that they could use a spreadsheet to develop a construction budget (Kushman, 2001).

When the groups completed their work, they were scheduled to defend their recovery plans before a hypothetical zoo "board of directors." Each student group gave a 15-minute presentation to the "board," complete with models, graphics, slides, video clips, and, in some cases, hypercard stacks and brochures. Board members, including zoo experts and teachers, critiqued the student works.

- *At the High School Level:* This activity is based on a problem given to engineering students at Massachusetts Institute of Technology. William McElroy, a former high school teacher of physics and current high school assistant principal, posed the same challenge to his students.

  The Problem: Design a vehicle that will climb a hill, cross the crest, and prevent your opponent from crossing in the opposite direction. The objective is to end the match with your vehicle and your opponent's on the other side of the hill.

The Rules:

1. You may use only the materials listed below to build your vehicle. It is not necessary to use all of them.
   - 2 coffee cans with plastic lids
   - 4 plastic soda bottles (1 or 2 liter)

- 8 rubber bands
- 2 mouse traps
- 1 12 x 24-inch piece of plywood
- 4 jar lids
- 2 wire coat hangars
- 1 3-foot wooden dowel (any diameter)
- 1 12 x 12-inch piece of cardboard
- 1 3-foot piece of string
- Any metal fasteners (paper clips, screws, bolts, nails, etc.)
- Any glue or cement

2. Your vehicle may use any means you can devise for reaching the other side of the hill and for preventing your opponent from reaching your side.

3. Your vehicle must be self-propelled. You may touch it to start, but you may not give it a push. You may not touch it after the match has begun. It may leave nothing at the starting line.

4. Your vehicle may be no longer than 12 inches and no wider than 8 inches at the moment it starts.

5. The hill will rise 3 inches from its base. The base, each side of the hill, will be 3 feet from the crest. The starting line on each side will be 2 feet from the crest. There will be sides 3 inches high to prevent either vehicle from falling off the hill and the inclines will be 10 inches wide.

6. Vehicles will compete two at a time. The winner will advance to the next round with other winners. The competition will continue to the championship round.

7. After 15 seconds or when all motion has stopped, whichever comes first, the vehicle that remains on the opposite side of the hill from its start will be declared the winner. If neither vehicle has crossed the crest or both vehicles finish on the sides opposite their starts, a draw will be declared and both vehicles will be disqualified.

Students may work individually or in teams to complete the construction of their vehicles. They have four weeks to complete the project and be ready for the competition. The students are encouraged to develop several approaches to their problems and weigh the probability of each design's success before deciding which to use. The materials specified may be used in any way. A vehicle may run on wheels or tracks. It may launch itself through the air. It may extend an arm, throw or drop an object, bulldoze the opponent, or take any action to prevent the opposing vehicle from crossing the crest. Plywood or flakeboard is used to make the double-inclined plane. The students work on their projects out of class, consulting with the teachers as needed.

This project asks students to apply principles of physics that they have studied for several weeks in class. The competition instills high interest in learning and often leads students to invest time well beyond regular class time.

Mathematics

A Constructivist Perspective.   Deborah Schifter (1996) describes a mathematics unit developed by Anne Hendry to introduce measurement to her first-grade students. Ms. Hendry created an outline of the Mayflower, 16 x 6 feet, on the classroom floor. One student was selected as a messenger from the King to carry an "edict" to the Pilgrims. The class was the Pilgrims. The edict said, "This ship cannot sail until you tell me how big it is." Thus, a problem was posed to the students.

The teacher began by asking the class, "What should we do? Who has an idea?" No one had a clue. Hendry reports that the silence was deafening. Finally, one child raised her hand and offered, "I think it is 3 feet long." Her estimate was based on her misinterpretation of the capital "E" in the word edict. The "E" looked like a three to several of the children. Another student volunteered, "I know it can't be 3 feet because the nurse just measured me last week and said I was 4 feet, and this boat is much bigger than me." This answered connected with the children's experiences and triggered further discussion.

Someone suggested, "Let's see how many times Tom can fit in the boat." The boat was four Toms long. The teacher then asked, "How can we tell this to the King if he does not know Tom?" "Send Tom to the King" was the easy solution. But the students wanted Tom to accompany them on the trip.

Then another student suggested that the boat could be measured by using hands just like horses are measured. The student making this suggestion was selected to try out his suggestion. He did it twice, but found a different answer each time. The children were puzzled, but concluded that he had to be careful to place his hands at the beginning of the boat and go all the way to the end without leaving gaps between the palms and the fingers.

"Great," said the students, "We now have an answer." Ms. Hendry then asked the smallest child in the class to see how many of her hands would measure the boat. Her answer differed from the first student. This discovery stimulated further discussion. The children rejected measuring by hands because everyone's hands were not the same size. This fact caused another student to suggest using feet. This approach was tried but was found to have the same problem as using hands.

After a day's reflection, one student suggested that because the King knew the messenger Zeb, Zeb's foot could be used. Using this approach, the students reported that the boat was 24 "Zeb's-foot" long and 9 "Zeb's-foot" wide. The children continued to explore this form of measurement the next day by measuring each other, the classroom, their desks, and the rug using a cutout version of Zeb's foot.

The teacher asked the children why they thought it was necessary to have a form of measurement that was always the same size, such as Zeb's foot, to measure everything. Through their discussions, they were able to internalize and verbalize the importance of a standard form of measurement. They saw the confusion in using different hands and feet because of size variability. The class then went on to explore rulers and the adoption of conventional units of measurement.

This unit built on the prior experiences of children in order to help them understand a concept that is usually presented straightforwardly on the specious assumption that students possess an appropriate background for the concept. In this first-grade example, Ms. Hendry skillfully posed questions to lead the students to conjecture about problems that are more complex. She concluded that in addition to learning about measurement, the children learned that it was up to them to offer their thoughts about questions posed. And, when faced with contradictions, it was up to them to discover a resolution (Schifter, 1996).

A Problem-Based Curriculum. The Interactive Mathematics Program (IMP) is a curriculum developed by researchers at the San Francisco State University with funding from the National Science Foundation (NSF). The curriculum is based on the belief that mathematics is best learned in the context of meaningful and interesting problems. Each unit is organized around a central theme.

Unit themes include such intriguing titles such as "Patterns," "The Game of Pig," "The Overland Trail," "The Pit and the Pendulum," "Shadows," "Do Bees Build It Best?" "Fireworks," "All about Alice," and "Pennant Fever." The various subjects of mathematics are integrated in studying the content of these units so that students experience algebra, geometry, probability, statistics, linear programming, and curve-fitting in the context of solving simulated real-world problems. They apply mathematical concepts and skills to problems in social science, the physical sciences, and music. Students work much of the time in learning teams of four. Because problems usually have more than one answer, the use of collaborative teams expands perspective and often uncovers misconceptions that students have about mathematical concepts. The teams tackle problems that are usually too complex to be solved by any one individual.

In a unit entitled "Meadows or Malls," student teams are asked to solve this problem:

> You're on a planning team, consulting with the city manager. Your task is to come up with a reasonable plan for the use of 550 acres of land recently obtained by the city. The acreage includes a recently closed army base, a 300-acre farm, and abandoned mining land.
>
> Two conflicting parties are interested in the property. The business community is pushing for development schemes, while environmental groups are advocating for recreational space. The two factions have arrived at a partial compromise, which is what you have to work with. They have agreed to the following two points: (1) a maximum of 200 acres from the army base and the mining land will be used for recreation and (2) the amount of army land used for recreation plus the amount of farm land used for development will together total 100 acres.
>
> Not only are you dealing with opposing factions but with improvement costs, ranging from $50 to $2,000 per acre, depending on which parcel of land is involved and how it will be used. You have to satisfy everyone while minimizing the total cost for improvement. To arrive at a reasonable allocation plan will demand careful analysis and attention to detail.[1]

The student teams work on this problem for six to eight weeks using algebra, geometry, and matrix operations. Group solutions to the unit problem must be explained both in writing and orally to the whole class. Solutions are reached by looking at similar but simpler situations in shorter problems. Along the way, students pose questions, look for patterns, and make connections between the current problems and the mathematics they have previously learned. "By solving a variety of problems, students deepen their understanding, and then begin to abstract the concepts and refine the techniques needed to apply to the complex original problem" (Alper et al., 1996).

At the end of each unit, students write reflective pieces on what they have learned about specific activities that best contributed to the depth of their conceptual understanding. These reflective papers are placed in student portfolios, along with other evidence of their learning. Students are free to update the contents of the portfolios at any time in order to capture a more valid picture of what they have learned.

The IMP curriculum challenges students to explore open-ended problems in ways that resemble the inquiry method used by mathematicians and scientists in their work. It gives students the opportunity to explore, conjecture, experiment, and reflect on their results. If they fail initially, they return to the problem and attempt to figure out what went wrong. They keep working cooperatively and individually to grasp the underlying mathematical ideas.

Research supported by NSF yielded several conclusions: (1) IMP students performed as well as, and often better, than cohorts in more traditional high school mathematics programs; (2) On tests focusing on quantitative reasoning and problem solving, IMP students outperformed their traditional peers; (3) IMP students enroll in more mathematics courses compared to peers in traditional programs (Webb, 2003); and (4) IMP has a positive effect on student achievement among diverse student populations (Webb & Dowling, 1996).

THE ARTS

Apprenticeships and Peer Teaching in the Performing Arts

At Germantown High School in Tennessee, theatre and media studies are more like internships than classes. The school's student-managed television studio operates 24 hours per day. The Poplar Pike Playhouse, Germantown's on-campus theatre facility, presents a full season of theatrical productions each year. Typically, the yearly schedule includes two main shows, several acting festivals, a touring children's theatre company, and several ensemble presentations. Students assume year-long positions as company manager, box office manager, costume coordinator, and sound and light coordinators, as well performers (Mann, 1998).

Starting in the ninth grade, students at Germantown begin a sequential fine arts curriculum with an introduction to theatre and studio, followed by courses in acting or technical theatre, and leading to film, video, or theatrical production workshops in 11th and 12th grade. The workshop/studio production experience is a two-year loop in which senior students mentor juniors prior to the latter accepting full responsibility for managerial positions.

A special feature of the school is a $3 million cable television studio on the school campus. Students are involved in producing the activities of their own local access station, GHS-TV. Over 400 hours of programming per month are cablecast to 16,000 community subscribers. The students produce a morning news show, "Wake Up Germantown," plus four original programs a week (Mann, 1998).

Frank Bluestein, chair of the fine arts department, writes, "People think theatre is about doing a play, but for us, it is serious study." Bluestein notes that everything about theatre demands research—studying the history of the period, the costumes, the design process, color, light, and human motivations. He describes how students in introductory theatre classes approach a play: they view a filmed version, they read it both as homework and together as a class, they critique it and act it out, they research the setting, and they attend a live performance. By the end of the course, they have encountered 30 different works. Bluestein believes that "theatre experiences are vital because they connect students to the world in ways that nothing else does" (Mann, 1998).

Art as Inquiry

The fifth grade students at Northwood Elementary School in North Canton, Ohio, examined two baseballs. The first was signed by Babe Ruth, the second by Earl Averill, a Hall of Fame outfielder who played for the Cleveland Indians. Their teacher asked what appeared to be an easy question to answer, "Which one of the two baseballs is the more valuable?" It was the students' introduction to the concept of provenance or authenticating the value and ownership of art (Khourey-Bowers & Croley, 2007).

The unit on provenance coincided with reading a novel about stolen artwork during World War II in Europe. The students learned that many Holocaust victims' family members had discovered paintings hanging in museums that allegedly were owned by their families and confiscated by the Nazis. The students read numerous articles, detailing cases where the ownership of artwork was in question. The teacher challenged the students to determine the rightful ownership of the stolen art from World War II. The focus of the inquiry was the work of Gustav Glint and specifically *A Portrait of Adele Bloch-Bauer*, whose provenance had been disputed (Khourey-Bowers & Croley, 2007).

With the work of Glint as model, the students replicated his style in their art creations using bridal magazine photos and wallpaper samples, touched up with gold paint. When the student completed their studio projects, they engaged in a lively debate about what to do with the portrait in question and who really owned it. They considered several possibilities without coming to a definitive answer. Many students continued their interest in provenance as an authentic question for art detectives after the unit was completed.

BUSINESS EDUCATION

Experiential Learning and Authenticity in Business Education

In the town of Rothsea, Minnesota, a teacher of business education at the local high school proposed that her students learn the principles and skills of management by taking over failed businesses. The class acquired a hardware store, a lumberyard, and a grocery store. They stocked all three businesses through bank loans and corporate grants totaling $100,000. Because the businesses were operated under the aegis of the school district, there were no taxes. Student labor was paid by school credit, with every student enrolled in the business department contributing a minimum of one hour per day. Each of the businesses turned a profit. In fact, they were so successful that the students have now taken on a fitness center. Family members frequenting these businesses feel that they are supporting their children. Rather than being concerned with grades, the students are more concerned with helping their businesses achieve success (*ABC World News Tonight*, 1993).

MicroSociety Schooling: Connecting Learning to Life

Talbot Hill Elementary School, a Title 1 school in Benton, Washington, adopted the George Richmond's MicroSociety philosophy 14 years ago. His philosophy averred that students learn best when they connect schooling to adding quality to their lives. At Talbot, three afternoons each week, every student participates in a profit business, a government agency, or a nonprofit organization. Students in grades K–2 work on their MicroSociety activities with their homeroom teachers. Students in grades 3–5 either go to their jobs or to their small business that they have launched as entrepreneurs (Dunton, 2006).

On a typical MicroSociety afternoon, a business owner graphs profits and loss on a spreadsheet. In a room across the hall, management trainees participate in a seminar on leadership. In another room, a loan officer evaluates the merits of an application for a new business loan. At the hall of justice, a judge briefs a group of citizens on the responsibility of jury duty. All business transactions use a school currency called "Cool Cash" (Dunton, 2006).

A Micro Academy is held every fall to orient students to their rights and responsibilities as citizens and about the basic concepts of the MicroSociety, economics, and governmental processes. A job fair where students fill out job applications and are hired follows the orientation.

A bicameral legislature is elected each year using a primary and general election model. It is not unusual for over 200 students to run for the offices. One representative from each classroom is elected and two senators are elected from each grade level. A president presides over the House of Representatives and a vice president over the Senate. Spirited campaigning precedes the elections, with students using PowerPoint presentations, closed circuit television, and pamphlets to influence the voters. Once elected, the legislature meets weekly to consider student suggestions for laws. One law suggested by a student group that was making and selling food products required all food handlers to pass a test each year (Dunton, 2006, p. 58).

Students desirous of starting a business are required to develop a mission statement for the business, a plan, and an operating budget. Students who receive a ticket for running in the hallways have their cases heard in the Hall of Justice. More serious violations are resolved through mediation or jury trials. In a specific case involving embezzlement from the student bank, the plaintiff was found guilty and required to repay the funds, as well as to perform community service. Students who serve as judges and lawyers must pass a bar exam assessing their knowledge of how the school's judicial system works.

Teachers at Talbot Hill do a great deal of coaching, removing supports for students as they are able to function more independently. They also develop rubrics for academic standards related to *Washington's Assessment of Student Learning* so that students can rate their own progress. Results of the state test in 2006 showed that Talbot Hill students far exceeded the school's adequate progress goals. Moreover, they were learning to apply academic skills in meaningful ways. Today, the MicroSociety program has been adopted by over 250 schools in 40 states.

PHYSICAL EDUCATION

A Cultural Approach Integrates Instruction

Keith Biggs, a physical education teacher at Ochwilla Elementary School in Palatka, Florida, introduced a variety of games and activities to his students. One of the most creative was the Highland Games, patterned after the Highland Games Festivals in Scotland that celebrate the Scottish and Celtic culture and heritage. The *Ochwilla Highland Games* came into being in 2006. The teacher was looking to broaden the activities for his physical education program in grades 3 through 5. Students' positive response to games such as "touch rugby" and "team handball" caused him to consider something a bit more complex. It was Halloween and a time when children like to dress up. So, he introduced the idea of the Highland Games.

In preparation for the games, the students read about and discussed the history of the games in Scotland, how they came about, and their rationale. They also talked about clans, the various tartan plaids that clans adopted, and the geography of Scotland. Their inquiry into the highland games led them to decide on four events: Turning the Caber, the Farmer's Walk, Tossing the Sheaves, and the Stone Throw. In the real highland games, the caber toss utilizes a tall tapered pine pole 18 to 21 feet long. The stone throw is similar to the modern-day shot put. Tossing the sheaves uses a 20-pound bundle of straw and a pitchfork, and the participants in the farmer's walk balance two heavy buckets on either end of a pole resting on their shoulders.

Obviously, the equipment for the *Ochwilla Highland Games* had to be constructed and adapted to the elementary environment. The teacher and the students began to think about ways the equipment could be developed to simulate the equipment used in the real games. They decided on the following:

- The caber was built out of a 12-foot piece of PVC pipe, six inches in diameter. They padded the bottom of the pipe with polyethylene foam to protect their hands.
- The Farmer's Walk used two plastic buckets partially filled with sand.
- Tossing the Sheaves was simulated by a burlap bag filled with sand and a pitchfork with the tines covered by plastic tubes. Styrofoam cups were placed in the mesh of the base backstop at different heights to determine the height of each throw.
- The Stone Throw used a twelve-pound medicine ball.

On the day of the event, the teacher wore a kilt with knee socks and sporran. The kilt created quite a stir and led to an animated discussion of how the wearing of kilts was banned by the British. And, since weapons were forbidden, how the Scots used the highland games to surreptitiously train for combat was also discussed.

The games were a huge success. The students enjoyed participating in the games, studying a different culture, and resolving some very real problems in adapting the equipment to the physical limitations of the elementary school.[2]

REFLECTION

The examples provided in this chapter offer insight into creative ways to apply personalized instruction to various instructional areas. The examples represent real strategies in school settings. In some cases, they draw explicitly on one of the strategies described in Chapter 4. In other instances, they appear to be multidimensional. We hope that the scope of the examples shows the breadth of the ways by which personalized instruction can be implemented.

In Chapter 7, we briefly describe how schools desirous of personalizing instruction can be structured and organized, with concrete examples from four different schools committed to developing a student-centered school culture.

NOTES

1. Interactive Mathematics Program, Key Curriculum Press, 1150 65th Street, Emeryville, CA 94608; 1-800-995-MATH; www.keypress.com.

2. Information for this example was provided by Mr. Keith Biggs, physical education teacher at Ochwilla Elementary School, in direct contact with the authors.

7

THE STRUCTURE AND ORGANIZATION OF PERSONALIZATION

Personalized schools are structured and organized differently than more traditional schools. In prior chapters, we presented a theoretical framework for personalizing instruction (see "Basic Elements of Personalized Instruction: Culture" [Chapter 2] and Figure 4.1), along with specific examples in subject areas. This chapter presents a brief description of the salient organizational structures of schools that are focused on personalization. In addition, four schools currently implementing their vision of personalization will be described. Each of these schools is a contemporary *quality exemplar* that clarifies the vision of what is possible at different levels of schooling.

If the present is a kind of prologue, the possibilities for the future are staggering. A journey into uncharted waters awaits the present school population and their future cohorts. How can schools prepare students for the unknown? Linda Darling-Hammond (1993) stressed the need for all students to learn at high levels and sees the job of instruction as that of enabling diverse learners to develop their talents in effective and powerful ways. The future, whatever it might bring, seems to demand flexible and thoughtful people unafraid to meet the unknown, whatever it might be.

Traditionally, schools have been lonely places for teachers. They spend their time in 750-square-foot classrooms with a prescribed number of students. Planning is usually done in these classrooms, an office, or a cubicle. Opportunities to meet regularly with colleagues to plan instruction and discuss problems are the exception rather than the rule. In addition, the current emphasis on high-stakes testing restricts curricular choices for students and teachers. Decisions about what to teach and when to teach it are made outside the school. Professional empowerment is valued in the abstract, but often absent in the application.

THE PLAN

One usually begins a new or different structure with a plan, an idea of where one is going. Personalizing a school is only conceptually different from constructing a building. In the latter, a set of architectural drawings usually precedes the actual construction. The plan should be practical, even visionary. It should look beyond the present to the future.

An excellent source for creating a forward-looking plan to personalize a school is Keefe and Howard's *Redesigning Schools for the New Century* (1997). The process these authors suggest begins with statements about mission and vision, a statement about culture and climate, and a list of student goals and outcomes. Keefe and Howard then describe the system components that must be addressed in order to achieve the vision, culture/climate change, and outcomes. These components are curriculum and instruction, school structure and organization, leadership, staffing and staff deployment, communication and political structures, school resources, and a plan for evaluation. All of these components must be realized if a one wishes truly to personalize a school.

SCHOOL BUDGET AND MANAGEMENT

In a personalized school, the budget gives high priority to the mission and goals of the school. Staff development is near the top of the list of priorities so that teachers can enhance the skills they need to work differently with students. Local control of funds becomes more of a reality. Some traditional concerns, such as the hiring of substitute teachers, are less important because teaching teams and student schedules are simply adjusted when teachers are absent. Monies saved are redeployed for instruction or advisement or other functions judged important by the school staff.

School organization is less hierarchical. Personalized schools benefit from engaging in a design process that includes consensus statements about the school's mission and vision, the school's culture and climate, and assumptions and beliefs about students and how they learn best. These basic statements provide a design and framework for development of all school components. Task forces composed of teachers, administrators, parents, students, and community members make critical decisions that impact the school's mission and vision. These task forces, with representative membership and approved by a committee of the whole, develop specifications for the key components of the school (Keefe & Howard, 1997).

Guided by the school design statement, teaching teams or smaller instructional units, such as schools-within-schools, have the freedom to provide appropriate experiences for students. Self-evaluation of teaching and learning are valued and supported. New staff members are employed only after affected teachers and the principal concur. Teacher-advisers (TAs) or advocates help students choose course offerings and plan their daily, weekly, and monthly schedules. Teacher-advisers monitor advisee progress and communicate salient information to teachers, administrators, and parents. Decision making is broadened as widely as feasible within guidelines established by the school district and state. As the instructional leader, the principal encourages those persons closest to a situation to make decisions in the best interests of students.

SCHOOL FACILITIES

Most schools have been constructed from specifications that reflect less than a personalized approach to instruction. The egg-crate structures with classroom next to classroom are sometimes modified slightly for elementary and middle-level schools, but instruction usually remains fixated on a traditional view. When districts do undertake new construction, decision makers typically do not begin with a design statement (Keefe & Howard, 1997).

School facilities supportive of personalized instruction ideally include resource areas, small group meeting rooms, workrooms for teachers to meet, discuss, and plan, offices for teacher-advisers with computers to access key databases about individual advisees, and perhaps even one or two larger meeting areas for large group presentations. Media centers are equipped with personal computers for student use and subscribe to a variety of databases. The center is available and used all day. Some students even have carrels or stations assigned to them on a continuing basis for research, long-term projects, or independent study. Hands-on labs and resource areas support the teaching of both the major disciplines and the practical arts. Appropriate software enables students to progress at their own pace. Large group areas are equipped with interactive whiteboards, LCD projectors, computer stations, and enhanced sound systems. The overriding consideration is to match the learning environment with the learning activity.

SCHOOL STAFFING CONSIDERATIONS

The typical ratio of classroom teachers to students is too large to foster serious attempts at personalized instruction. In a conventional secondary school schedule, it is not unusual for teachers to be assigned 150 or more students throughout the school day. In self-contained elementary classrooms, teachers are often assigned 30–35 students. The sheer weight of the numbers can preclude any meaningful attempt to work with students more closely. As a matter of survival, teachers standardize their lesson plans and strategies for most students and rely on special teachers and pull-out programs to accommodate individual differences. Attempts to lower class sizes to 20–25, while well meaning, do not ensure personalization.

An analysis of staffing assignments, especially at the secondary level, reveals that a sizable number of building-level educators have few or no instructional assignments. Principals, assistant principals, guidance counselors, deans of students, behavioral specialists, curriculum resource specialists, student activities directors, athletic directors, and teachers on special assignment rarely, if ever, teach students on a regular basis. When schools have a high number of nonteaching faculty members and a conventional staffing pattern, small student-teacher ratios are virtually impossible to achieve unless the school district increases the staffing allocations. Under conventional staffing patterns, smaller student-to-teacher ratios can be realized only by deciding that all staff will work with students for some part of the school day.

Some type of differentiated staffing can help teachers reduce the number of students with whom they work at any given time and facilitate an accommodation of student differences. Simply adding more personnel in a traditional classroom does not necessarily improve student achievement. Teacher aides should be deployed carefully. Aides who work directly with students should be competent in the specific subject field. Clerical and technical aides can relieve teachers of paperwork, maintain student records, and operate equipment. General aides can be used to supervise cafeterias, corridors, restrooms, and bus-loading areas. This kind of differentiated staffing was seen as a way to professionalize the role of the teacher in the NASSP Model Schools Program, 1969–1974.

TEAMING

One form of teacher assignment with many potential benefits is teacher teaming. When teachers are assigned by teams to groups of students, greater flexibility in student grouping can be achieved. Team composition can take several forms. Usually, a team is composed of several teachers with either single or double subject matter responsibilities. A guidance counselor or resource teacher may be assigned to specific teams, either full or part time. A teacher trained in special education or as a cognitive skills specialist can assist students with special needs and work with individuals or small groups. Student teachers may be assigned to teams, plus volunteers from the community. In addition, at the elementary level, teaming allows students to interact with a variety of caring adults as opposed to the typical self-contained classroom.

Assigning students to a teaching team for the major portion of the school day can enable teachers to accommodate student differences more effectively. Teams readily form small learning communities where students and teachers become well acquainted. Teachers within a learning community interact daily and plan instruction for individual students and groups. The proximity of teachers to each other offers an opportunity for continual dialogue, consultation, and expanded learning. When teams facilitate students' daily schedules, they can place students in more appropriate learning environments. Team members may also serve as advisers to students within the team and remain with them throughout their years at the school.

FLEXIBLE SCHEDULING

Student and teacher schedules are important components in personalized instruction. Elementary teachers usually meet with students for a full day, with pull-out programs for special needs students and enrichment programs at specific times during the school day. When special education and resource teachers work directly with a teacher or team of teachers, pull-out programs can be avoided and additional resources are available for all students. Personalization, of course, requires more than simple contact. Elementary classrooms focused on personalized instruction make regular use of differentiated instruction, cooperative small groups, learning centers, student projects, reciprocal teaching, and cognitive apprenticeships.

At the secondary level, block schedules have become popular vehicles for encouraging flexibility and enabling teachers to vary instruction. Block scheduling is particularly appropriate for student projects, team learning, community-based experiential learning, and practical problem-solving activities. The 4-x-4 schedule offers students and teachers longer class periods and fewer classes. Teachers in the 4 x 4 usually teach three classes each semester with a period each day for planning. Students take four classes rather than six or seven each semester and, over the course of a year, can complete eight credits toward graduation. Class periods in the 4-x-4 are 85 to 90 minutes in length. This and other block scheduling alternatives do provide some opportunity for teachers to personalize instruction, but the time periods are usually of uniform length each day. Students who need an extended time frame to work on a presentation or project are frequently not accommodated.

The student-driven schedule can facilitate greater personalization and support a continuous progress approach to instruction. Students in this arrangement have a teacher-adviser with whom they meet each day. The teacher-adviser helps individual students with long-range planning, weekly planning, and daily scheduling. The TAs are empowered to schedule students into appropriate learning environments for group and individual study.

The student-driven schedule, however, assumes a curriculum organization that permits students to progress at their own rates. The school staff organizes the curriculum into units or segments and prepares learning guides for each sequence. Learning guides usually focus on common objectives with various activities to achieve them. Students select the activities that best fit their learning styles and their interests. They work on the activities either individually, in pairs, or in learning teams—in resource centers created for each subject or group of subjects. The student-driven schedule enables students to budget the time necessary to complete a learning task. Time use is under the control of the TA and the student. The TA monitors student progress academically and socially. If students are not using their time wisely, restrictions are imposed.

COMMUNITY INVOLVEMENT

James Comer of Yale University and Joyce Epstein of Johns Hopkins University have written extensively about the importance of parental involvement in helping children succeed in school. Comer's School Development Program has been successful in involving urban school parents and community members in student learning. Comer contends that children's experiences at home and at school deeply affect their psychosocial development, which in turn shapes their academic performance (Comer, 1997). Epstein (1995) asserted "the way schools care about children is reflected in the way schools care about families" (p. 701). She believes that when schools form partnerships with parents, opportunities for children to succeed academically are greatly enhanced.

Diagnosis is the foundation of a personalized approach to education and instruction. Certainly, parents know much about their children's experiences, interests, and work habits by virtue of their association in their children's formative years. Parents can help schools create valid individual profiles of students' knowledge levels, skills, and interests. Working with parents in Baltimore, Maryland, Epstein (1995) also established that parents and children can effectively work together in completing homework assignments.

Communities can create school-like opportunities that support student projects, apprenticeships, experiential learning, and community service. Community surveys conducted by the school can identify available community talents and resources that can provide teachers with additional options in their quest to personalize instruction. In the early 20th century, John Dewey's Laboratory School at the University of Chicago frequently used the community as a suitable learning environment for young children. It was a way for the children to connect what happened in school with the life of the community. Dewey's school focused on the centrality of the individual student. The forming of meaningful school, parent, and community partnerships with students as the center extends Dewey's idea into the new century.

QUALITY EXEMPLARS

Thomas Haney Secondary School, 8–12

The Thomas Haney Secondary School (23000 116th Avenue, Maple Ridge, BC V0R 2P0; Telephone: 604-467–9081; www.thss.ca/) is a public high school in Maple Ridge, British Columbia. The school opened in 1992 and currently serves 1,000 students in grades 8–12. Haney replaced traditional secondary school classrooms with spaces designed for innovative programs. It is one of six schools in the Canadian Coalition of Self-Directed Learning.

Haney identified a set of principles to shape a personalized instructional model and to design the facilities of the school. These principles are as follows:

- Students learn at different rates and in different ways.
- Students learn better if they assume responsibility for their own learning.
- Current learning should support life-long learning.
- Students can learn and want to learn.
- School facilities should support, not hinder, innovation.

The Thomas Haney building features a large, open-space area, called the Great Hall, where students obtain study guides and work either alone, with another student, or in learning teams. Students work here on mathematics, English, and social studies. They work on second languages in the school media center, near the spaces where these classes meet periodically. Other spaces are more specialized for small-group work, labs, or practicums in science, technology, art, music, drama, physical education, and business education.

Each student develops a personalized educational plan (PEP) in collaboration with his or her teacher-adviser. Students earn credit in eight different subjects per year (sometimes more than eight) and do so in a variety of formats. Teacher-advisers monitor student progress in all subjects in which advisees are seeking credit.

The teacher-adviser uses information from past student achievement and other personal data to create an appropriate educational plan for each advisee. The plans are subject to modification based on student progress, interests, and needs. Students use a planner developed by the school to decide the areas where they will study during the day and week. The weekly schedules are developed with the help of the adviser and approved in advance. Students are able to change schedules in light of new information or unplanned contingencies. Advisees keep the planners with them at all times and use them in conferences with their advisers to assess the amount of time spent on specific areas of the curriculum and their academic progress in each of the areas.

The curriculum is organized into learning guides to permit self-direction and independent learning. Each course is divided into guides with most courses having a total of 20 units. The learning guides are written by teachers and address the course objectives. Varying activities are offered so that students can meet the objectives in accord with their interests, knowledge, skills, and developmental needs. The amount of independent time generally varies with the demonstrated maturity of the student. As a rule of thumb, students spend two-thirds of their time on self-selected activities. Time estimates are flexible, however, to correspond with the requirements established by the British Columbia Ministry of Education. In reality, students work at their own pace and move more quickly or slowly depending on their prior knowledge, interests, and willingness to commit time. Eighth grade students begin in fairly structured classes in which they are introduced to learning guides and to the responsibilities of self-directed learning.

Learning guides follow a common format regardless of the subject or course. They begin with an introductory paragraph that offers students an overview of the guide, followed by outcome statements detailing what students are expected to attain upon completing the guide. An evaluation section provides a description of what students must complete and to what standard. The next section lists the resources to be used or consulted. Learning activities and an activity checklist complete the guide.

The learning activities section leads students to textbooks, outside reading, interactive videos, laser discs, hands-on materials, field studies, community-based experiences, computer activities, and skill shops aligned with the guide's objectives. The guides also list special seminars for information that can only be gleaned from a teacher or guest lecturer. A variety of activities are offered for each objective to accommodate individual students.

Students are assigned "teacher-markers" in subjects they are pursuing for credit. The teacher-markers meet with the students one-on-one as needed, review test results, and give feedback on student progress. As students work to complete learning activities, they interact with teacher-markers and other teachers of the same subject. The open facilities of the Great Hall, the media center, and other spaces enable teachers to move about the areas, observing students at work and intervening as appropriate (Jenkins & Keefe, 2002, p. 452).

Creative independent or group projects are built into the learning guides. Students negotiate with subject teachers for projects based on individual interests. A typical project contracted by an eleventh grade student involved building a portfolio of original poetry that later served as a one-person show for an audience of approximately 200 students. Another student wrote an op-ed piece for the school newspaper based on the reading of several historical novels. Several students are currently involved in a joint project on salmonid enhancement at a regional park. They are learning how to propagate salmon eggs to breed healthier, more environmentally sound species.

The Haney technology programs involve students in graphics, metals, robotics, video editing, and communications technology. Rather than create their own learning guides, teachers in the technology programs modify commercially developed materials. Tech students work independently, in pairs, or in learning teams on these guides, with teachers coaching as needed.

The physical education program is different, as are choral and instrumental music, drama, and science. In PE, music, and drama, students meet in class groups two or three times per week. Physical education is divided into four units: team games, individual events, personal development, and outdoor pursuits. For individual events, students choose activities such as cross-country, aquatics, bowling, tennis, curling, racquetball, wrestling, and golf. In outdoor pursuits, students receive credit for skiing (with the ski club), hiking, cycling, or providing a community service. Personal development includes weight training, aerobics, running, and walking.

In choral and instrumental music, students work individually and in sectional groupings when the total performance group is not scheduled. The individual and sectional time allows teachers to work more intensely with students in guided practice experiences. In science, students check-out kits to complete experiments. They work in a large laboratory with a team of teachers who monitor progress and provide help.

At Thomas Haney, students can advance at their own pace with as much teacher help as necessary. Students spend most of their time working alone or in teams in places appropriate to the chosen or assigned learning activities. Students are encouraged to search out information from many sources, including the school's technologically equipped library, the Internet, and from the district teachers' resource center. Students take tests when they are ready and not in accordance with a teacher's schedule. Tests are graded and the results reviewed with the individual student in order to map further direction. Students may redo any unsatisfactory work. They are only in competition with themselves. Other forms of assessment include presentation to faculty members and to other students, musical recitals, art shows, and project exhibitions.

Self-directed learning may not touch all students equally at first, but, in time, it makes them work harder and prepares them for life. As one teacher observed, "These kids work through breaks, they work through lunch, they even follow me to the washroom . . . . These kids do it all themselves. I'm just here for assistance" (*Sunday Province*, 1997, p. A11).

The Key Learning Community, K–12

The Key Learning Community (777 South White River Parkway, West Drive, Indianapolis, IN 46221; Telephone: 317–226–3048; www. 616.ips.k12.in.us), a K–12 heterogeneous nontracked program located on two campuses in Indianapolis, Indiana, began as the vision of a small cadre of elementary teachers and gradually expanded to include middle and high schools. The school serves 446 students on a year-round basis. The design was a complex blend of ideas drawn from the work of several educational theorists. From James MacDonald, Key educators borrowed and expanded on the idea of using themes as organizing centers for an interdisciplinary approach to curriculum (Bolanos, 1994). They also built on the works of Howard Gardner (multiple intelligences), Mihaly Csikszentmihalyi (intrinsic motivation), and David Feldman (developmental standards). Every student receives equal emphasis in each of the eight areas of intelligence identified by Gardner: musical, logical-mathematical, linguistic, naturalist, bodily kinesthetic, spatial, interpersonal, and intrapersonal.

Generally, in the K–8 levels learning revolves around themes chosen by the faculty, usually two per year. At the high school level, one theme per semester is chosen from Ernest Boyer's Eight Commonalities (1995). The themes help students make intrapersonal choices in line with their strengths, inquire deeply into the topic, and become quite proficient in an area. Some students develop original pieces of work as an extension of the topic. Examples of themes for K–8 are: "let's make a difference," "heritage," and "renaissance—then and now." Themes can be repeated and expanded as new information and more resources are added. The themes span all grades and all subjects and provide focus for the academic subjects (Bolanos, 1994).

Every student, regardless of age, is required to develop and complete a project related to the themes. The student presentations are video-taped and become a part of the student's academic portfolio. Because students complete two independent projects each year that they attend the school, the video portfolio documents progress longitudinally. The theme of renaissance, then and now, spurred one eight-year-old to investigate the role of jester in the medieval court, complete with appropriate costume and several magic tricks to keep the student and adult audience entertained. In another instance, a kindergarten student's interest in the degree of heat on Venus led him to create a large cardboard thermometer that compared the temperature of tap water, soup, chocolate chip cookies, his own body, and the surface of Venus. Later, when in the fifth grade, he investigated the history of the Macintosh computer. He made an Adobe Acrobat presentation about each model's debut, cost, speed, memory, and hard-disk space (Armstrong, 2002). Projects allow students to explore their interests and strengths, and thus, their intrapersonal intelligence.

Instead of the typical class structure, primary-aged students (grades 1–3) are grouped together, as are students from grades 4, 5, and 6. Multi-aged classes allow students who excel in one area but lag in another to learn at their own pace. A typical schedule differs from day to day, but linguistics, Spanish, math/science, and social studies are treated as fundamental. In addition to academic classes, students receive the equivalent of daily instruction in music, art, physical education, and computers. Every student learns to play a musical instrument, beginning in grade 1 with the violin.

Each day, K–12 students spend time in their "pods," a term adopted from the phrase "peas in a pod," where they work with a qualified teacher and peers of different ages. Every student selects a "pod" from the ones offered. Pods are developed by teachers and span all the multiple intelligence areas. One pod stresses the "math pentathlon" where students play board games that exercise their logical, spatial, and mathematical skills. In the architecture pod, students adopt houses and buildings in the immediate neighborhood for walking tours (Olson, 1988). In addition, students in the middle and high school are assigned to a teacher-adviser who remains with them throughout high school.

Three days per week elementary students are scheduled in the "Flow Room." Based on the theory of optimal experience developed by Mihaly

Csikszentmihalyi, "The Flow Center" provides a semi-structured type of free play where students choose from several activities in different intelligence areas to develop their intrapersonal intelligence. Teachers observe the activities that students select over time, carefully noting in which areas students are "happily concentrated." The identified strengths are then used to structure learning activities in all the content areas and to build experiences on individual student strengths.

Developmental performance descriptors serve as criteria for student assessment. Criteria are written at three levels: universal, cultural, and discipline based. The universal level (UL) describes what all students in all cultures can do. The cultural level (CL) identifies what students are expected to do in the Key Learning Community culture. Key students create projects for each of the curricular themes. The discipline-based level (DL) depicts quality of work at the three levels of a discipline: novice (DL-N), apprentice (DL-A), and journeyman (DL-J). The novice level indicates that the student has a basic understanding of the subject. The apprentice level represents that a student has a deep understanding of the subject. The journeyman level indicates that a student has an ability to perform at a high level that surpasses expectations. Students are not recommended for high school until they reach the beginning novice stage of a discipline (Key Learning Community, 2005–2006, p. 9). Teachers make professional judgments about student progress based on class work, school developmental descriptors, and the chronological age of the student. Assessment does not compare one student against another; rather, student work is considered a benchmark for a particular student at a particular point in time.

One goal of the Key Learning Community is to connect students with the city of Indianapolis and encourage active participation in both service and apprenticeship activities. Partnerships with businesses and organizations have been established that enable students to spend extended time in an apprenticeship with a community mentor. Apprenticeships exist in law, auto mechanics, music, visual arts, sports, finance, banking, social work, history, and research. The apprenticeship is tailored to fit the needs of both the student and the mentor (Bolanos, 1994).

At the high school level, all seniors must complete a community-based apprenticeship focused on their areas of interest. Placement alternatives include professional, educational and cultural institutions, community service organizations, legal and medical offices, and arts organizations. The students receive no remuneration or credit for participation in the apprenticeship program. During the junior year, students begin to investigate areas of interest in which they would like to fulfill the senior apprenticeship requirement (see their website for further information).

Seniors spend four mornings each week (Monday–Thursday) in their apprenticeships supervised by the Key Apprenticeship Supervisor and return to the K–12 campus for classes in the afternoon. One student, for instance, expanded his interest in Native American pottery by apprenticing in an art studio in downtown Indianapolis. Another student helped destitute families at The Children's Bureau. She located and found appropriate community resources for people who needed them. She also learned grant writing skills and increased funding available to the Bureau (see their website for further information).

Graduation from the Key Learning Community is based on successfully completing 52 credits of course work and the apprenticeship. Students also must document, in a multimedia portfolio, their participation and applied knowledge regarding eight human commonalities. Table 7.1 lists Boyer's eight commonalities with examples of applications.

The success of the Key Learning Community can be measured in a number of different ways. All students take the accountability tests required of all public school students in Indiana. The results show that

Table 7.1. Ernest Boyer's Eight Commonalities and a Sample Application

Commonalities	Applied Knowledge
Shared Use of Symbols	Major multimedia composition with sound, graphics, and text
Shared Life Cycle	In-depth work with elderly or children
Shared Membership in Groups	Participation in School Governance, teams, and community
Shared Producing and Consuming	Major project related to marketing or economics
Shared Sense of Time and Space	Major project on the history of Indianapolis
Shared Relationship with Nature	Major project on environmental concerns
Shared Values and Beliefs	Major project related to diversity, mutual trust, respect, and responsible citizenship
Shared Sense of the Aesthetic	Major composition, exhibition, or performance

Source: Data from Key Learning Community, 2004. Available at: www.616.ips.k12.in.us/

they do well when compared with their cohorts in other schools. But the important measure of the Key Learning Community goes beyond these statistics. One measure is the degree of intrinsic motivation that students exhibit in the pursuit of learning. As one student succinctly stated, "We do more than just memorize stuff for a test and write it down and forget it. We actually understand the stuff we are talking about" (Armstrong, 2002). Teacher turnover at the school is practically nonexistent, and their enthusiasm can be seen in the time spent in professional activities. One of the many visitors to the school remarked, "Teachers at Key Learning are not only subject matter experts, but they participate in ongoing discussions about assessment, learning, and aspects of the school" (Armstrong, 2002).

Francis W. Parker Charter Essential School, 7–12

According to their 1994 Charter, the Francis W. Parker School's (49 Antietam Street. Devens, Massachusetts 04134; Telephone: 978–772–3293; www.parker.org) mission is "to move the child to the center of the education process and to interrelate the several subjects of the curriculum in such a way as to enhance their meaning for the child." Parker, in Devens, Massachusetts, is a grade 7–12 public charter school serving approximately 400 students. The academic disciplines are integrated under three academic domains: the arts and humanities, mathematics, science, and technology, and Spanish and wellness. The course work centers on an essential question that cuts across traditional disciplinary lines. The essential question is addressed school-wide at all levels and generates subquestions that invite active learning of both thinking skills and content-area knowledge. As faculty and students address the essential question, the perspectives that various disciplines bring to the collective inquiry are pursued. Students are helped to see the connections between and among disciplines, as their understanding is raised to a higher level. The following is a list of the school-wide essential questions for several different years (Francis W. Parker Charter Essential School, 2005–2006):

- What is community? (1995–1996)
- What is change? (1995–1996)

- What is balance? (1996–1997)
- What are the patterns? (1998–1999)
- What's the limit? (1999–2000)
- What really matters? (2000–2001)
- Where's the truth? (2001–2002)
- What are the possibilities? (2002–2003)
- What's next? (2003–2004)
- What is unique? What is universal? (2004–2005)

The use of an essential question each year tends to establish the precedent that Parker curriculum and learning tasks will be inquiry-based.

Small class size, low student-to-teacher ratio, and a focus on active learning are staples of the Parker community. The school is organized into three divisions: I (roughly seventh and eighth grades), II (roughly ninth and tenth grades), and III (roughly eleventh and twelfth grades). Standards have been developed for each division derived from the wisdom of the faculty, the content and skills of specific disciplines, and the Massachusetts Curriculum frameworks. Students are held accountable for achieving the standards of each division. They present evidence to the faculty, and often to the community, in what are known as *Gateway Portfolios*, to advance from one division to another (Francis W. Parker Charter Essential School, 1999).

Students also take an active role in school governance. They serve on important school operations committees, a school-wide community congress, and a student justice committee. Student life is framed by a Parker School Constitution written and ratified by the students. Service is a key ingredient of the school philosophy. Peer tutoring is widely practiced, as well as hosting visitors to the school. According to their website, students also volunteer in the Devens community—in hospitals, nursing homes, and community centers.

The school does not rank students nor does it use an A-to-F traditional grading scheme. Teachers appraise student work in narrative form and assess their progress toward meeting specific standards in terms of three levels of competence—Just Beginning (JB); Approaches (A); and Meets (M)—all in relationship to division standards. Assessment narratives are produced twice each year, at midpoint and at the end of the year (Francis W. Parker Charter Essential School, 2005–2006).

Class size ranges from 15 to 50 multiage students with one or two teachers. A flexible block-type schedule allows more time for in-depth learning activities, as well as giving teachers substantial time to plan during the school day. The student-teacher ratio enables faculty to know students well and to generate thoughtful and accurate assessments of student learning.

Student work is assessed using portfolios, school-wide standards, and scoring rubrics. Students advance at a rate commensurate with their individual development and their Personal Learning Plans. They demonstrate their learning in individual assignments, projects, exhibitions, and portfolios. Each student receives a *Year-End Assessment* in narrative form from his or her teacher for each domain. For each of the key skills and content areas, the report indicates whether a student is "JB," "A," or "M" in satisfying standards in the appropriate division. Students are promoted from one division to another on the basis of a "Gateway Exhibition," in which they document meeting the school standards for their Division. Students may advance to another Division at any time during the school year based on their academic progress and in consultation with their teacher-adviser and their parents (see their website for further information).

Every Parker student is assigned a teacher-adviser each year and placed in a group based on age. Other secondary considerations for placement are a student's preference for a teacher in a domain, a request from the student or teacher, or to balance gender or diversity in an advisory group. The advisee ratio is 1:12. Advisers help students develop yearly personal learning plans (PLPs), monitor student progress, discuss teachers' assessments with advisees and parents, and help build competencies in the eight "Parker School Habits of Learning" (inquiry, expression, critical thinking, collaboration, organization, attentiveness, involvement, and reflection). Advisory groups meet approximately four hours per week (30 minutes at the start of the school day for connection and 10 minutes at the end of the day for reflection). They meet for one hour each Wednesday afternoon.

Division III students attend more seminars and laboratory courses in the three domains than Division I and II students. All Division III students must commit two hours per week to in-school service. Some repair computers in the tech lab; some serve as an aide in Division I classes; others tutor lower division students or serve as community ambassadors or help with hosting visitors or answer the office telephone or do custodial work. The senior seminar is a year-long course dedicated to developing and fostering critical thinking, inquiry, collaboration, and life after Parker. It is also the focus for the Senior Project (Francis W. Parker Charter Essential School, 2005–2006). Division III students also have a Capstone Senior Project, a topic that they choose to investigate independently with the help of an outside mentor or learning preceptor. The project can take many forms, from community internships to apprenticeships to science projects to academic inquiries, all resulting in a formal paper. The project focuses on a question crafted by the student. In every case, the student is required to make a public presentation of his or her findings and conclusions (Francis W. Parker Charter Essential School, 2005–2006).

Visitors to the school give Parker high marks for its positive school culture, the challenges provided students, the respectful atmosphere, and the staff members' ability to know each student well. One visitor wrote, "I was especially impressed by the students who worked on a research project, the students' portfolio presentations, the climate of respect and intellectual rigor." Another commented, "I observed teachers truly acting as facilitators for perhaps the first time in my life. They guided discussions and steered activities back on track, but allowed students to follow their own interests and curiosities" (Francis W. Parker Charter Essential School, 2005–2006, p. 37).

The Parker School is a total experience. Named for Francis W. Parker, whom John Dewey called "the father of progressive education," the school focuses on ideas rather than content coverage. Parker attempts to live by the Coalition of Effective Schools' principle "less is more," and the other "Nine Common Principles of Essential Schools." The school culture and climate reflect the value each individual brings to the school family. No one is unspecial. When queried about the difference between Parker and his previous school, one student remarked, "They give you more feedback here. Feedback helps you improve yourself. There is a lot of revision here [at Parker]. You just don't do an assignment and turn it in." Another said, "A lot of whys are asked and how-comes. Why is this important; so-what and who-cares questions. We have our opinions and facts, but so what? Tell me why that's important" (McVicar, 1998, p. 3).

Francis W. Parker, the man, was committed to organizing schools as democratic communities. Before the turn of the 20th century he wrote, "I am trying to apply well established principles of teaching, principles derived directly from the laws of the mind. The methods springing from them are found in the development of every child. They are used everywhere except in school." Francis W. Parker, the school, seems a living and developing tribute to the wisdom of its namesake.

The Met Center, Multi-Campus High School

The Met School (325 Public Street, Providence, RI 02905; Telephone: 401–752–2634; www.themetschool.org) is a public high school of 700 students located in the city of Providence, Rhode Island. Its structure and organization are the brainchild of Dennis Littky and Elliot Washor. Opening its doors in 1996, the success of the school can be seen in such common school indicators as 94% average daily attendance, a 95% graduation rate, and a record of 99% of the graduates being accepted to college over seven graduating classes. Seventy percent of the college attendees have graduated or are still in attendance. Most are from low-income families and the first in their family to go to college (Castleman & Littky, 2007).

The Met, officially known as the Metropolitan Regional Career and Technical Center, is composed of six different school sites with approximately 100 students at each site with a separate principal. It is the flagship school of a network of 45 similar schools around the country called the *Big Picture Schools*, all committed to personalizing the high school experience. There are no required courses, no paper-and-pencil tests, and no grades. "The school takes a "one-student-at-a-time" approach that seeks to capitalize on each student's strengths, interests, and learning style (Arnold, 2006). Students spend three days on one of the campuses and two days in a community internship.

A typical day on campus begins with a meeting of the entire school in a 30-minute "pick-me-up assembly." The assembly agenda consists of staff and student presentations, announcements, and an occasional outside speaker. Students then go to their advisory groups for 45 minutes, in which they discuss anything, from current events to Shakespeare. For the next one hour and 45 minutes they work on the independent projects coached by their teacher-adviser. After the lunch break, everyone engages in 30 minutes of silent reading. The next one hour and 30 minutes is devoted to independent projects. Advisory groups reconvene at the end of the day to review the day's work and to allow each student to comment on what he or she accomplished (Arnold, 2006).

On Tuesdays and Thursdays, students spend the entire day in internships with mentors in the Providence community. The internships are based on student interests and occur in settings as diverse as hospitals, graphic design studios, and a bakery. One student actually developed a DVD explaining the high rate of asthma cases among Latinos. Another built a classic wooden boat under the watchful eye of a master boat builder. Students are visited every two weeks on site by their teacher-advisers.

Students are assigned to advisory groups of 15 in grade nine and remain with the same adviser throughout their high school careers. Teacher-advisers are generalists, who guide their advisees in every academic area and help the advisory group to develop a sense of trust and teamwork. In a very real sense, advisers serve as coaches, diagnosticians, and liaisons with parents and community mentors. They gather as many resources as possible to help students explore their interests (Castleman & Littky, 2007, p.60). They also meet with individual advisees and his or her parents every quarter to develop and refine an individual learning plan.

One student, for example, centered his entire high school experience on studying the Japanese language and culture. His adviser helped him enroll in a class in Japanese at another high school in the area and later in a class at Brown University. With the help of a local church, the student was able to travel to Japan and live with a host family during his junior year at The Met. During his senior year, he was hired by an on-line comic book company to translate Japanese comics into English. Upon graduation from high school, he was admitted to Brown University, where he is now a junior majoring in anthropology (Castleman & Littky, 2007).

Students document every aspect of their projects in portfolios, which are later refined during their senior year and presented with their applications to colleges. Students defend their work each quarter in hour-long presentations to a panel composed of their adviser, their parents, their community mentor, and their peers. The panel offers feedback to help the students improve the projects and to revise their individual learning plans for the next quarter. Advisers prepare a two-page narrative describing the student's highlights for the nine weeks, goals met, and areas for further development. The last section of the narrative specifies additions and modifications to the student's learning plan.

The Met has adopted the following five learning goals that students are expected to meet through rigorous projects and internships:

1. Empirical Reasoning: The goal is to think like a scientist—to use empirical evidence and a logical process to make decisions and to evaluate hypotheses.
2. Quantitative Reasoning: The goal is to think like a mathematician— to understand numbers, to analyze uncertainty, to comprehend the properties of shapes, and to study how things change over time.
3. Communication: The goal is to be a great communicator—to understand your audience, to write, to read, to speak and listen well, to use technology and artistic expression to communicate, and to be exposed to another language.
4. Social Reasoning: The goal is to think like an historian or anthropologist—to see diverse perspectives, to understand social issues, to explore ethics, and to look at issues historically.
5. Personal Qualities: The goal is to be the best you can be—to demonstrate respect, responsibility, organization, leadership, and to reflect your abilities and strive for improvement (see their website for further information).

Many traditional school educators fight the annual battle of "senioritis," where many graduating seniors do little work in the second semester. The seniors at The Met are busy completing a 75-page autobiography and a Senior Thesis Project and in some cases, traveling to distant lands. For example, one senior designed and led a college-accredited course for six Met students, culminating in a trip to Nicaragua to study the influence of education on democracy. Two other seniors collected medical supplies to send to a small hospital in the Dominican Republic. They gathered thousands of dollars worth of gloves, trays, first-aid kits, masks, sheets, surgical gowns, and surgical scissors from medical supply companies in New England and sent them to the hospital in the small town of Bonao (Fields, 2006). According to their website, an advisory group traveled throughout the southern United States investigating the history of the civil rights movement, prompting one student to remark, "I did more the past two weeks than in the 16 years I've been alive. We'll remember this for the rest of our lives. We have done the impossible."

Met educators have dramatically demonstrated that student interest is a superior motivator for learning and that the appropriate place for learning to occur is not necessarily the school building or campus. During the 1970s, the late Dr. J. Lloyd Trump, then the Director of Research for NASSP, recommended that high school buildings be constructed to house only two-thirds of a school's population at any one time. He asserted that the money saved in construction should be used to purchase vans to transport the other one-third of the students into the community. Nearly forty years later, the Met is proving the soundness of his recommendation.

RETROSPECTIVE

All of the schools described in this chapter exist today. These schools are dynamic; they are in motion. Undoubtedly they will continue to change as the result of new discoveries in learning theory, instructional strategies, organization, and so forth. The four schools are somewhat different in philosophy and structure, but they do share several characteristics in common. All are committed to a personalized form of instruction, whether it is apprenticeships, self-paced learning, project learning, immersion, coaching and mentoring, advisement, experiential learning, community-based learning, or many of these in combination. These schools care for students as persons. Congeniality and cooperation permeate the school culture—between teachers and administrators, teachers and teachers, teachers and students, and teachers and parents. These schools operate under the same rules and the same constraints as their more conventional cohorts. But they are blazing new frontiers in K–12 personalized education for other educators to emulate and to adapt to local circumstances.

POSTSCRIPT

At the beginning of his book *How Children Fail* (1968), the late educational provocateur John Holt included the following quote from William Hull, "If we taught children to speak, they'd never learn." In the text of his book, Holt commented that all children learn to speak the languages and dialects of their immediate surroundings without apparent difficulty. Ostensibly, they do so by observation and mimicry. Yet, the attempt of our schools to teach all children literacy skills has been unsuccessful regardless of the methods employed. Perhaps the problem is trying too hard to make children learn in ways that adults learn best and not in accord with the strengths and proclivities of individual students.

Peter Senge's notion of the school as a learning organization makes sense to anyone trying to change a social institution that has resisted serious change for almost a century. Schools are organizations with interrelated parts. When educators contemplate changes in the existing organization, they must also implement changes in all the related components if the changes are to be effective. Personalization does not occur in a vacuum. It is a symbiotic process of change both in underlying attitude and spirit and in the school's key components. If a school staff does not honestly believe that all children can learn when offered appropriate learning environments, then no matter what is done or how small the student-teacher ratio may be, very little improvement will occur.

Traditional school organizations and structures are still the practice in most public schools. Using a rear-view mirror approach, some school policy makers propose back to basics, tougher standards, increased standardized testing, more emphasis on academics, less time for art, music and other "frills," and more remedial programs. These "reformers" forget the drudgery and boredom that are the by-products of conventional school programs and practices. Is it any wonder that recess and vacation are the most anticipated events in the day and the year of many schools past and present?

In a recent issue of the *Phi Delta Kappan*, Steven Wolk (2007) asked,

> Why Go to School? When our children's school experiences are primarily about filling in blanks on worksheets, regurgitating facts from textbooks, writing formulaic five-paragraph essays, taking multiple-choice tests, and making the occasional diorama—that is, when they are devoid of opportunities to create an original thought—we should expect the obvious outcome: children—and later adults—who are unable to think for themselves. None of this should surprise us. Passive schooling creates passive people. If we want people to think, learn, and care about the many dimensions of life, if we want neighbors who accept the responsibility of tending to the world and making it a better place, then we need schools and curricula that are actually about life and the world. (pp. 648–649)

What might the future of schooling and personalized instruction look like? Futurists speculate about the trends that will influence life and times in our 21st century. Gary Marx (2006), for example, describes sixteen trends affecting the world that will influence educational policy. Prominent among these trends is movement from "standardization to personalization." He anticipates that "standards and high-stakes tests will fuel a demand for personalization in an education system increasingly devoted to lifelong human development" (pp. 6–7).

Your authors will not hold our collective breath until this hopeful prophecy comes true, but the basis for the prediction is surely defensible and likely inevitable. Blackbourn et al. (2007–2008) also predict

> a shift away from the standardization of procedures and performances to individualization among all institutional activities. . . . To be successful, educational organizations will have to provide their stakeholders with indi-

vidualized and personalized services. . . . Those individuals, groups, and educational organizations that are unwilling to adapt to the needs of those they serve, and cling stubbornly to established, traditional practices, may well find themselves marginalized. (pp. 10–11)

So the future will be different; education will be different; and individual students will be its principal beneficiaries. But if this is going to happen, a new or different kind of No Child Left Behind legislation and implementation will have to be passed. A number of national educational associations have currently joined ranks to lobby for "certain fundamental changes in the law, vastly improved implementation, and adequate funding" (NASSP, 2007). The American Association of School Administrators, the American Federation of Teachers, the National Association of Elementary School Principals, the National Association of Secondary School Principals, the National Education Association, and the National School Boards Association have urged Congress to enact important changes in the NCLB, in five significant areas:

1. A redesign of the federal accountability framework to improve public schools rather than abandon them;
2. Valid, reliable, unbiased assessment systems that are aligned with state standards;
3. Maximum flexibility for states and school districts to address the assessment and learning needs of English language learners and students with disabilities;
4. Helpful interventions tailored to the needs of schools and communities rather than the current system of punitive sanctions; and
5. Determination of the qualifications of principals, teachers, and other education professionals by states and local districts.

But notwithstanding this strong appeal to Congress, our traditional educational system will not change unless the public, parents, and educators all commit themselves to the goal of the personalization of learning and instruction. We have been at this point in the change cycle too many times in the past. Just ask survivors of any of the earlier school reform efforts. Something more is needed than interest from Congress or strong statements of intent or better assessments.

We must have the *resolve* to make real and substantive changes in all schools this time around, not just those with enough local resources or enthusiastic communities and school staffs. There are a number of very promising contemporary school renewal initiatives already under way, with the promise of more to come, but it is the *culture of renewal* that must change this time or our momentum will wind down as it has done so often before. *We must establish a culture of school renewal in communities throughout the nation, one that recognizes that all students have a right to learn according to their own best talents and interests, and the claim to a school program that supports and assists them in their efforts.* As hip-hop entrepreneur Russell Simmons observes in his book, *Do You* (2007): "Education in America today has become very much about rules, about passing standardized tests rather than exploiting the talent you have inside of you" (p. 28). His message to the members of the educational establishment is that it is their responsibility to help students connect with the talents which are uniquely theirs.

We believe that personalization can and should be the basis of this new culture of school renewal. Most of our schools are not bad; they are just average, perhaps mediocre. They can be much better. It is the system itself that prevents them from really improving. The system must change so that our schools can change. We believe that a vital personalization must become the cornerstone of school renewal, if educators and the communities they serve, hope to change, in any significant way, the basic grammar of schooling. Only then will school renewal truly take hold and schools become all that they can be for all students.

REFERENCES

ABC World News Tonight. 1993. Small town renewal.

Adler, M. 1982. *The Paideia Proposal.* New York: Macmillan Publishing.

Allen, D. 1995. *The Training Protocol: A Process for Reflection.* Providence, RI: Coalition of Essential Schools.

Allen, D. 1998. *Assessing Student Learning: From Grading to Understanding.* New York: Teachers College Press.

Alper, L., Fendel, D., Fraser, S., and Resek, D. 1996. Problem-based mathematics—not just for the college-bound. *Educational Leadership* 53(8): 18–21.

Alt, M. N. 1997. How effective an educational tool is student community service? *NASSP Bulletin* 81(591): 8.

American Psychological Association (APA), Presidential Task Force on Psychology in Education. 1993. *Learner-Centered Psychological Principles: Guidelines for School Redesign and Reform* (4th ed.). Washington, DC: APA.

Anderson, R. C. 1977. The notion of schemata and the educational enterprise: General discussion of the conference. In *Schooling and the Acquisition of Knowledge,* eds. R. C. Anderson, R. J. Spiro, and W. E. Montague. Hillsdale, NJ: Erlbraum.

Armstrong, S. 2002. The Key Learning Community: Cultivating multiple intelligences. *Edutopia.* Available at: www.edutopia,org/node/957

Arnold, M. S. 2006. Innovation in education: One student at a time. *RIEIDC Focus.* Available at: www.riedc.com/riedc/blue_sky

Barr, R., and Tagg, J. 1995. From teaching to learning. *Change* (November/December): 13–25.

Barrs, M., Ellis, S., Hester, H., and Thomas, A. 1988. *The Primary Language Record.* London: Inner London Education Authority/Centre for Language in Primary Education.

Beyer, B. K. 1992. Teaching thinking: An integrated approach. In *Teaching for Thinking,* eds. J. W. Keefe and H. J. Walberg. Reston, VA: National Association of Secondary School Principals.

Blackbourn, J. M., Fillingim, J., Kritsonis, M. A., Campbell, J., Rader, D., Schillinger, J., and Ray, J. (2007–2008). The road ahead: Ten trends that will impact education in this century. *National Forum of Educational Administration and Supervision Journal* 24(3): 4–22.

Bloom, B. S. 1976. *Human Characteristics and School Learning.* New York: McGraw-Hill.

Bloom, B. S. 1984. The search for methods of group instruction as effective as one-to-one tutoring. *Educational Leadership* 41(8): 4–17.

Bolanos, P. J. 1994. The Key Renaissance Middle School: Extending the notion of multiple intelligences. In *World Class Schools: An Evolving Concept,* eds. J. Jenkins, K. S. Louis, H. J. Walberg, and J. W. Keefe. Reston, VA: National Association of Secondary School Principals.

Boyer, E. L. 1995. *The Basic School: A Community for Learning.* San Francisco: Jossey-Bass.

Bracey, G. 2006. Things fall apart: No Child Left Behind self destructs. *The Huffington Post.* Available at: www.huffingtonpost.com/gerald-bracey/things-fall-apart-no-chi_b_35935.html

Bransford, J. D., and Vye, N. J. 1989. A perspective on cognitive research and its implications for instruction. In *Towards the Thinking Curriculum: Current Cognitive Research,* eds. L. B. Resnick and L. E. Klopfer [ASCD Yearbook]. Alexandria, VA: Association for Supervision and Curriculum Development.

Bruner, J. 1998. *The Culture of Education.* Cambridge, MA: Harvard University Press.

Carnegie Corporation of New York, Council on Adolescent Development. 1989. *Turning Points: Preparing American Youth for the 21st Century.* Washington, DC: Carnegie Corporation.

Carroll, A. W. 1975. *Personalizing Education in the Classroom,* 20–25. Denver: Love Publishing.

Carson, C. C., Huelskamp, R. M., and Woodall, T. D. 1992. *Perspectives on Education in America* [Final draft]. Albuquerque, NM: Sandia National Laboratories.

Case, R. 1992. On the need to assess authentically. *Holistic Education Review* 5(4): 14–23.

Castleman, B., and Littky, D. 2007. Learning to love learning. *Educational Leadership 64*(8): 58–61.

Champagne, A. B., Klopfer, L. E., and Gunstone, R. F. 1982. Cognitive research and the design of science instruction. *Educational Psychologist 17*(1): 31–48.

Civil Rights Project. 2006. Tracking achievement gaps and assessing the impact of NCLB on the gaps: An in-depth look into national and state reading and math outcomes. Available at: www.civilrightsproject.harvard.edu/news/pressreleases/nclb_report06.php

Clark, D. 1999. *Fred Keller: The Personalized System of Instruction (PSI).* Available at: www.nwlink.com/~donclark/hrd/history/history.html

Clark, D. C. 1991. Developmental traits. In *Instructional Leadership Handbook,* 2nd ed., eds. J. W. Keefe and J. M. Jenkins. Reston, VA: National Association of Secondary School Principals.

Clement, J. 1979. Mapping a student's causal conceptions from a problem-solving protocol. In *Cognitive Process Instruction,* eds. J. Lockhead and J. Clement. Philadelphia: Franklin Institute Press.

Clerk, F. E. 1928. *A Description and Outline of the Operation of the Adviser-Personnel Plan at New Trier High School.* Winnetka, IL: New Trier High School.

Cobb, R. B., Abate, S., and Baker, D. 1999. Effects on students of a 4x4 junior high school block scheduling program. *Education Policy Analysis Archives* (February). Available at: http://epaa.asu.edu/epaa/v7n3.html

Cohen, D. L. (1991). Flow room: Testing psychologist's concept introduces learning in disguise at Key School. *Education Week* (June): 6–7.

Cohen, M. D., March, J. G., and Olsen, J. 1972. A garbage can model of organizational choice. *Administrative Science Quarterly 17*(1): 1–25.

Cohen, R. 1987. High (school) anxiety [Critic at Large column]. *Washington Post Magazine,* November 15.

Collins A., Brown, J. S., and Newman, S. E. 1989. Cognitive apprenticeship: Teaching the craft of reading, writing, and mathematics. In *Knowing, Learning, and Instruction: Essays in Honor of Robert Glaser,* ed. L. B. Resnick. Hillsdale, NJ: Lawrence Erlbaum.

Comer, J. P. 1997. *Waiting for a Miracle: Schools Can't Solve Our Problems—We Can.* New York: E. P. Dutton.

Creswell, J. 1997. *Creating Worlds, Constructing Meaning.* Portsmouth, NH: Heinemann.

Csikszentmihalyi, M. 1990. *Flow: The Psychology of Optimal Experience.* New York: Harper & Row.

Cunningham, W. G., and Gresso, D. W. 1993. *Cultural Leadership: The Culture of Excellence in Education.* Needham Heights, MA: Allyn and Bacon.

Cushman, K. 1996. Looking collaboratively at student work: An essential toolkit. *Horace* 13(2): 7.

Cushman, K. 1997. Demonstrating student performance in essential schools. *Horace* 14(2): 5.

Daniel, B. S. 1991. Contract learning. In *Instructional leadership handbook,* eds. J. W. Keefe and J. M. Jenkins. Reston, VA: National Association of Secondary School Principals.

Darling-Hammond, L. 1993. Reframing the school agenda: Developing capacity for school transformation. *Phi Delta Kappan* 74(10): 752–761.

Darling-Hammond, L. 1996. The right to learn and the advancement of teaching: Research, policy and practice for democratic education. *Educational Researcher* 25(6): 5–17.

Darling-Hammond, L. 1997. *The Right to Learn: A Blueprint for Creating Schools that Work.* San Francisco: Jossey-Bass.

Darling-Hammond, L. Ancess, J., and Falk, B. 1995. *Authentic Assessment in Action: Studies of Schools and Students at Work.* New York: Teachers College Press.

Deming, W. E. 1993. *The New Economics for Industry, Government, Education.* Cambridge, MA: Massachusetts Institute of Technology.

Dewey, John. 1900/1990. *The School and Society.* Chicago: The University of Chicago Press.

Dewey, John. 1902. *The Educational Situation.* Chicago: University of Chicago Press.

Dunn, R., and Dunn, K. 1978. *Teaching Students Through Their Individual Learning Styles.* Reston, VA: Reston Publishing.

Dunton, S. 2006. Building a microsociety. *Educational Leadership* 63(8): 56–60.

Edmonds, R. 1982. Programs of school improvement: An overview. *Educational Leadership* 40(3): 4–11.

Educational Research Service (ERS). 1978. *Class Size: A Summary of the Research.* Arlington, VA: ERS.

Ellis, A. K., and Fouts, J. T. 1993. *Research on Educational Innovations.* Larchmont, NY: Eye on Education.

English, F. W. 1994. *Theory in Educational Administration.* New York: Harper Collins.

English, F. W., and Hill, J. C. 1990. *Restructuring: The Principal and Curriculum Change.* Reston, VA: National Association of Secondary School Principals.

Epstein, J. R. 1995. School/family/community partnerships: Caring for the children we share. *Phi Delta Kappan* 76(9): 701–712.

Falk, B. 1998. Looking at students and their work: Supporting diverse learners with the Primary Language Record. In *Assessing Student Learning: From Grading to Understanding*, ed. D. Allen. New York: Teachers College Press.

Farnham-Diggory, S. 1992. *Cognitive Processes in Education*, 2nd ed. New York: HarperCollins.

Farnham-Diggory, S. 1994. Paradigms of knowledge and instruction. *Review of Educational Research* 64(3): 463–477.

Fazio, B. 1992. Students as historians—Writing their school's history. *The Social Studies* 82(2): 64–67.

Featherstone, H. 1998. Studying children: The Philadelphia Teachers' Learning Cooperative. In *Assessing Student Learning: From Grading to Understanding*, ed. D. Allen. New York: Teachers College Press.

Ferguson, S. 2005. Breathing life into foreign language reading. *Educational Leadership* 63(2): 63–65.

Feuer, M. J., and Fulton, K. 1993. The many faces of performance assessment. *Phi Delta Kappan* 74(6): 478.

Francis W. Parker Charter Essential School. 1999. Curriculum and instruction. Available at: www.parker.org

Francis W. Parker Charter Essential School. 2005–2006. *Annual Report.* Devens, MA: Francis W. Parker Charter Essential School.

Francis W. Parker Charter Essential School Website (2007). Available at www.parker.org

Galang, S. 2007. New design for learning. *The Salem News.* May 7.

Geertz, C. 1973. *The Interpretation of Cultures.* New York: Basic Books.

Georgiades, W. D. 1969. *The Pontoon Transitional Design for Curriculum Change.* Los Angeles: Center for Excellence in Education, University of Southern California.

Georgiades, W. D., Keefe, J. W., Lowery, R. E., et al. 1979. *Take Five: A Methodology for the Humane School.* Los Angeles: Parker and Son.

Gibboney, R. A. 1994. *The Stone Trumpet: A Story of Practical School Reform 1960–1990.* Albany, NY: State University of New York Press.

Glass, G. V., and Smith, M. L. 1978. Meta-analysis of research on the relationship of class size and achievement. *Educational Evaluation and Policy Analysis* 1:2–16.

Glasser, W. 1986. *Choice Theory in the Classroom.* New York: Harper Perennial.

Glasser, W. 1986. *Control Theory in the Classroom.* New York: Harper and Row.

Glasser, W. 1998. *The Quality School*. New York: HarperCollins.

Goodlad, J. I. 1984. *A Place Called School*. New York: McGraw-Hill, p. 242.

Goodlad, J. I. 1999. Flow, eros, and ethos in educational renewal. *Phi Delta Kappan* 80(8): 571–578.

Gores, H. B. 1976. The habitats of education. In *A Nation of Learners* ed. L. V. Goodman. Washington, DC: U.S. Government Printing Office.

Gottfredson, G. D., and Daiger, D. C. 1979. *Disruption in GOD Schools*. Baltimore: Center for Social Organization of Schools, Johns Hopkins University.

Gregorc, A. F. 1978. *Transaction Ability Inventory*. Columbia, CT: Author. [Currently the Gregorc Style Delineator, Gabriel Systems, Maynard, MA, 1982].

Gruwell, E. 1999. *The Freedom Writers Diary*. New York: Broadway Books, pp. 1–8.

Guskey, T. R. 1996. Reporting on student learning: Lessons from the past— Prescriptions for the future. In *Communicating Student Learning* [1996 ASCD Yearbook], ed. T. R. Guskey, pp. 13–24. Alexandria, VA: Association for Supervision and Curriculum Development.

Hamilton, S. F., and Zeldin, S. R. 1987. Learning civics in the community. *Curriculum Inquiry* 17(4): 407–420.

Hatch, T. 1998. How comprehensive can comprehensive form be? *Phi Delta Kappan* (March): 518–522.

Hess, B. 1992. Unpublished manuscript. New York: SUNY at Stony Brook.

Holt, J. 1968. *How Children Fail*. New York: Pitman Publishing.

Houston, P. D. 2007. The seven deadly sins of No Child Left Behind. *Phi Delta Kappan* 88(10): 744–748.

Howley, C. B. 1989. Synthesis of the effects of school and district size: What research says about achievement in small schools and school districts. *Journal of Rural and Small Schools* 4(1): 2–12.

Hunt, D. E., Butler, L. F., Noy, J. E., and Rosser, M. E. 1978. *Assessing Conceptual Level by the Paragraph Completion Method*. Toronto: Ontario Institute for Studies in Education.

Jenkins, J. M. 1994. Thomas Haney Centre: A school for all reasons. In *World Class Schools: An Evolving Concept*, eds. J. Jenkins, K. L. Louis, H. J. Walberg, and J. W. Keefe. Reston, VA: National Association of Secondary School Principals.

Jenkins, J. M., and Keefe, J. W. (2002). Two schools: Two approaches to personalized learning. *Phi Delta Kappan* 83(6): 449–456.

Jones, B. F., Palinscar, A. S., Ogle, D. S., and Carr, E. G., eds. 1987. *Strategic Teaching and Learning: Cognitive Instruction in Content Areas*. Alexandria, VA: Association for Supervision and Curriculum Development.

Jones, R. 1995. Wake up! *The Executive Educator* 17(8): 15–18.

Joy, A. 2007. Anzar students show what they know. *Hollister Freelance*. Available at: www.freelancenews.com/news/contentview.asp?c=215396

Joyce, B., and Showers, B. 1982. The coaching of teaching. *Educational Leadership* 40(1): 3–10.

Keefe, J. W. 1977. *Taxonomy of School Schedules for Continuous Progress* [Learning Environments Consortium International, Position Paper]. Unpublished.

Keefe, J. W. 1983. Advisement—A helping role. *The NASSP Practitioner* 9(4): 1–16.

Keefe, J. W. 1989. Personalized education. In *Organizing for Learning: Toward the 21st Century*, eds. H. J. Walberg and J. J. Lane. Reston, VA: National Association of Secondary School Principals.

Keefe, J. W. 1991a. Assessing, reporting student progress. In *Instructional Leadership Handbook*, 2nd ed., Edited by J. W. Keefe and J. M. Jenkins. Reston, VA: National Association of Secondary School Principals.

Keefe, J. W. 1991b. *Learning Style: Cognitive and Thinking Skills*. Reston, VA: National Association of Secondary School Principals.

Keefe, J. W. 1994. School evaluation using the CASE-IMS model and improvement process. *Studies in Educational Evaluation* 20: 55–67.

Keefe, J. W., and Howard, E. R. 1997. *Redesigning Schools for the New Century: A Systems Approach*. Reston, VA: National Association of Secondary Principals.

Keefe, J. W., and Jenkins, J. M. 1997. *Instruction and the Learning Environment*. Larchmont, NY: Eye on Education.

Keefe, J. W., Jenkins, J. M., and Hersey, P. W. 1992. *A Leader's Guide to School Restructuring* [Special report of the National Association of Secondary School Principals Commission on Restructuring]. Reston, VA: National Association of Secondary School Principals.

Keefe, J. W., Monk, J. S., Letteri, C. A., Languis, M. L., and Dunn, R. 1986, 1989. *The National Association of Secondary School Principals Learning Style Profile*. Reston, VA: National Association of Secondary School Principals.

Keller, F. S. 1968. Goodbye, Teacher. *Journal of Applied Behavior Analysis* 1: 83.

Key Learning Community (2005–2006). *Handbook*. Indianapolis, IN: Key Learning Community.

Khourey-Bowers, C., and Croley, C. B. 2007. Art detectives. *Educational Leadership* 64(8): 51–52.

Klausmeier, H. J., Lipham, J. M., and Daresh, J. C. 1980. *The Renewal and Improvement of Secondary Education: Concepts and Practices*. Madison, WI: Wisconsin Research and Development Center for Individualized Schooling.

Kolb, D. A. 1976. *Learning Style Inventory: Technical Manual*. Boston: McBer and Co.

Kosanovic, G. E. 1994. *Retooling the Instructional Day: A Collection of Scheduling Models*. Reston, VA: National Association of Secondary School Principals.

Kovalik, S., and Olsen, K. D. 1998. The physiology of learning—Just what does go on in there? *Schools in the Middle* (March/April): 32–37.

Kulik, C-L. C., Kulik, J. A., and Cohen P. A. 1990. Instructional technology and college teaching. In *Teaching Psychology: A Handbook: Readings from Teaching of Psychology*, eds. J. Hartley and W. J. McKeachie. Hillsdale, N.J.: Lawrence Erlbaum Associates.

Kulik, J. A., Kulik, C-L. C., and Cohen, P. A. 1979. A meta-analysis of outcome studies of Keller's Personalized System of Instruction. *American Psychologist* 34: 307–318.

Kushman, J. W. 2001. *Integrating Middle School Curriculum around Real-World Issues*. Portland, OR: Northwest Regional Educational Laboratory.

Lasley, T. J., II. 1998. Paradigm shifts in the classroom. *Phi Delta Kappan* 80(1): 84–86.

Lee, V. E., and Smith, J. B. 1995. *Effects of High School Restructuring and Size on Gains in Achievement and Engagement for Early Secondary Students*. Madison, WI: Wisconsin Center for Educational Research, University of Wisconsin.

Letteri, C. A. 1980. Cognitive profile: Basic determinant of academic achievement. *Journal of Educational Research* 77(4): 195–199.

Letteri, C. A. 1985. Teaching students how to learn. *Theory into Practice* 14(2): 112–122.

Levin, H. M., and Hopfenberg, W. S. 1991. Don't remediate, accelerate. *Principal* 70(3): 11–13.

Lewin, K. 1936. *A Dynamic Theory of Personality*. New York: McGraw-Hill.

Lezotte, L. W., and Bancroft, B. A. 1985. Growing use of the effective schools model for school improvement. *Educational Leadership* 42(6): 23–27.

Lindquist, M. M., Dossey, J. A., and Mullis, I. V. S. 1995. *Reaching Standards: A Progress Report on Mathematics*. Washington, DC: U.S. Department of Education.

Little Dust Productions. 2007. Available at: www.littledust.com/films/freedom_writers.php, pp. 1–6.

Lounsbury, J. H., and Clark, D. C. 1990. *Inside Eighth Grade: From Apathy to Excitement*. Reston, VA: National Association of Secondary School Principals.

Madaus, G. F., and O'Dwyer, L. M. 1999. A short history of performance assessment—Lessons learned. *Phi Delta Kappan* 80(9): 688–695.

Mann, L. 1998. Theatre education: A dramatic tool for learning. *Education Update* 40(5): 1, 6–7.

Marx, G. 2006. *Sixteen Trends, Their Profound Impact on Our Future: Implications for Students, Education, Communities, Countries, and the Whole of Society.* Alexandria, VA: Educational Research Service.

Marzano, R. J. 2006. *Classroom Assessment and Grading That Works.* Alexandria, VA: Association for Supervision and Curriculum Development.

McDonald, J. 1996. *Redesigning School: Lessons for the 21st Century.* San Francisco: Jossey-Bass.

Meier, D. 1992. Reinventing teaching. *Teachers College Record* 93(4): 594–609.

Meier, D. 1998. Can the odds be changed? *Phi Delta Kappan* 79(5): 358–362.

Messick, S., et al. 1976. *Individuality in Learning.* San Francisco: Jossey-Bass.

Met School Website. 2006. Available at www.themetschool.org/home

Metzger, M. 1998. Teaching reading beyond the plot. *Phi Delta Kappan* 80(3): 240–246, 256.

National Association of Secondary School Principals (NASSP). 1996. *Breaking Ranks: Changing an American Institution.* Reston, VA: NASSP.

National Association of Secondary School Principals (NASSP). 2004. *Breaking Ranks II: Strategies for Leading High School Reform.* Reston, VA: NASSP.

National Association of Secondary Principals. 2007. Joint statement on the reauthorization of the Elementary and Secondary Act (ESEA). Available at: www.principals.org/joint_recommendations

National Commission on Excellence in Education. 1983. *A Nation at Risk: The Imperative for Educational Reform.* Washington, DC: U.S. Department of Education.

National Diffusion Network. 1992. *Educational Programs That Work*, 18th ed. Longmont, CO: Sopris West.

Neill, D. M. 1997. Transforming student assessment. *Phi Delta Kappan* 79(1): 34–40, 58.

New Hampshire Department of Education. 2007. *New Hampshire's Vision for Redesign: Moving from High Schools to Learning Communities.* Available at: www.ed.state.nh.us/education/doe/HSvision.pdf

Newman, D. 1992. Technology as support for school structure and school restructuring. *Phi Delta Kappan* 74(4): 308–315.

Newmann, F. M., Marks, H. M., and Gamoran, A. 1995. Authentic pedagogy: Standards that boost student performance. *Issues in Restructuring Schools* 8. Center on Restructuring of Schools, University of Wisconsin-Madison.

Newmann, F. M., Secada, W. G., and Wehlage, G. G. 1995. *A Guide to Authentic Instruction and Assessment: Vision, Standards and Scoring.* Madison, WI: Wisconsin Center for Education Research, University of Wisconsin-Madison.

Niguidula, D. 1993. *The Digital Portfolio: A Richer Picture of Student Performance* [Studies on Exhibitions no. 13]. Providence, RI: Coalition of Essential Schools, Brown University.

Niguidula, D. 1997. *A Digital Portfolio Sampler* [CD-ROM]. Providence, RI: Annenberg Institute for School Reform, Brown University.

Niguidula, D. 1998. A richer picture of student work: The digital portfolio. In *Assessing Student Learning: From Grading to Understanding*, ed. D. Allen. New York: Teachers College Press.

Oakland Aviation High School Website. 2007. Available at www.aviationhigh school.org/methodsofassessment.html

O'Connor, K. 1995. Guidelines for grading that support student learning and student success. *NASSP Bulletin* 79(571): 91.

Olsen, S. 2007. Handhelds help turn kids into marine biologists. Available at: www.CNET.com

Olson, L. 1988. Children flourish here. *Education Week* 7: 18.

O'Neil, J. 1992. Wanted: Deep understanding: Constructivism posits new conceptions of learning. *ASCD Update* 34(3): 1, 4–5, 8.

O'Neil, J. 1995. On schools as learning organizations: A conversation with Peter Senge. *Educational Leadership* 52(7): 20–23.

O'Neill, J., Wagner, R., and Gomez, L. M. 1996. Online mentors: Experimenting in science class. *Educational Leadership* 54(3): 39–43.

Onosko, J. J. 1992. An approach to designing thoughtful units. *The Social Studies* 83(5): 193–196.

Palinscar, A. S., and Brown, A. L. 1984. Reciprocal teaching of comprehension-fostering and comprehensive-monitoring activities. *Cognition and Instruction 1*: 117–175.

Parker Annual Report, 1996–97.

Pate-Bain, H., Achilles, C. M., Boyd-Zaharias, J., and McKenna, B. 1992. Class size makes a difference. *Phi Delta Kappan* 74(3): 253–256.

Peel, J., and McCary, C. E., III. 1997. Visioning the "little red schoolhouse" for the 21st century. *Phi Delta Kappan* 78(9): 702–705.

Perkins, D. 1992. *Smart Schools: Better Thinking and Learning for Every Child*. New York: Free Press.

Prospect Center. 1986. *The Prospect Center Documentary Processes: In Progress*. North Bennington, VT: The Prospect Archive and Center in Education and Research.

Reeves, D. B. 2004. *Accountability for Learning: How Teachers and School Leaders Can Take Charge*. Alexandria, VA: Association for Supervision and Curriculum Development.

Rosenshine, B. 1984, 1991. Direct instruction. In *Instructional Leadership Handbook*, eds J. W. Keefe and J. M. Jenkins. Reston, VA: National Association of Secondary School Principals.

Rosenshine, B., and Guenther, J. 1992. Using scaffolds for teaching higher level cognitive strategies. In *Teaching for Thinking*, eds. J. W. Keefe and H. J. Walberg. Reston, VA: National Association of Secondary School Principals.

Ross, A. and Olsen, K. 1993. The Way We Were . . . The Way We Can Be: A Vision for the Middle School through Integrated Thematic Instruction. Second Edition. Kent, WA: Books for Educators, Covington Square.

Rutter, R. A., and Newmann, F. M. 1989. The potential of community service to enhance civic responsibility. *Social Education* 53(1989): 371–374.

Ryan, J. M., and Miyasaka, J. R. 1995. Current practice in testing and assessment: What is driving the changes? *NASSP Bulletin* 79(573): 1–10.

Sarason, S. B. 1989. *The Creation of Settings and the Future Societies*. San Francisco: Jossey-Bass.

Schifter, D. 1996. In *Constructivism: Theory, Perspectives, and Practice*, ed. C. T. Fosnot. New York: Teachers College Press.

Schrag, F. 1992. Nurturing thoughtfulness. In *Teaching for Thinking*, eds. J. W. Keefe and H. J. Walberg. Reston, VA: National Association of Secondary School Principals.

Seidel, S. 1991. *Collaborative Assessment Conferences for the Consideration of Student Work*. Cambridge, MA: Harvard Project Zero.

Sergiovanni, T. J. 1987. *The Principalship: A Reflective Practice Perspective*. Boston: Allyn and Bacon.

Shields, P. M., and Knapp, M. S. 1997. The promise and limits of school-based reform: A national snapshot. *Phi Delta Kappan* 79(4): 288–294.

Shoreham-Wading River Middle School Friday Memo No. 4D. n.d. *Students Work with the Aged*. Shoreham, NY: Shoreham-Wading River Central School District.

Silver, H. F., and Hanson, J. R. 1980. *User's Manual: The Learning Preference Inventory*. Moorestown, NJ: Hanson Silver and Associates.

Simmons, R. 2007. *Do You*. New York: Gotham Books.

Singham, M. 1998. The canary in the mine: The achievement gap between black and white students. *Phi Delta Kappan* 80(1): 8–15.

Sirotnik, K. A. 1999. Making sense of educational renewal. *Phi Delta Kappan* 80(8): 606–610.

Sizer, T. R. 1984. *Horace's Compromise: The Dilemma of the American High School*. Boston: Houghton Mifflin.

Sizer, T. R. 1992. *Horace's School: Redesigning the American High School*. Boston: Houghton Mifflin.

Sizer, T. R. 1996. *Horace's Hope: What Works for the American High School*. Boston: Houghton Mifflin.

Slavin, R. E. 1991. Synthesis of research of cooperative learning. *Educational Leadership* 48(5): 71–82.

Slavin, R. E. 1995. *Cooperative Learning: Theory, Research and Practice*, 2nd ed. Needham Heights, MA: Allyn and Bacon.

Smith, M. L. 1993. *The Role of High-Stakes Testing in School Reform*. Washington, DC: National Education Association.

Sternberg, R. J. 1996. Myths, countermyths and truths about intelligence. *Educational Researcher* 25(2): 11–16.

Stiggins, R. J. 1995. *Student-Centered Classroom Assessment*. New York: Macmillan.

Stiggins, R. J. 1997. *Student-Centered Classroom Assessment*, 2nd ed. Columbus, OH: Merrill.

Stiggins, R. J. 2007. Assessment through the student's eyes. *Educational Leadership* 64(8): 22–23.

Stolp, S., and Smith, S. C. 1995. *Transforming School Culture: Stories, Symbols, Values and the Leader's Role*. Eugene, OR: ERIC Clearinghouse on Educational Management.

Strenge, R. 2007. WSU cyber tutoring research gives pre-service teachers virtual experience. *WSU News Service*. Pullman, WA.

Stufflebeam, D. L., et al. 1971. *Educational Evaluation and Decision Making* [Phi Delta Kappa National Study Committee on Evaluation]. Itasco, IL: F. E. Peacock.

Swanson, J. 1997. Hey, teachers: Leave those kids alone. *Sunday Province* [Vancouver, BC], February 16.

Tanner, D., and Tanner, L. 1990. *History of the School Curriculum*. New York: Macmillan.

Tanner, L. 1988. The path not taken: Dewey's model of inquiry. *Curriculum Inquiry* 18(41): 472–479.

Tanner, L. 1997. *Dewey's Laboratory School: Lessons for Today*. New York: Teachers College Press.

Thelen, H. 1954. *Dynamics of Groups at Work*. Chicago, IL: University of Chicago Press.

Tomlinson, C.A. 1999. *The Differentiated Classroom*. Alexandria, VA: Association for Supervision and Curriculum Development.

Tomlinson, C.A. 2006. Reconcilable differences? Standards-based teaching and differentiation. *Educational Leadership* 58(1): 6–11.

Tomlinson, C.A. and Jarvis, J. 2006. Teaching beyond the book. *Educational Leadership* 64(1): 16–19.

Torp, L., and Sage, S. 1998. *Problems as Possibilities*. Alexandria, VA: Association for Supervision and Curriculum Development.

Treisman, P. U. 1992. Studying students studying calculus. *College Mathematics Journal* 23: 362–372.

Trump, J. L. 1977. *A School for Everyone.* Reston, VA: National Association of Secondary School Principals.

Tyack, D., and Cuban L. 1995. *Tinkering toward Utopia.* Cambridge, MA: Harvard University Press.

Ubben, G. C. 1976. A fluid block schedule. *NASSP Bulletin* 60(397): 104–111.

Voss, J. F. 1979. Organization structure and memory: Three perspectives. In *Memory, Organization and Structure*, ed. R. C. Puff. Hillsdale, NJ: Academic Press.

Walberg, H. J. 1984. Improving the productivity of America's schools. *Educational Leadership* 41(8): 19–27.

Wang, M. C., and Lindvall, C. M. 1984. Individual differences and school learning. In *Review of Research in Education*, ed. E. W. Gordon. Washington, DC: American Educational Research Association.

Wardman, K. T. 1994. From mechanistic to social systems thinking [A digest of a talk by Russell L. Ackoff]. *Systems Thinker* 5(1): 1–4.

Washburne, C. W., and Marland, S. P. 1963. *Winnetka: The History and Significance of an Educational Experiment.* Englewood Cliffs, NJ: Prentice-Hall.

Webb, N. L., 2003. The impact of the interactive mathematics program on student learning. In *Standards-Based School Mathematics Curricula: What Are They? What Do Students Learn?* eds. S. Senk and D. R. Thompson, pp. 375–398. Mahwah, NJ: Lawrence Erlbaum Associates.

Webb, N.L. and Dowling, M. 1996. Impact of interactive mathematics program on the retention of underrepresented students: Cross-school analysis of transcripts for the class of 1993 for three high schools. *Project Reports* 96(2). Madison: University of Wisconsin-Madison, Wisconsin Center for Education Research.

Weick, K. E. 1982. Administering education in loosely coupled schools. *Phi Delta Kappan* 27(2): 673–676.

Wiggins, G. 1989. Teaching to the (authentic) test. *Educational Leadership* 46(7): 141–147.

Wiggins, G., 1998. *Educative Assessment: Designing Assessments to Inform and Improve Student Performance.* San Francisco: Jossey-Bass.

Wiggins, G. and McTighe, J. 2005. *Understanding by design*, 2nd ed. Alexandria, VA: Association for Supervision and Curriculum Development.

Willis, S. 1997. Field studies—Learning thrives beyond the classroom. *ASCD Curriculum Update* (Winter): 1–2, 6–8.

Wolk, S. 2007. Why go to school? *Phi Delta Kappan* 88(9): 648–658.

Wood, G. H. 1992. *Schools That Work*. New York: Plume.

Wood, P., Bruner, J., and Ross, G. 1976. The role of tutoring in problem solving. *Journal of Child Psychology and Psychiatry 17*: 89–100.

Worthen, B. 1993. Critical issues that will determine the future of alternative assessment. *Phi Delta Kappan 74*: 444–454.

Yale Child Study Center. 1998. *Overview of the School Development Program (K–12)*. New Haven, CN: School Development Program.

ABOUT THE AUTHORS

James W. Keefe is the author of more than 60 books, articles, and assessment tools. He is the former director of research for the National Association of Secondary School Principals and president of the Learning Environments Consortium International, a nonprofit coalition of individuals, schools, and districts committed to school renewal in the United States, Canada, and Europe. He taught at the junior high and the senior high school levels and served as a high school assistant principal and principal. He also taught graduate education courses at the University of Southern California and Loyola Marymount University in Los Angeles.

John M. Jenkins has authored or coauthored eight books, edited several monographs, and written some 30 articles and book chapters. He was a high school principal for more than four decades and served as the director of the P. K. Yonge Development Research School on the campus of the University of Florida. Jenkins also taught graduate-level courses at the University of Florida and the University of Miami. He had previously taught at elementary, middle, and high school levels. He is vice president of the Learning Environments Consortium International and a certified quality assurance review chair for AdvancED, the newly formed accrediting association combining the Southern and North Central Accrediting Associations.